INDIGENOUS FUTURES

Tim Rowse is in the History Program, Research School of Social Sciences, at the Australian National University. He studied at the University of Sydney and the Flinders University of South Australia, and has taught and researched at Macquarie University, the University of Melbourne, the Menzies School of Health Research and the ANU. In pursuit of his academic and practical interests in Indigenous affairs, he lived for several years in Central Australia. Among his books are *Remote Possibilities* (1992), *After Mabo* (1993), *Traditions for Health* (1996), *White Flour, White Power* (1998) and *Obliged to be Difficult* (2000). He has recently published a biography of Dr HC Coombs.

INDIGENOUS FUTURES
CHOICE AND DEVELOPMENT FOR ABORIGINAL AND ISLANDER AUSTRALIA

Tim Rowse

UNSW PRESS

A UNSW Press book

Published by
University of New South Wales Press Ltd
University of New South Wales
UNSW Sydney NSW 2052
AUSTRALIA
www.unswpress.com.au

© Tim Rowse 2002
First published 2002

This book is copyright. Apart from any fair dealing for the purpose of private study, research, criticism or review, as permitted under the Copyright Act, no part may be reproduced by any process without written permission. Inquiries should be addressed to the publisher.

National Library of Australia
Cataloguing-in-Publication entry:

Rowse, Tim, 1951– .
Indigenous futures: choice and development for Aboriginal and Islander Australia.

Bibliography.
Includes index.
ISBN 0 86840 605 8.

1. Aborigines, Australian — Social conditions. 2. Aborigines, Australian — Economic conditions. 3. Aborigines, Australian — Land tenure. 4. Aborigines, Australian — Government policy. 5. Aborigines, Australian — Politics and government. 6. Aborigines, Australian — Government relations. 7. Australia — Politics and government — 1965– . 8. Australia — Race relations — Political aspects. I. Title.

305.89915

Cover illustration Rod Moss *Rectangular Visions,* 2000, graphite on Arches paper
Printer Griffin Press

CONTENTS

Foreword by Professor Jon Altman, Director, CAEPR   vii
Acknowledgments   xiii
Introduction: From assimilation to self-determination   1

PART 1
  INTERPRETING THE ABORIGINAL EMPLOYMENT DEVELOPMENT POLICY
     Introduction   25
  1   Some outcomes of the Aboriginal Employment Development Policy   29
  2   Indigenous culture and Indigenous choice   36
  3   The problem of motivation in education, training and employment   50
  4   Indigenous institutions and the labour market   65

PART 2
  LAND, SEA AND ECONOMIC DEVELOPMENT
     Introduction   81
  5   Hunting, gathering and tourism   85
  6   Mining incomes   92
  7   Native title   103
  8   Representing the land-owner interest   111

PART 3
  DOMESTIC CHOICES: CHILDREN, GENDER AND IDENTITY
    Introduction   127
  9 Families and welfare   130
  10 Gender reforming   152
  11 Households, individuals and the Indigenous population   167

PART 4
  INDIGENOUS AGENCIES OF COLLECTIVE CHOICE
    Introduction   175
  12 ATSIC's regions: the 'equity' issue   184
  13 ATSIC's regions: the identity issue   191
  14 Modernising Indigenous political culture   204

PART 5
  MAKING GOVERNMENTS ACCOUNTABLE
    Introduction   219
  15 The Indigenous Sector and relations within and   220
     among governments

Conclusion: CAEPR and the Indigenous Sector   230

Notes   237
References   252
Index   265

FOREWORD

by Professor Jon Altman
Director, CAEPR

In this foreword, I provide some background on the project that resulted in *Indigenous Futures: Choice and development for Aboriginal and Islander Australia*. I also explain why Tim Rowse was selected to write it. But first, I say something about the Centre for Aboriginal Economic Policy Research (CAEPR).

CAEPR is a multidisciplinary social sciences research centre established at the Australian National University (ANU) in 1990. The Centre did not have a virgin birth: it grew from a combination of two developments. In 1985, the Committee of Review of Aboriginal Employment and Training Programs, chaired by the late Mick Miller, concluded with a final recommendation (No. 164) calling for the establishment of a Bureau of Aboriginal Economic Research. This recommendation was greatly influenced by the dearth of such research — noted by the Miller Committee as a handicap on its work — in an important area of public policy. The Miller recommendation was for a public service bureau with internal research capacity and a program to fund external research projects. In 1986, discussions and strategic planning at the ANU, impelled by the Miller Inquiry recommendation, also highlighted the need for such a centre. Setting up CAEPR took another three years. The federal Department of Aboriginal Affairs (DAA), having secured additional resources from Treasury to sponsor research on the multi-million-dollar Aboriginal Employment Development Policy, administered a selective tendering process that was won by CAEPR.

CAEPR's main funding now comes from the ANU, the Aboriginal and Torres Strait Islander Commission (ATSIC) and the Department of Family and Community Services (DFACS). Its major goal is to contribute to better outcomes for Indigenous people by independently monitoring changes in socioeconomic status, influencing policy formation and constructively informing public and policy debates. Through research that combines academic excellence with policy relevance and realism, CAEPR's intent is to be the foremost national research centre on Indigenous economic and social policy. From the outset, CAEPR was multidisciplinary, initially combining economics, anthropology, human geography and demography, more recently expanding with staff qualified in political science, law and health.

CAEPR has been subject to three independent reviews to date and has undergone three associated development phases. The first, which I now think of as 'CAEPR Mark I', extended from 1990 to 1993. During this initial phase, CAEPR was primarily funded by ATSIC (which replaced the DAA in 1990) and was affiliated with the Department of Archaeology and Anthropology in the Faculty of Arts. The second phase, 'CAEPR Mark II' extended from 1994 to 1998. In this five-year period, CAEPR consolidated as a stand-alone research centre within the Faculty of Arts with enhanced ANU support. 'CAEPR Mark III' is the current phase. It began in 1999 when CAEPR was established as a university centre with its own strategic plan and a raised profile, both within the ANU and nationally.

What has all this got to do with this book? Well, just as CAEPR's genesis had its partial origin in the Miller Review recommendation, so this book had its origin in the second review of CAEPR undertaken in September 1996 and chaired by Emeritus Professor Peter Karmel. In recommendation 2 (iv) the review Committee suggested that 'the Centre give priority to the production of a major publication in order to present an overview of its work to date'.

From the outset, as Foundation Director of CAEPR, I was keen for the author of this major publication to be someone from outside CAEPR's established staff. This would ensure an independent perspective: such a project might result not only in a synthesis and dissemination of CAEPR research, but also in an element of critical review.

In 1999 I approached Tim Rowse, who was then a visiting fellow at the Centre completing his Nugget Coombs biographical project, to undertake this task. My hope was that the book would fittingly mark CAEPR's tenth anniversary in April 2000. I approached Tim for a number of reasons. First, I knew that he was an avid reader of CAEPR's publications; indeed, he had formally and rigorously reviewed a number in the anthropology journal *Oceania*. Secondly, Tim is a disciplinary polyglot and I believed that this was essential for any scholar reviewing CAEPR's multidisciplinary work. Thirdly, Tim is very politically engaged and has a keen interest in

Indigenous institutions and public policy. I thought this was extremely important for a meaningful synthesis of CAEPR publications. And finally, he has a justified reputation for productivity, and I knew this was going to be an extremely challenging task.

It transpired that Tim was able to start in July 2000 and so it was agreed that the project would be undertaken during CAEPR's eleventh year, but would focus on the first decade of work, 1991 to 2000. It was Tim who early on coined the term the 'CAEPR corpus' to refer to the subject he would write about. The term 'corpus' was used in the Concise Oxford sense of 'body, collection of writing'. There are at least two ways in which this could be defined: it could either be the work that is published and badged by CAEPR — that is, the CAEPR monographs, discussion papers and working papers; or it could be all publications produced by CAEPR staff. A problem with the former definition is that ten of CAEPR's monographs are edited volumes, with many of their 142 chapters written by non-CAEPR authors. By the end of 2001, the corpus defined in this way consisted of nearly 400 publications. The corpus in the second sense consists of an even greater number — nearly 600 publications. Tim and I agreed that to be manageable, the CAEPR corpus should be limited to the body of work published by CAEPR and by CAEPR authors, although somewhat heroically Tim chose to include many individual chapters in edited volumes, irrespective of author affiliation.

Tim was appointed a fellow at CAEPR for a 12-month period. His methodology primarily involved reading the CAEPR corpus. He presented a number of work-in-progress seminars that allowed critical intellectual engagement with authors and others. Indeed, like a good participant observer, Tim immersed himself fully in CAEPR, so much so that by 2001 he himself had become an active contributor to the corpus (something he had also done in 1999 as a co-editor and contributor to the CAEPR monograph *Land Rights at Risk: Evaluations of the Reeves Report*). As draft chapters of this book rolled out, Tim made them available to all those he had cited, seeking to ensure that he had accurately represented research findings.

It is not surprising, given the breadth of CAEPR's work, that Tim has had to select a particular lens through which to view it. He has focused on what CAEPR's research tells us about the existence, role, functions and growth during the 1990s — under the policy umbrella of self-determination, more recently self-management — of what he terms 'the Indigenous sector'. In providing a tertiary analysis based on secondary sources — using the CAEPR corpus as data — it has been understandably difficult for him to take fully into account the institutional and political contexts in which CAEPR has emerged and operates. These, however, are important issues precisely because CAEPR's work is undertaken in a vibrant and highly contested environment. Hence, I now make a few brief comments about some of the issues and tensions that CAEPR faces as a university-based research organisation examining Indigenous economic and social policy.

CAEPR has always been an unusual institution, mediating as it does the interests of three core sets of stakeholders: the academy; the bureaucracy (and government); and the Indigenous sector. Each of CAEPR's stakeholder groups has different priorities. To generalise somewhat, the academy values scholarship, independence and longer-term pure research; the bureaucracy values practical short to medium-term applied research that fits strategically within party-partisan policy frameworks; and the Indigenous sector values practical research focused on outcomes, preferably conducted as advocacy. A big challenge for CAEPR has been the juggling act: how to be relevant and applied; independent and scholarly; and politically informed and engaged. Meeting diverse, and at times competing, requests for research is never easy, especially when the demand for research always exceeds the supply of researchers (somewhat paradoxically, given frequently articulated Indigenous concerns about over-research) and when the issues to be addressed are usually urgent and worthwhile.

Judgments about which issues to pursue and how to pursue them require both internal and external negotiation. CAEPR is made up of a group of committed researchers. In 1990, the Centre started with only six staff; it now has nearly twenty. Some CAEPR staff were recruited with already distinguished academic careers and established research interests, others are new to this area, yet all now have robust and productive professional engagements with Indigenous policy research. CAEPR's multidisciplinary establishment is one of its strengths, but this also creates challenges for internal communications. Academic staff themselves face trade-offs between maintaining disciplinary integrity and research linkages, and publishing policy-oriented discussion papers (that are the primary subject of this book) quickly and in a language accessible to a range of stakeholders. There is no one corporate CAEPR view, but a diversity of views, something that from an 'ideas' perspective is healthy; although at times this is poorly understood by more politicised external interests.

Negotiations with stakeholders about research priorities have often been influenced by broader policy frameworks. In 1990, when it was established, CAEPR had a contractual research agenda defined by the parameters of the Aboriginal Employment Development Policy, and focused on labour market issues and evaluation. Notwithstanding this obligation, CAEPR's research was far wider from the outset because of the personal research interests of its academic staff. During the 1990s, in response to a series of political and policy changes, its research agenda widened to include a range of emerging socioeconomic issues: demographic transitions and population growth; native title and land rights; reconciliation; the contested issue of welfare dependence and proposed welfare reform; education reform; economic and community development; and, most recently, governance. CAEPR's existence since 1990 has not been uncontested, but it has managed to survive a number of federal and ATSIC elections and a change of federal government. With time, the intellectual capital vested in CAEPR grows and its value seems to be increasingly recognised.

These comments are provided primarily to highlight the enormous challenge that Tim faced in reviewing the work of a complex organisation embedded in the vexed, apparently intractable, unresolved and highly contested area of Indigenous policy research. And because Tim approached his task in a very fair way, trying to give maximum coverage to the CAEPR corpus in all its diversity, without 'fear, favour or affection', this task was made even more difficult.

The commissioning of this research has resulted in a highly informed critical reading of CAEPR's corpus that provides, from a particular perspective, some insights into where we have been (sometimes unwittingly) and where some of our research may be going. Tim has used the lenses of political science and history that animate his own long-standing research on self-determination and the institutions of Indigenous Australia — what he terms here 'the Indigenous sector' — through which to view CAEPR's work. But these are not the only lenses that could have been used, nor are these the ones through which CAEPR has predominantly oriented or viewed its own work. CAEPR's economic policy orientation has been its primary lens, leading to the focus on labour markets, welfare and development issues. Yet any lens, in providing focus on a particular object or field, necessarily leaves other objects or fields out of view. Consequently, one should ask not only what the lens allows us to see, but also what it blinds us to. For example, one could question whether Tim's lens was wide enough. By focusing on the Indigenous sector, does he under-emphasise the larger nation-state of which this sector is a part? Does this lens highlight or shade the complex linkages, articulations and comparisons between Indigenous and non-Indigenous Australia that so much CAEPR research examines? Ultimately, it may be impossible, when reviewing a body of work of this size, to use more than one synthesising lens, to wear more than one pair of spectacles, whatever their political or disciplinary hue. But it is important to remain alert to the inevitability that different lenses provide different views as well as different insights.

Undoubtedly, a valuable benchmark has now been established for further intellectual auditing of CAEPR research, and this development is warmly welcomed by all of us at the Centre. As more research is produced and disseminated (especially via our Website) I encourage others, Indigenous and non-Indigenous, from whatever perspective or discipline, to use and to challenge our research findings, for this is precisely why they are placed so visibly in the public domain. Indigenous policy issues are complex and often seemingly intractable, yet they are clearly of enormous national importance, and independent rigorous research and open debate and analysis will continue to be vital. Researchers at CAEPR will continue to employ their various disciplinary lenses in further expanding the CAEPR corpus. We look forward to an ongoing critical dialogue with Indigenous and non-Indigenous researchers and colleagues who share our concerns about the vitally important issues of national significance in this policy arena.

ACKNOWLEDGMENTS

Jon Altman, Director of the Australian National University's Centre for Aboriginal Economic Policy Research, made this book possible by employing me for one year (July 2000–June 2001). My brief was to write a 'synthesis' of CAEPR's published research. Synthesis requires interpretation. Jon made it clear that there was no CAEPR 'line' that I should follow. It was for me to decide how to interpret and to criticise the CAEPR corpus. I am grateful to him for the physical and intellectual space.

My CAEPR (and ex-CAEPR) colleagues were always available to explain and argue, in the friendliest atmosphere, the points of their works. Bill Arthur, Diane Smith, Julie Finlayson, Boyd Hunter, John Taylor, Will Sanders, David Martin, Anne Daly, Siobhan McDonnel, Matthew Gray, Shirley Campbell, Robert Levitus, David Pollack, Frances Morphy and Jerry Schwab — all played their parts in the formulation of my 'synthesis'.

Elaine Thacker and Mark Champion did me the additional service of reminding me that beyond the university was an Indigenous constituency. I was no less encouraged by conversations with: Nic Peterson, Yasmine Musharbash, Rosita Henry, Peter Sutton, Martin Krygier, Francesca Merlan, Bruce Buchan, Elspeth Young, Anna Yeatman and Katherine Gibson. Nic Peterson, Jon Altman and Robert Levitus made such effective criticisms of my first draft that I reconstructed the book, its sequence and its themes.

Sally Ward, Ilona Crabb, Deborah Mitchell and Jelena Kovac took care of bibliographic and administrative requests. Robert Lindsay edited the manuscript with sympathy and accuracy.

INTRODUCTION: FROM ASSIMILATION TO SELF-DETERMINATION

Since the early 1970s, the Australian system of government has been changed by the rise of the Indigenous Sector.

The Indigenous Sector consists of thousands of publicly funded organisations. Some are statutory authorities (for example, the Land Councils in New South Wales and in the Northern Territory, and the Aboriginal and Torres Strait Islander Commission — ATSIC), some are incorporated 'councils' performing the functions of local governments in remote parts of the continent, some are employers and job placement agencies (the Community Development Employment schemes), and there are Indigenous health services, legal services, housing associations, schools and sporting clubs. The rise of the Indigenous Sector, I will argue in this book, is the most important product of the policy era known as 'self-determination'.

As Commonwealth government policy, 'self-determination' began some time (it is difficult to be precise) between Prime Minister McMahon's Cairns Statement of April 1971 and the earliest decisions of the Whitlam government in December 1972 and January 1973.[1] Its characteristic public policy moves have been two: affirming Indigenous land rights and publicly subsidising Indigenous organisations. Enacted through programs centred on land and on Indigenous organisations, 'self-determination' is usually understood as being based on rejection of the assumptions and practices of 'assimilation', the official policy philosophy in the years (again roughly) 1950–70.

Recent public debate has questioned whether Indigenous Australians have benefited from the shift from 'assimilation' to 'self-determination'. Among those sceptical of its worth two proposals can be found. One confidently suggests a return to 'assimilation'; the other searches for a new set of terms for a new strategy of Indigenous 'empowerment'. Let us suspend for a moment our judgment about whether Indigenous welfare has been raised, lowered or left the same by the policy and programs of the last thirty years. Let us instead agree on the facts that, for good or ill, one of the outstanding results of 'self-determination' policy has been the rise of the Indigenous Sector and that the institutions of this sector now form parts of the apparatus by which Australians (especially Indigenous Australians) are governed. In what terms are we to understand and judge the Indigenous Sector?

THE HISTORIC RATIONALE OF THE INDIGENOUS SECTOR

In Australia, at the moment, there is no easy answer to the question of how we should assess the achievements of the Indigenous Sector. In this introductory chapter, I will argue that our ways of seeing the Indigenous Sector are mediated by unresolved issues in Australian liberalism.

By the end of the decade of 'Reconciliation', 2000, it was clear that that term had taken on two competing meanings. In one vision, the differences between Indigenous and other Australians were to fade away; the nation's unity would be predicated on the elimination of 'difference'. In the competing view, 'reconciliation' would enact and enshrine the different ways that Indigenous and non-Indigenous Australians belonged to 'Australia'. Difference, in this second view, was reconciliation's fundamental principle; in the first view, it was its nemesis. These contrasting perspectives on reconciliation are echoed by three contrasts in the ways that Australians have been talking and writing recently about 'assimilation' and 'self-determination' policies.

What is the problem that these policies were meant to address? Here are two contrasting answers. One starts by acknowledging that Indigenous Australians are different from other Australians, but insists that this is primarily so in ways that bring shame on all Australians. That is, this response takes seriously the fact that Indigenous Australians are disadvantaged, as measured by certain social indicators such as employment, income, health, levels of education. To relieve disadvantage, governments have devised special Indigenous programs, many of them delivered by Indigenous agencies. The intended effect of these programs is to allow Indigenous Australians to 'catch up' with non-Indigenous Australians, in terms of the above social indicators. In principle, when the social indicators show equality of well-being between Indigenous and other

Australians, these special programs will no longer be necessary and will be phased out. This perspective has an honourable lineage in Australian public policy debate. Some of the advocates of the 'Yes' vote in the 1967 referendum hoped that when the Commonwealth acquired national powers in 'Aboriginal affairs' its policies would positively discriminate between Aboriginal and other Australians, so as to deal effectively with the disadvantage of the former.[2] Reducing 'disadvantage' is the basic task of what the Howard government has been calling 'practical reconciliation'.

The alternative view is that 'practical reconciliation' is not nearly enough. In this perspective Indigenous Australians are a colonised people who remain 'different' from post-1788 immigrants in many ways that are positively affirmed in the language and imagery of Aboriginal and Torres Strait Islander identities. Insofar as Aborigines and Torres Strait Islanders remain distinct 'peoples', governments should concede to them the right to look after their own affairs, to practise self-determination. Part of that practice will be to devise Indigenous solutions to the problems of 'disadvantage', but that is not the end of the story. In this alternative perspective, the Indigenous Sector actualises the Indigenous right to self-determination. Whether it takes a long or a short time to relieve disadvantage, these Indigenous structures must be entrenched in the machinery of Australian government — by recognising Indigenous regional authorities (and securing a share of public revenue for their use), and by negotiating some kind of framework agreement (covering land tenure, public revenue and other substantive issues) between Australian governments and representatives of the Indigenous Australians. Some people would call this agreement a 'treaty'. The Senate took this idea sufficiently seriously in 1981 to ask its Standing Committee on Legal and Constitutional Affairs to look into the legal feasibility of such an agreement.[3] The High Court's judgments in Mabo (1992) and Wik (1996) have been taken by some to imply that Indigenous Australians retain a substantial measure of unextinguished sovereignty that should be acknowledged in a treaty and practically embodied in the design of our public institutions.

These two contrasting responses to Australia's colonial legacy are associated with contrasting ways of thinking about public policy.

In the first perspective, there is no long-term future for separate publicly subsidised Indigenous institutions. The success of government policies, as measured in changed social indicators, would make them unnecessary. Once that condition of equality of welfare is reached, it would simply be a matter of private choice, not a responsibility of government, were Indigenous Australians to maintain their many associations, councils and corporations. In the second perspective, Indigenous people will always maintain their own institutions, for these are the apparatuses of their self-determination, expressing their destiny as a people emancipated from a colonised condition. It is likely, and certainly acceptable in principle, that these Indigenous institutions will be funded, at least partly, by transfers from Consolidated Revenue. One of the matters to be negotiated in a compact or 'treaty' would be security of access to public funds that underwrite a permanent suite of Indigenous institutions.

Another difference between the two perspectives is less a difference of principle than of emphasis and perspective. The two perspectives tend to value 'Indigenous culture' differently. Those who think in terms of the first perspective are more likely to dwell on the ways that contemporary Indigenous beliefs and behaviour are a hindrance to the development of happier and healthier lives. Indeed, the term 'disadvantage' may have more than one meaning, referring not only to measurable inequalities in socio-economic conditions and health status but also to the inherent 'disadvantages' of a life shaped by Aboriginal or Torres Strait Islander custom.[4] That is, if the Indigenous condition is problematic and in need of remedial programs, one of the lines of corrective action will be that Indigenous Australians will reconsider the ways that they see themselves, their obligations to one another, and their aspirations for their children. In the process of being uplifted — in terms of their measured employment, education, health and income — Indigenous Australians will review established behaviours and beliefs critically, leaving behind inhibiting and self-destructive ways and embracing new ones. There might not be any future for 'Indigeneity', in this perspective, other than as a fond memory of one's ancestry (for example, in the same way that it is possible for me to say that I am of Irish and Cornish descent). In this way of thinking, Indigenous institutions either have no place or must resemble non-Indigenous organisations in all operational respects.

In the second perspective, Indigenous Australians are assumed already to have the basic capacities for self-government, whether these capacities are of ancient origin ('tradition') or have recently been acquired through adaptation to colonial pressures. The responsibility to change beliefs and practices thus falls much more heavily on non-Indigenous Australians, who must now review critically their established approaches to government. Non-Indigenous authority is exhorted and invited, in this second perspective, to enable Indigenous Australians to experiment in the design of their own institutions. Indigenous Australians are to be enabled, as well, to make their own autonomous judgments about what counts as their 'well-being'. That is, this perspective challenges the assumption that the well-being of all Australians can and should be judged according to the same criteria.

The third difference that troubles or enlivens Australia's postcolonial liberalism has to do with the way Indigenous 'choice' is imagined. It is not necessary to suppose that Indigenous Australians are simply driven by the inexorable logic of 'modernity' (in one perspective) or by the noble imperatives of 'tradition' (in the alternative perspective). Indigenous Australians, like other humans, make choices, and their agency must be taken into account by any policies that are intended to effect changes in the ways they live. But what kinds of subjects of choice are they supposed to be? In one perspective, the tendency is to assume that when Indigenous people make choices about how they will adapt to or resist the pressures of modern Australia they will do so as individuals or possibly as households. In the second perspective, Indigenous choice is imagined as a matter not only for individuals and households but also for larger collective agents: 'communities', councils, associations, regions, even 'nations'. Of course, it is logically possible to imagine that Indigenous Australians are 'choosing subjects' in both the individual and the collective senses. However, those who are sceptical of 'self-determination' are much less likely to see value in collective Indigenous agency. After all, it was the ambition of 'assimilation' to emancipate the Indigenous individual or household from the wider communal loyalties that were understood to hold them back. Those more positively disposed towards 'self-determination' need not discount the importance of individual choice, but they argue that individuals and households are enabled more than disabled by being part of a wider Indigenous community that has corporate powers of action and decision.

In an unavoidably abstract fashion, I have evoked the contemporary antinomies in the ways that Australians now imagine the Indigenous predicament. In the rest of this introduction I will introduce the reader to the ethical and analytical framework that I have applied in reading the work produced by the Centre for Aboriginal Economic Policy Research (CAEPR) at the Australian National University. As the reader will see, I strongly sympathise with the self-determination perspective. However, I will make a plea in this book for understanding self-determination as a realisation of the fundamental value that, in human rights, we attach to the individual.

DIFFERENCE AND CHOICE

In April 2001, Robert Manne published a critical comment on what he saw as the rapid 'right' turn in discussion of Indigenous policy in Australia. He worried that the tendency of discussion was towards a rebirth of 'assimilationism'. He objected to 'assimilationism' in the following terms:

> ... if the traditional communities are indeed destroyed, one distinctive expression of human life — with its own forms of language, culture, spirituality and sensibility — will simply become extinct. Humanity is enriched and shaped by the diversity of its forms of life. It is vastly impoverished as this diversity declines. If contemporary Australians allow what remains of the traditional Aboriginal world to die, we will be haunted by the tragedy for generations.[5]

I thought that Manne's argument against 'assimilation' did not state the most important principle of self-determination policy. Accordingly, I wrote the following letter in reply (which the *Sydney Morning Herald* did not publish):

> It would be more in keeping with liberal-democratic principle to ask whether being 'assimilated' is good from the point of view of the individual subjected to it. The answers to this question will vary from person to person, and household to household. Some Indigenous Australians have wanted to assimilate, and some have not. And 'assimilate' has meant different things to different people. When some Indigenous Australians choose to remain in remote regions, despite there being little demand for their labour and poor provision of public services, they are making a choice in favour of a way of life in which attachment to kin and to country are central values.
>
> Some people now condemn the results of this choice. Seeing Indigenous social pathologies in these remote places, they explain them as the sad harvest of 'separatism' — a policy philosophy imposed, they say, on Indigenous Australians since the 1970s. I see it differently. In replacing 'assimilation' policy with 'self-determination' policy, governments have provided for an unprecedented variety of Indigenous ways of life in Australia. Remote communities are publicly subsidised in many ways, but their residents are no longer obliged to live on them. A great many Indigenous Australians choose to take their chances in towns and cities, making use of mainstream institutions. When that proves difficult, as it often does, they can turn to kin who have kept their distance, physically and culturally, from the conditions that our society imposes on those who would be 'successful'.
>
> In short, the best feature of a policy of Indigenous self-determination is not that it perpetuates human diversity, but that it maintains the real possibility of choice by Indigenous Australians. 'Assimilationism', as practised in the past, was often coercive in its methods and patronising in its assumptions. By embracing self-determination policy in the 1970s, Australia became a more liberal society.
>
> No option available to Indigenous Australians is without cost. That is their fate as colonised people. We uphold their dignity, as humans and as citizens, if we maximise their ability to make judgments of cost and benefit for themselves. To enable choice is a worthy goal of public policy.

The difference between Manne's argument and mine is simple and fundamental. He wants to assess policy with the question: what is good for society? His answer is 'cultural diversity'. I wanted to assess policy with the question: what is good for the individual? My answer was 'choice'. No doubt, despite our different philosophical positions, Robert Manne and I could agree in our judgments about many issues of Indigenous policy. However, the difference between his communitarian argument and my libertarian response remains significant. If the result of Indigenous Australians' choices over the next few generations is that there is a reduction in cultural diversity, then from the point of view outlined in my letter I would not see it as a 'tragedy', but as an acceptable consequence of maximising Indigenous choice.

I now want to reflect on three difficulties that I might have in holding that position.

First, there is an ethical issue for the state. Is the state abandoning its responsibilities by leaving so much to Indigenous choice?

Second, there is a practical issue. Is it possible for Indigenous people to have a choice about their way of life, if the government has not given financial and other kinds of support to sustaining Indigenous Australians values and practices that are alternative to the ways of most other Australians? Putting this another way, is not Manne right to emphasise the maintenance of cultural diversity as a goal of public policy, because only with the achievement of that goal will Indigenous choice (whether individual or collective) be possible?

Third, there is an issue that we might call 'scientific' — whether it is realistic to regard people's behaviour as a manifestation of their choices. Is not people's behaviour determined by the structures of opportunity that they face? Do people ever really have much 'choice'?

I will discuss these issues in reverse order.

CHOICE AND SOCIAL DETERMINATION

In understanding human behaviour, the social sciences offer a range of intellectual traditions. Some theories of social action emphasise its structurally determined character, so that to understand what people do we must understand the *powerful structures* of which they are the knowing or unknowing bearers. An alternative approach is to assume a high degree of self-determination, so that structures are best explained as effects of decisions made by individuals who are 'rational actors' dealing with a world of *scarcity*. These alternative emphases are both challenged by an approach to human behaviour that asks what *meanings* actors attach to features of their world and to their actions within it. In a recent survey of trends in historiography, William Sewell suggests that we respond to this intellectual variety with a cheerful eclecticism:

We must imagine a world in which every social relationship is simultaneously constituted by meaning, by scarcity and by power. This would imply, for example, that all social relations are discursive but that social relations are never exhausted by their discursivity. It also implies something much more radical: the discursive features of the social relationship are themselves always constitutively shaped by power relations and conditions of choice under scarcity. It further implies that this constitutive shaping is reciprocal — just as meanings are always shaped by scarcity and power, so scarcity is always shaped by power and meaning, and power is always shaped by meaning and scarcity [6].

Sewell's advice helps me to introduce the theme of this section — that when researchers have tried to examine systematically some of the conditions of Indigenous living, it has not been easy to come up with explanatory accounts that clearly delineate the contributions of powerful structures, rational choices and socially constructed meanings.

Much of CAEPR's early research was stimulated by the need to evaluate the Aboriginal Employment Development Policy (AEDP), announced in 1987. The AEDP was the Hawke government's response to the Miller Report of 1985.[7] Miller's schemes for Indigenous economic development portrayed Indigenous Australians as having the opportunity and the 'right' to *choose a lifestyle*. The Report did not limit the exercise of that right to Indigenous Australians living in certain regions or in certain ways, though it implied that 'remote' Aboriginal people would benefit most from the exercise of that right.

Outlining the AEDP, the Hawke government acknowledged 'the different aspirations and employment needs of Aboriginal people arising from markedly different social circumstances and cultural values'.[8] The AEDP defined its outcomes as 'equity' — equality between Indigenous and non-Indigenous Australians in terms of some standard socio-economic indicators, such as employment and income. Other socio-economic indicators, such as school retention rates, have also been understood to be relevant. Putting it rather crudely: education leads to employment which yields income. However, 'equity' or 'equality' in these measured outcomes was to be pursued by measures that enabled Indigenous 'choice'. This duality of policy aims, 'equality' *and* 'choice', made program outcome indicators difficult to interpret. Indigenous people's continuing poor labour market status could be understood partly as a reflection of their different 'aspirations', 'values' and choices. If the Indigenous rate of employment continued below the non-Indigenous rate, were we to conclude that the AEDP was *failing* to achieve employment equity? Or was it rather that the policy was *succeeding* in allowing Indigenous peoples' choice not to be educated, employed and rewarded in the same ways that non-Indigenous Australians were? I offer some examples of AEDP evaluations that evoked this conundrum.

There is a very high rate of 'unemployment' on outstations. As John Taylor wrote in 1991, it is clear that 'outstation residents display far less tendency to have school-based skills'.[9] However, he added, this explanation begs the question of 'whether this reflects cultural choice or problems of accessibility or a mixture of both'. Was policy failing (in that outstation residents lacked schooling), or was policy succeeding (in that people were enabled by land tenure and welfare policies to choose to live on outstations, far from jobs and schools)?

Confronted by the same statistics of high unemployment in remote locations, Altman and Smith in 1992 discussed some interpretive possibilities:

> Among some sections of the Aboriginal population the statistical goal of employment equality may already be met. For example, it has been argued that [on] many outstations Aboriginal people are already fully employed. But as a result of the statistical exclusion of people participating in subsistence from the ranks of the employed and the failure to count their production as income-in-kind this contribution is not officially acknowledged. If welfare income at outstations was classified as CDEP wages, with economic work being subsistence production, then residents would immediately be reclassified as employed within the labour force with payment of UB equivalents being interpreted as wages for that work.

They then noted a consequence of that reclassification. Those now understood to be 'employed' would be limited to low incomes; the AEDP goal of non-Indigenous and Indigenous income equality would be forfeited. They thus suggested that:

> Such a reclassification could mean that the goal of income equality may not be appropriate in the outstations context if *people make a conscious choice* to reside in locations that are remote from mainstream economic opportunities'.[10]

My third example comes from the work of labour economist Anne Daly. She found from her regression analyses of 1986 Census data that, even when Aborigines were equal in education to non-Aborigines, they were less likely to have a job. Referring to this result as 'a strong negative Aboriginal effect', she speculated about its possible behavioural constituents:[11]

> [M]any Aborigines living traditional lifestyles may not be interested in entering the formal labour market. Alternatively, those in remote areas may have been discouraged by the absence of jobs in these regions and ceased to think of themselves as members of a formal labour market. This 'discouraged worker' effect may also apply in the more settled parts of Australia if employers discriminate against Aborigines and are unwilling to employ them at the award wages set by the Industrial Relations Commission.[12]

Daly acknowledged that her data and mode of analysis could not lead her to any firm conclusions about the significance of Indigenous people's *choices* as a determinant of their 'welfare dependency'. She speculated that Indigenous welfare recipients 'may not be interested in entering the formal labour market'.[13] While allowing the possible significance of Indigenous choices, her comments also invoke structures (such as the mismatched spatial distributions of job demand and of the Indigenous population) and meanings (employers' ascription of negative qualities to Aboriginal applicants, and vice versa).

My fourth example of Indigenous choice playing a part in their labour-market outcomes is an observation made by John Taylor about the industrial and occupational distribution of Indigenous people who are employed in the formal labour market:

> On the surface, industries that under-employ Aborigines and Islanders appear to share high human capital requirements, such as medicine, education, accounting, and various trades-based industries. Equally, however, there are many examples, such as cafes and restaurants, department stores, and banks, where this is less likely to be the case and where factors such as *discrimination or personal choice* may be more responsible. In some industries, therefore, the general thrust of the Aboriginal Education Policy towards upgrading Aboriginal and Islander skills may be beneficial in bringing about greater equality in employment distribution. In other cases, however, attempts at raising the level of human capital may prove ineffective owing to *Aboriginal and Islander preferences* in the labour market.[14]

In short, it would appear that the outcomes of programs to increase Indigenous training, employment and income are affected by choices that Indigenous people make. Indigenous choice is not the whole story, but it is of some significance in explaining the outcomes of Indigenous policies.

For my second set of examples I turn to more recent CAEPR work on housing. In their paper measuring Indigenous housing needs, Neutze, Sanders and Jones warn that their composite index of need incorporates 'standards drawn from the non-Indigenous world. Indigenous Australians may not all aspire to these standards or value housing in quite the way implied in them. It is difficult to know to what extent differences in housing conditions may be a result of these different aspirations and values, as opposed to differences in opportunity and capacity to pay'.[15] In acknowledging that Indigenous people may not share non-Indigenous standards about housing, these three authors were careful not to imply that all Indigenous people think about housing in the same way. That is, they do not imply a single Indigenous set of standards. That was wise, for recent ethnographic research published by CAEPR suggests that Indigenous communities vary in their ways of thinking about housing.

In Yuendumu, Musharbash found that Warlpiri crowd into dwellings:

> Large households satisfy people's desire to be close to their kin. From a Warlpiri perspective to be close to one's kin is desirable not only so that one has *malpa* ['company'], but also support. The latter is expected to be both social and financial. Sharing responsibilities such as child care as well as money and other resources is easiest when co-residing. However, the pressure to share may also contribute to and intensify the 'boom and bust' cycles of households ... [T]he provision of new houses does not lead to the formation of nuclear family households, but to 'overcrowding' which occurs for social reasons and for the sharing of resources.[16]

Consider the contrasting situation in Kuranda, observed by Henry and Daly:

> Mobility and overcrowding in Kuranda are partly a consequence of the dire shortage of housing available for Indigenous people. Although Indigenous people utilise extensive kin networks, and emphasise the fact that they 'live extendedly' (as one key reference person put it) as being what makes them different from non-Indigenous Australians, there is nevertheless a contemporary cultural preference for nuclear family units to have separate dwellings or to keep separate 'hearthholds'. For example the 20 members in household 36 live in a three-bedroom house. That the adult children of the tenants, with their conjugal partners and offspring, are 'usual residents' in this house is *not a matter of cultural choice but of social necessity.*[17]

One CAEPR researcher has generalised that when Indigenous Australians make decisions about how they use the houses available to them, they are making trade-offs between competing values:

> Whilst some Aboriginal households benefit from subsidised rentals and access to State and Territory specially-funded Aboriginal housing, the costs associated with housing represent significant outlays for many Aboriginal people. Larger household size, the compositional complexity of many households and their internal dynamism aggravate the financial difficulties associated with Aboriginal expenditure on housing, so that *some households opt for the lower financial burden associated with substandard housing. Such a decision*, however, can have consequences for the educational performance of children, and for the health status and employment prospects of household members.[18]

My final example of social scientists trying to infer the choices of Indigenous Australians comes from the sphere of education. It is well established that Indigenous Australians who go to school or get vocational training do so, for the most part, in 'mainstream' institutions. Does this state of affairs reflect Indigenous aspirations or does it reflect the failure of governments to provide an Indigenous alternative to the mainstream service?

National Aboriginal and Torres Strait Islander Survey data

collected in 1994 show that a clear majority of respondents (85.5 per cent) indicated that they are happy with the education their children are receiving at school; a further 10.3 per cent were unhappy while 4.0 per cent said they did not know. The majority of Indigenous parents (84.0 per cent) indicated they feel welcome in their children's schools; only 2.6 per cent felt unwelcome. Nearly half (46.8 per cent) of the rural parents reported that they were involved with decision-making at their children's school; this compared to 37.6 per cent of capital city parents. Jerry Schwab comments:

> These data could be interpreted as showing Indigenous parents' high levels of satisfaction with mainstream. However, when people appear 'satisfied' with what they have got, it may reflect resignation that their real preferences are never likely to be met. This seems to be the case among a large minority of NATSIS respondents. One third (33.2 per cent) of them said that they would have preferred to send their children to an Aboriginal community-controlled school. Nearly half expressed a preference for the mainstream schooling that was provided and more than one in ten said that they did not know.[19]

By distinguishing real from apparent preferences, Schwab raises the issue of how people's thinking about choice is affected by what they are used to being able to do — that is, by structures. He has speculated on the reasons that Indigenous families may have been able to accommodate themselves to, and even come to prefer, a 'mainstream' education or (as he puts it) to be 'sceptical of the path of empowerment through educational separation'. Indigenous parents may perceive a vast improvement, within their own lifetimes, in the system's readiness to include Indigenous children and to address their needs sympathetically. Their sense of what 'community-controlled' education might mean in practice may be affected by sad memories of the segregated, 'mission'-based schools that they or their parents had to suffer. They might lack confidence in the democratic processes of their local Indigenous 'community', and they might not have been exposed to positive models of community-controlled schooling. Having constructed this speculative history of Indigenous preference formation, Schwab recommends that governments do more to support the 'Indigenous-controlled' option, so that its strengths and weaknesses could become better understood. That is, he implies that Indigenous preferences, having been formed by a perverse history, may be reformed by a more benign regime of service provision, in particular, by public funding of Indigenous-controlled education and training.

My quotations from the CAEPR researchers demonstrate that although social scientists give great weight to the structural and historical limitation of Indigenous peoples' choices, they do not present Indigenous people's behaviour as completely structurally determined.

The CAEPR researchers attach unweighted explanatory significance to Indigenous choices, and they imply or assert explicitly that public policy can shape both the options available to Indigenous people and their choices from among those options.

SOURCES OF DIVERSITY

Schwab's argument leads me to the second of the problems that I acknowledged in my argument against Robert Manne's communitarian justification for post-assimilation policies. Is not Manne right to emphasise the maintenance of cultural diversity as a goal of public policy, if we know that only social diversity allows genuine Indigenous choice (whether individual or collective) about how to belong to Australian society?

To answer this question I want to distinguish between two sources of cultural diversity, and to make the point that one of them is much more an effect of public policy than the other.

I suggested above that the rise of the Indigenous Sector is the main product of the self-determination era. It amounts to a substantial challenge to the forms both of Australian government and of Indigenous sociality. The Indigenous Sector is neither the 'state' (though it is almost entirely publicly funded), nor is it 'civil society' (though its organisations are mostly private concerns in their legal status). Rather the Indigenous Sector is a third thing created out of the interaction — sometimes, but not always, frictional — of government and the Indigenous domain. The Indigenous Sector is an important source of Indigenous choice. That is, Indigenous individuals and households in many regions can choose whether to get basic services such as health, housing and education from either a mainstream or an Indigenous Sector provider.

Lest I seem complacent about this, I acknowledge the possibility that in some regions, in respect of some needs, Indigenous people do not yet have sufficient choice between mainstream and Indigenous providers. Where choice exists, it is important to celebrate it as a benefit of wise public policy. In particular, I would celebrate the CDEP scheme. CDEP, chosen by a community as a local alternative to individual entitlements to unemployment payments, enables Indigenous Australians to choose a work environment in which they are socially comfortable, even if they do not earn as much as they might in a non-CDEP job. (In many regions, the choice is not between CDEP and non-CDEP jobs, but between CDEP and no job, since nearly all jobs are generated by CDEP.) There is a view in government (including among some Indigenous people) that CDEP is merely a stepping-stone to 'real' or 'proper' employment. I would rather celebrate CDEP as the institutional framework that allows individuals a choice about the kind of social experience that a job makes possible.[20]

That is one kind of social diversity, enabling choice — a direct effect of government action. However, there are other sources of social and cultural diversity that effectively create conditions in which Indigenous choice is possible. The Indigenous milieu is internally differentiated, and it is possible for individuals and households to live in different ways, at different times, as they move from one Indigenous milieu to another.

In what terms may we imagine this Indigenous diversity? In many generalisations about the ways that Indigenous Australians remain different from other Australians, the most important cultural difference to which people refer has to do with family and kinship. That is, it is sometimes asserted that Indigenous people think and act differently from non-Indigenous people when it comes to understanding how people are related and to weighing the importance of kin-relatedness, compared with other kinds of relatedness. Yet do all Indigenous Australians think about kinship in the same way? Is kin-relatedness the primary way in which all Indigenous Australians figure their social relationships? Recently, Peter Sutton has remarked on the differences between Indigenous people for whom kinship is but one sphere of life (and a 'private' sphere, at that) and Indigenous people for whom the most important relationships are those defined by the customs of kinship.[21] For Sutton, 'modernisation' entails greater involvement with people who are not your kin and a consequent displacement (but not replacement) of kinship by other values and practical considerations.

To the extent that 'integration with kin'/'integration with non-kin' is an axis of variation among the social milieux that Indigenous Australians find themselves in, there is a range of Indigenous milieux. The significance of kinship in the Indigenous social order varies across regions and generations.

It is important to distinguish analytically the two different kinds of diversity that I have just evoked. The first — mainstream as against Indigenous providers of services — depends a great deal on whether governments support organisations of the Indigenous Sector. The second kind of diversity — the significance of Indigenous kinship as a social ordering principle — is much less affected by public policy. Much cultural variation among Indigenous Australians is a product of the history of colonisation itself: different kinds of colonial institutions, in different regions, enforced at different times, meeting different Indigenous reactions.

So, another way for me to state my disagreement with Robert Manne is that his notion of cultural diversity seems to dwell on the Indigenous non-Indigenous difference and to overlook the significance of cultural diversity, resulting from acculturation, within Indigenous Australia; and that he implies an exaggerated role for public policy in sustaining Australian cultural diversity. In my emphasis on the centrality of Indigenous choice to good policy, I attach more importance than Manne does to intra-Indigenous diversity. Individuals and families can move about within a culturally differentiated Indigenous world. Second, I estimate less than Manne does the degree to which governments can be held responsible for maintaining cultural diversity. Indigenous people retain much scope for managing in their own ways (sometimes uneasily) the different demands made by different Indigenous milieux.

THE ETHICAL STATE

One of the right-wing thinkers that Robert Manne warned us against, as leading us back to 'assimilationism', was Roger Sandall. In his recent book *The Culture Cult*, Sandall argued that Australian policies have effectively neglected the educational needs of Indigenous Australians living in the remote communities of the Northern Territory. He cites the opinion of one Northern Territory educator that (in Sandall's words) 'literacy will only result when Aboriginal parents want it for their children'. I understand Sandall to be questioning the wisdom not only of parents who do not make a commitment to their children's literacy, but also of Northern Territory government policies that (effectively, if not intentionally) allow the parents' unwise choices to blight their children's future. The combination of parental and governmental neglect, says Sandall, has left many Indigenous Territorians 'illiterate, vocationally disabled, unpresentable outside the ethnographic zoos they live in'.[22]

Peter Sutton, in his much-quoted inaugural Berndt Lecture, also takes aim at what he considers to be a misplaced emphasis on choice. Sutton acknowledges that by citing cultural differences in values, one can question the pertinence of this or that measure of Indigenous disadvantage and suffering. I gave examples earlier of the cultural relativity of measures of housing 'overcrowding'. Sutton thinks that too much has been made of such differences. He has heard people argue 'for example, that people are "free to go to hell their own way", that people "have the right to make their own mistakes" and to set their own standards of what constitutes a social problem …'. Sutton is not swayed by such promotions of choice and difference because 'we do not normally apply such an argument to the care or neglect of infants, the elderly, the mentally handicapped, and many other potential victims of abuse. That is, Australians generally assert through the state a duty of care towards others …'.[23]

Sandall and Sutton are questioning one of the foundations of post-assimilationist Indigenous policy: the necessity for pathways of Indigenous adaptation and development to be open to choice by Indigenous people themselves. They are arguing that the state cannot justify its persistent concession of choice to Indigenous Australians when the apparent effects of their choices are so disabling and self-harming. In that persistence the state fails in its duty of care. They are not lone voices. As I show in Chapter 2, CAEPR researchers have been developing an in-principle distinction between wise and unwise Indigenous choices.

I am generally sympathetic to arguments that the state has a responsibility to protect the vulnerable from their incapacity to manage their own lives. However, it is not enough simply to assert this principle and hope that everyone will agree about who is vulnerable, and what is the best way to protect them from their own unwise choices with the least infringement of their autonomy. (Anna Yeatman has recently argued persuasively that social policy be founded on respect for individual autonomy.[24]) Because neither Sandall nor Sutton have much to say in answer to these two questions, they are not programmatically 'assimilationist'. But if they have little if anything to say about the design of future government programs, their arguments nonetheless cast doubt on the principle of Indigenous choice. Their counter-principle seems to be that Indigenous choice should be restricted to certain options that, in the judgment of an authority such as the state, would lead to their collective betterment.

However, Sutton's views on Indigenous choice are not so simple as my summary, so far, would suggest. His Berndt lecture was a plea for acknowledgment that the culture of Indigenous people was not entirely a blessing to them in their efforts to deal with the modern world. We must 'rethink' Indigenous culture, he urges, lest in our romanticism we ignore its ill-effects. He intends his phrase 'rethinking culture' to refer not only to what non-Indigenous authorities (such as anthropologists, politicians, and supporters of self-determination) should do with their conceptions, but also to what Indigenous people themselves might do with their behaviour, values and attitudes. Urging their 'cultural self-reassessment', he offers his qualified endorsement of the principle of Indigenous choice:

> The old culturally oppressive, chauvinist and racist policies both of churches and the state, under which even the most private aspects of life were in many places subject to Whitefella scrutiny and control, are happily past. If it is to happen in generations rather than centuries, the kind of cultural redevelopment I have referred to is something that, in the final analysis, only Indigenous people themselves can make effective, *if indeed that is a realistic and conceivable option for them*. But cultural change does not proceed, as it were, by committee. Deep changes in culture are normally and in most of human history unintentionally generated in contexts such as significant economic change, radical ideological shifts such as mass conversion to a proselytising religion, or major environmental catastrophes.[25]

The way that the state can act responsibly towards Indigenous people, Sutton seems to be arguing, is not by directing their cultural renovation, but by promoting a context — 'significant economic change' — that makes 'deep changes in culture' more likely. With this argument, it becomes clearer what Sutton means by the state taking responsibility for the vulnerable — not the direct co-option of Indigenous powers of choice, but the promotion of new contexts of Indigenous choice.

CONCLUSION

After reviewing my three doubts about my critical response to Manne's communitarian case against 'assimilation', I am led to two conclusions.

My unpublished reply was right to emphasise choice, rather than cultural diversity, as the value underpinning a defence of Indigenous self-determination. However, I think that it was misleading that I exemplified choice as if it were necessarily a matter for individuals. The subjects of Indigenous choice are individual *and* collective. Households, families, communities and organisations make choices. As I said in the beginning of this Introduction, the rise of the Indigenous Sector — agencies of collective choice — is (along with land rights) the defining achievement of the self-determination policy era.

Second, in highlighting choice as the fundamental value of self-determination policy, I cannot avoid saying something about the significance of individual choice. Here I will adopt a useful distinction made by Charles Taylor between 'ontological issues and advocacy issues'.[26]

Ontologically, individuals may be relatively unimportant. That is, my approach to understanding society and history places great emphasis on the structural determination of patterns of human behaviour. Without denying altogether the creativity of individuals, I understand the scope for creativity to be determined by pressures and limits that are not explained as simply the sum total of the choices of many individuals. Those constraining and enabling determinations of behaviour are best understood as deeply embedded structures and processes. I am committed to an ontology of structures. I welcome such analytic respect for structure, for example, in CAEPR writers' accounts of the demand for and supply of Indigenous labour. Anyone concerned with Indigenous performance in the labour market must acknowledge as a deep structure that (a) private investment in labour-hungry industry is not a feature of many localities where Aboriginal people live, and (b) many Aboriginal people's strategies of social reproduction require that they spend a large part of their life in places and engaged in activities that remove them, effectively, from labour markets. While neither (a) nor (b) are immutable, they are not easily transformed. They are the deep structures that condition the success and failure of certain government programs.

In terms of 'advocacy', however, I am strongly 'individualist'. That is, I subscribe to an understanding of human rights in which individual autonomy is the supreme value. I want to judge governments and societies according to the criterion that they should be maximising the autonomy of human individuals. I see collective action — whether by 'nation-states', 'peoples', corporations, or associations — as open to this judgment. When nation-states or 'peoples' assert their sovereign rights to self-determination, I support their assertion to the extent that it enables their members ('citizens') and the members of other nations or peoples to enjoy autonomy as individuals. However, I am hostile to claims that human rights can be realised only through individuals' inclusion within any particular nation-state or people. As Anna Yeatman puts it, 'The individual as the subject of human rights belongs nowhere as far as any particular jurisdiction goes, but represents the substantive claim in relation to which any jurisdiction may be judged'.[27] Nation-states and 'peoples' asserting their rights to sovereignty and self-government I see as contingent and imperfect attempts to realise or mediate human rights.

'Human rights' is a relatively new moral framework in which to evaluate the claims of this or that collective entity to give effect to human well-being. Equally new is the discourse of 'Indigenous rights'. Both have gained purchase on law and moral reasoning only since 1945. They provide much of the conceptual material by which Australians now ponder the quality of their settler–colonial society. Any careful consideration of 'self-determination' policy must try to come to an understanding of the relationship between Indigenous rights and human rights. That has been the most challenging part of my research project within CAEPR, for CAEPR's research agenda has hugely privileged the descriptive over the normative. Yet no discussion of public policy can take place in a normative vacuum, and CAEPR aspires to policy relevance. So I have tried to work out my normative framework. In doing so, I have attended to how Indigenous Australians now speak and write normatively.

To describe the emerging terms of Indigenous political discourse in Australia requires a book of its own. However, my impression is that Indigenous Australians experience their struggle for human rights in more than one way. The sense of individual and family entitlement and autonomy is very strong, as it is for other Australians. For historical reasons and now for institutional reasons, the sense of collective entitlement is also strong. As I see it, the modern political culture of Indigenous Australians is a complex layering of elements.

The strong sense of individual entitlement (for example, to litigate, to vote and to receive welfare benefits) is a lasting result of the assimilation era — in both its benign and its harsh manifestations. Indigenous Australians' continuing affirmation of communal or collective entitlement (and here I mean more than their affirmation of Indigenous identity) has been answered, more recently, in the state's deliberate soliciting of incorporation, communal title and Indigenous representation, giving rise to what I am calling the Indigenous Sector. Defending 'self-determination' from 'neo-assimilationists' should not blind Indigenous and non-Indigenous Australians to the complexity of this normative heritage.

In order to read CAEPR's research with questions of value in mind, I have returned to a descriptive framework based on a taxonomy of 'choosing selves'. In two previous publications I have suggested that 'self-determination' has been actualised — in the last thirty years and continuing — as innovations in Indigenous choosing behaviour. To state a truism, 'self-determination' has required the formation of Indigenous 'selves'. I understand the 'self' in 'self-determination' to have three levels of existence: the individual/person/citizen, the family/household and the organised communal agency. My book attempts to focus on these levels, one at a time, to show some of the ways that governments and social scientists 'construct' them.

In Part I, I portray the Aboriginal Employment Development Policy (AEDP) as an attempt to realise one of the most common forms of individual autonomy in Australian society: being a waged or salaried worker. Starting in 1987, the AEDP — whose evaluation was partly the original rationale for CAEPR's existence — tried to increase the proportion of Indigenous Australians who had a full-time or part-time job. Without a job, they were 'welfare-dependent'; with a job they were fulfilling one of the conditions of 'independence' as modern Australia understands that term. After summarising the disappointing outcomes of the AEDP (Chapter 1), I highlight three themes in CAEPR research that are relevant to understanding that failure in a constructive way. In Chapter 2, I trace the changing terms in which CAEPR researchers have imagined putative Indigenous 'workers' as having a choice about their entry into the labour market. In Chapter 3, I highlight the impressive body of CAEPR writing about one of the forms of Indigenous employment: participation in CDEP schemes. In this chapter I put forward my own interpretation of CDEP as a political institution, not just a labour-market device. CDEPs, I suggest, are one of the outstanding features of the burgeoning 'Indigenous Sector', their strengths perhaps underappreciated. In Chapter 4, I take up yet another theme occasioned by the evident 'failure' of the AEDP: the question of what is an appropriate training for Indigenous Australians. Does it not make a difference, I ask, whether we see education and training from the individualist standpoint of the labour market, or from the standpoint of the collective Indigenous political project?

In Part II, I continue the emphasis of Part I on 'economic development', but without the labour market as the focus. Rather, In Chapters 5–8, I have examined the economic utility of the natural and cultural resources that Indigenous people own collectively. Here 'communal selves', rather than 'individual selves' are the issue. Again, it is impossible not to deal with the institutions of the Indigenous Sector — land councils, royalty associations, Native Title Representative Bodies — the apparatuses made necessary by land rights and 'native title'. The problems of realising the economic value of Indigenous property are in part problems of political development.

In Part III, I turn to the intermediate 'selves' so far neglected in my exposition of CAEPR's research: the family/household'. CAEPR has tried to give an account of the 'domestic' units of Indigenous social life, as the units to which 'responsibility' and 'choice' can be affixed in social policy. In Chapter 9, I have traced the difficulties of substantiating such categories as 'household', 'family' and 'single parent', when the researcher feels obliged to draw on both ethnographic and Census data. In Chapter 10, I interpret sex differences in Indigenous labour market outcomes, in order to speculate on the pressures that Indigenous people might now be feeling on the system of gender relations. In Chapter 11, I review CAEPR's considerations of the growth in the Indigenous population, arguing that the 'problem' of its reliable enumeration is in part a reflection of the way that the Census empowers the household as the locus of identity choice.

Although my analytic framework takes seriously the three modes of 'self' in 'self-determination' — the individual, the domestic and the communal selves — I acknowledge that my tendency is to emphasise the third of these as defining the new threshold to which Indigenous Australians have moved in the era of 'self-determination'. In my introduction to Part IV, I have stated my theoretical rationale for considering Indigenous Australians' 'collective agency' as a phenomenon of 'organisation'. In three chapters, I review what CAEPR has said about some of these experiments. In Chapter 12, I examine ATSIC as an attempt to reconcile Indigenous regionalism with a political imperative to aggregate the Indigenous interest at a national level. In Chapter 13, I examine the Torres Strait (on which much good work has been done at CAEPR), in order to question the utility of 'identity' categories in such experiments. In Chapter 14,

I return to a theme introduced earlier in this Introduction: the innovative pressures on Indigenous political culture

In Part V, I reverse the presumption that Indigenous culture must change in order to make the Indigenous Sector fit into the wider structure of government. Instead I examine work by CAEPR, recently reiterated by the Commonwealth Grants Commission, which points to necessary changes in the relations among all government agencies. How does the Indigenous Sector articulate with a system of government that distributes sovereignty between national, State, Territory and local government agencies?

PART I

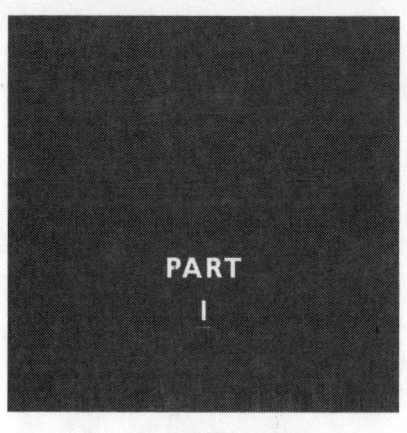

INTERPRETING THE ABORIGINAL EMPLOYMENT DEVELOPMENT POLICY

INTRODUCTION

In 1984, the Hawke government convened a Committee of Inquiry into labour market strategies for Indigenous Australians, appointing a Queensland Aboriginal man, Mick Miller, to chair it. The Committee's findings were published in 1985 as the *Report of the Committee of Review of Aboriginal Employment and Training Programs*. Miller cited research showing that 71 per cent of total national Aboriginal income was derived from government; 22 per cent of these government transfers was made up of 'primary economic assistance', the rest being 'welfare'. Miller saw opportunities to get more Indigenous Australians off welfare and into jobs and small businesses by public investment in Indigenous economic development.

While advocating new and better government programs, Miller was notably cautious in his assessment of what governments could achieve. Governments needed to take stock of the legacies of colonisation: 'dispossession, dispersal, destruction of the traditional economic base and its replacement by a tenuous relationship with the wider economy'. Under these pressures, Indigenous Australians had adopted 'new forms of Aboriginal life-style which are still in conflict with the wider society in many ways'. This legacy set limits to what government labour market programs could achieve, Miller warned. 'Aboriginal unemployment is as much a result of those historical processes and the continuing relationship with white Australian society as it is a function of structural difficulties in the labour market as a whole. It should not be expected therefore that the labour market problems of Aboriginal people will necessarily respond to measures designed to correct or ameliorate those general labour market difficulties.'[1]

Miller rejected the assumption that, from the point of view of Indigenous Australians, 'work for wages and salaries is the most appropriate and practicable basis for earning a livelihood'. To live by receipt of a wage or a salary entailed commitment to certain lifestyles:

> In the more remote areas which were not colonised to the extent of others, and where Aboriginal traditional custom and law remain very strong, people have removed themselves from *the enforced change of life-style encompassed by a western style economy*. In so doing they have not rejected entirely any relationship with the wider society and economy, but have chosen to maintain a life-style compatible with their traditional culture.[2]

Miller found two reasons to support such people's efforts to combine hunter-gatherer subsistence with selected elements of the market economy: they had a 'right to seek such a mix' and the mix 'makes economic sense'. 'We consider it important that the Australian community recognises the right of Aboriginal people to this option.'[3]

That is, the Miller report saw Indigenous Australians as people endowed with the opportunity and the right to *choose a lifestyle*. Accordingly:

> The whole question of the way in which Aboriginal people can *provide for their livelihood in accordance with the life-style they choose* raises structural matters which need to be addressed. These include access to and control of land and other resources, local government arrangements for Aboriginal towns, relationships with other forms of local government, access to development capital and involvement in particular industries.[4]

In policy initiatives flowing from the Miller Report this valuation of Indigenous 'choice' was complicated by the government's striving for 'equality' in the socio-economic indicators of Indigenous and non-Indigenous well-being. When the Hawke government responded to Miller by formulating the Aboriginal Employment Development Policy (AEDP) in 1987, it claimed to support Indigenous Australians' 'aspirations to gain employment and provide for their own livelihood wherever they live and in accordance with their traditions, chosen way of life and cultural identity'.[5] However, the language of the AEDP added some new terms: 'employment and income *equity* for Aboriginal and Torres Strait Islander Australians', 'redress the severe *imbalances* between Aboriginal society and the rest of Australians society'.[6] Altman and Sanders have noted that 'equity' was then becoming central to the Hawke government's conception of 'social justice'.[7] In the Hawke government's view 'equity' could be judged simply from a statistical comparison of Indigenous and other Australians' rates of employment, unemployment, self-employment and their levels of income. These specifications of 'inequity' and 'imbalance' were reflected in a clear statement of policy objectives — to achieve:

- employment equity with other Australians, that is to increase the proportion of Aboriginal people aged 15 and above who are employed from 37% to around 60%;
- income equity with other Australians, that is a doubling of the median income of Aboriginals;
- equitable participation in primary, secondary and tertiary education; and
- a reduction of Aboriginal welfare dependency to a level commensurate with that of other Australians, that is a reduction in Aboriginal dependency on the unemployment benefit from the current level of around 30% of the working age population to only 5%.[8]

In stating these objectives, the Hawke government did not repudiate the Miller Report's emphasis on choice. It acknowledged 'the different aspirations and employment needs of Aboriginal people arising from markedly different social circumstances and cultural values'.[9] However, the AEDP statement now posed governments with a question: to what extent was Indigenous people's 'inequity' of labour market status and income a reflection of their different 'aspirations', 'values' and choice? If the Indigenous rate of employment continued to be below the non-Indigenous rate, were we to conclude that the AEDP was failing to achieve what it called 'equity' or that it was succeeding in allowing a choice not to be employed?

In hoping to reconcile 'choice' with 'equity' the AEDP was raising (but hardly resolving) one of the unresolved issues within postcolonial liberalism that I described in my Introduction. On the one hand, Indigenous people were being conceived as lacking in well-being, and the state had a responsibility to lift them to the levels of well-being measured among non-Indigenous Australians. On the other hand, Indigenous people were being presented as historically and culturally different; they had a right to enact their difference by choosing their 'way of life'. What if some of the effects of that choice included staying 'below' Australian standards of well-being?

In the next four chapters I discuss CAEPR's efforts to deal with this policy conundrum. After Chapter 1 outlines the disappointing results of the AEDP, I ask to what extent can we account for the Indigenous rates and patterns of employment and unemployment as the outcome of Indigenous 'choice'? Much of CAEPR's research has understood 'choice' as an activity of the individual. He/she is understood as optimising well-being by making rational decisions about his/her 'investment' in education and his/her subsequent attachment to, or aloofness from, the formal labour market. When CAEPR researchers have used this analytic framework, they have tried to understand what makes the Indigenous chooser different from the (implicitly) 'normal' Australian chooser. Thus, CAEPR researchers have drawn on ethnographic literature in order to imagine the cultural context of the Indigenous individual's choices. 'Culture' appears in this way of representing Indigenous Australians as a series of constraints and opportunities. In Chapter 2 I have reviewed the terms in which CAEPR writers have described these constraints and opportunities. In Chapter 3, I have traced CAEPR researchers' attempt to apply critically 'human capital' theory — in particular, that theory's notion of the individual as a rational 'investor' in education.

In the CAEPR literature there is an alternative perspective on the significance of Indigenous choice in determining their labour market outcomes. In this perspective, it is not the attributes of the Indigenous individual that matter so much as the properties of new institutions that mediate Indigenous Australians' relationship with the labour market. Chapter 4 is about the CDEP schemes. I argue that CDEPs are political institutions to which the government has granted limited but real autonomy. CDEPs create a demand for labour that is sensitive to the cultural characteristics of the Indigenous suppliers of labour. To understand CDEPs it is not necessary to put forward a model of the Indigenous individual 'choosing subject', as in the studies summarised in Chapters 2 and 3; rather the point is to understand the political and economic conditions under which CDEPs survive as anomalous but enduring institutions.

Applying that institutional perspective, I conclude Chapter 4 by returning to the issues of education and training raised in Chapter 3, but this time from an institutional, rather than individual, perspective. I highlight a critical point made in CAEPR's studies of Australia's recently reformed Vocational Education and Training (VET) system: the lack of recognition of the Indigenous Sector as an 'industry' interest.

1
SOME OUTCOMES OF THE ABORIGINAL EMPLOYMENT DEVELOPMENT POLICY

Using the Censuses of 1986, 1991 and 1996, John Taylor has measured changes in the labour market status of Indigenous Australians. His 1993 monographs revealed two of the most important features of the initial impact (1986–91) of the AEDP: the prominence of the Community Development Employment Projects (CDEP) scheme, and the depth of regional variation.[10]

1986-91

Taylor began by reviewing some overall trends in the Indigenous population. Though there is a long-standing tendency for the Indigenous population to become more urban, it remained in 1991 more 'rural' than other Australians (Indigenous 32.8% compared to 14.6% for non-Indigenous Australians). The demand for labour tended to be stronger in the cities. As well, he found that there had been a disproportionate expansion of the Indigenous working-age population. The combined effect of these two features of the Indigenous population was to make it more difficult to reduce the rate of Indigenous unemployment.

By 1991 there had been a slight convergence in the overall rate of employment of the Indigenous and non-Indigenous populations, but Aborigines were still 0.51 and Torres Strait Islanders 0.77 of the non-Indigenous figure (1.0) in 1991. The rise (1986–91) in the employment rate had been better for Indigenous females (5.8 per cent) than males (2.7 per cent). The female labour force participation rate had risen by 5 per cent in 1986–91, while remaining the same for males.

These changes were most pronounced in rural areas. Indeed, Indigenous job growth 1986–91, had been 'predominantly a rural phenomenon involving mostly part-time work with an increasing emphasis on labouring and para-professional jobs in community services' — a reflection of the importance of CDEP, Taylor infers.[11] The Northern Territory had showed one of the most marked reductions in Indigenous unemployment rates from 35 per cent (1986) to 25 per cent (1991); the national fall had been 35.3 to 30.8 per cent, and in ACT, Victoria and Tasmania the rate of Indigenous unemployment actually rose. These regional variations in Indigenous labour force status could be described as an entrenched South-East versus North-West divide (with rural NSW falling into the North-West). In the North-West Indigenous unemployment rates were relatively high, but falling rapidly as an effect of the spread of CDEP. In the South-East the unemployment rates were low relative to the national Indigenous average, but a deteriorating demand for labour was not being offset by CDEP growth. The underlying sources of this regional variation, according to Taylor, were the different histories of economic development and the cultural circumstances of the 'North-West' Indigenous Australians — their attachment to remote lands, their intermittent supply of labour. Noticing that these regional disparities were evident in the labour force status of Indigenous youth, Taylor inferred that they were likely to persist.

Though the 1991 Census did not specifically ask respondents whether their employment was in a CDEP scheme, Taylor attributed 58 per cent of the Indigenous job growth in 1986–91 to the spread of CDEP. The Northern Territory was the fastest-growing CDEP zone, the numbers involved expanding almost sixfold (compare Queensland five-fold, national 3.6 fold). The Northern Territory was the only State/Territory where CDEP accounted for *all* employment growth.

Taylor distinguished full-time from part-time jobs. Indigenous employment had been increasingly part-time, Taylor found, a tendency most pronounced in the Northern Territory and South Australia. In this respect, there had also been a gross regional difference, with the Eastern States (except Queensland) showing the least tendency towards part-time work.

Indigenous Australians increased their skills and qualifications at a much greater rate (across a range of levels) than did other Australians. However among Indigenous Australians an increasing rural/urban skills gap had become evident. In this respect, the Northern Territory contrasted markedly with other States/Territories. CDEP, a program designed to accommodate a labour force with low skills, was probably a significant factor in this difference.

Taylor's study paid attention to incomes, as well as to employment. 'Mean employment incomes for Aborigines and Torres Strait Islanders have increased at a considerably slower rate than for other employed Australians.'[12] Where Indigenous incomes had increased most, there had also been the greater increase in the gap between male and female incomes. The ratios of Indigenous to non-Indigenous mean incomes showed wide regional variations. The greatest contrast between Indigenous and non-Indigenous incomes was to be found in the Northern Territory. The Northern Territory ratios (of Indigenous to non-Indigenous incomes) were much lower than the national average Indigenous ratios and only a little more than half the Indigenous ratios in major urban parts of the ACT, Tasmania and Victoria, where Indigenous people were, relative to non-Indigenous people, the best off.

Like other CAEPR researchers, Taylor defined 'welfare dependency' to include all transfer payments by the Australian government to Indigenous citizens, not only Unemployment Benefits. His study showed the persistence of high levels of welfare dependence, despite the AEDP. That is, the proportion of all Indigenous incomes deriving from employment in 1991 had risen only slightly since 1986, notwithstanding the rise in the proportions employed. To the extent that job creation 1986–91 had been based on the expansion of CDEP, it had not generated higher incomes. The regional pattern of 'welfare dependency' was similar to the regional pattern of income level: the Northern Territory and Western Australia showed the least proportion of Indigenous income coming from employment. 'The income returns from employment for Indigenous people are likely to fall increasingly behind those for the rest of the population, at least in certain regions', he predicted.[13]

Taylor showed that because so much of employment growth in 1986–91 had been due to CDEP, the Australian government had not moved Indigenous Australians towards 'economic equality', as it is usually measured, with other Australians by 1991. In particular, CDEP employment set limits to Indigenous income growth. His regional analysis enabled him to describe two rather different social environments to which governments were delivering labour market programs. In one, programs other than CDEP were of limited effectiveness 'where labour supply is often determined by culturally-based priorities, such as preference for intermittent employment, or where residential choices and lack of rural-urban labour migration limit access to mainstream labour markets'.[14] In the other environment, governments were likely to get better outcomes for labour market programs. 'Where low human capital is the main constraint on access to formal employment opportunities', it was reasonable for government to promote 'an upgrading of skill levels to ensure higher occupational status'.[15] It followed that the AEDP goal of statistical equality 'may be appropriate for some sections of the population but not for others'.[16]

Taylor was careful to discourage readers from thinking that he was simply calling for a regionally differentiated approach, as there were 'complexities ... in areas where a whole spectrum of community and cultural types co-exist'.[17] The success or failure of policy should be measured 'in a manner that reflects ... regional priorities, the variability of participation in formal and informal economies, and the restricted options in many remote locations'.[18]

In these observations, Taylor queried the national, statistical terms in which AEDP was being evaluated. Realistic policy evaluation demanded attention to the particularities of regions.

In a further argument for realism, CAEPR researchers pointed out that any consideration of the *rates* of employment, unemployment and labour force participation should take into account changes in the size of the base population. Before the results of the 1996 Census became available, Taylor and Altman surveyed 'the job ahead' for any government wishing to pursue the AEDP goal of equality of labour market status. Projecting the rapid growth of the working-age Indigenous population (29 per cent from 1996–2006), they predicted that the Indigenous demand for jobs would be likely to continue to exceed the supply, and by an ever greater gap. To achieve employment equality by 2001 would require an 80 per cent increase in Indigenous employment over the years 1996–2001. To achieve equality with non-Indigenous employment-to-population ratio by 2006 would require the number of jobs to more than double (103 per cent increase) over ten years. If the measure of policy success were not jobs, but full-time jobs, the task was even more difficult, because a higher proportion of Indigenous than non-Indigenous jobs in the 1990s were part-time. Income equality between Indigenous and non-Indigenous Australians would be no less elusive, they predicted, owing to the high proportion of Indigenous income that would come from welfare payments and from CDEP, and due to the low occupational status and high Indigenous engagement with part-time work.[19]

1991–96, AND BEYOND

When Taylor studied the 1996 Census data, he found that he had first to consider what the 1996 Census told him about the Census of 1991. The rate of growth of the Indigenous population 1991–96 had been six per cent per year — so far above expectations that it provoked the question, had thousands of Indigenous people been overlooked in the 1991 enumeration?[20] For a number of reasons, the

CAEPR researchers decided that they had. The 1996 Census was credible. First, Taylor's analysis of the social composition of the 1996 population showed that the housing needs and job requirements of those counted as Indigenous Australians in 1996 were no different *in kind* — if far greater in number — from those revealed in the 1991 count.[21] Second, by considering the Indigenous responses not only to the Census questions but also to the 'Post-Enumeration Surveys' conducted in 1991 and 1996, Hunter concluded that there was more stability than was at first apparent in the numbers identifying as Indigenous Australians. As well, his comparison of three successive Censuses, in respect of the revealed educational qualifications and place of residence, did not demonstrate that the 'new' people were of a different socio-economic character from the 'old'. He warned against doubting that these newly identified people were Indigenous. The 1996 Census was 'sufficiently credible ... to be taken at face value'.[22] Taylor thus made the 1996 Census the basis for a revised estimate of the number of working-age Indigenous Australians in 1991. He used this new 1991 figure not to recalculate the comparison of 1986 with 1991 (this has never been done), but to compare 1991 with 1996 employment outcomes.

Taylor analysed the 1991–96 employment and income trends for five States (not South Australia) and for both Territories.[23] The national expression of these trends was that the Indigenous employment rate grew from 37.0 to 40.7 per cent, the unemployment rate fell from 30.8 to 22.7 per cent, while the labour force participation rate held steady (falling slightly from 53.5 to 52.7 per cent).[24] This represented a 15 per cent increase in the number of employed Indigenous people. Most of this increase in employment was due to CDEP growth of an estimated 68 per cent, compared with a 6.6 per cent rise in the number of non-CDEP Indigenous jobs.[25] Taylor's State- and Territory-based analyses showed minor variations on this national theme. In some States/Territories the growth in non-CDEP jobs matched or slightly exceeded the growth in numbers of working-age Indigenous Australians (Tasmania, Western Australia, Queensland) and in others (Victoria, New South Wales, Australian Capital Territory) the Indigenous population grew faster than Indigenous jobs.

If CDEP was the 'saviour' of an otherwise stagnant or deteriorating job market, it was also the damnation of the government's striving for income equality. The income poverty of Indigenous Australians, relative to non-Indigenous Australians, Taylor pointed out in each of his State/Territory papers, cannot be relieved by employment growth that is so dependent on CDEP.

Taylor and Hunter projected two labour market outcomes by 2006: one which took only 'mainstream' employment as important and thus classed CDEP participants among the unemployed, the other recognising CDEP as 'employment'. They drew two conclusions:

> First, without the contribution from CDEP scheme employment, labour force statistics for Indigenous Australians would be ... far worse. Second, even with relatively high growth in employment, which allows for an expansion of CDEP scheme work, the employment rate will continue to fall and employment will not improve due to sustained growth in labour supply. Thus, simply to prevent Indigenous labour force status from slipping further behind it will be necessary to maintain a commitment to special employment programs as well as to generate additional outcomes in the mainstream labour market. However, to move beyond this, and attempt to close the gap between Indigenous and other Australians, will require an absolute and relative expansion in Indigenous employment that is without precedent.[26]

Taylor and Hunter considered different ways that the government could define its Indigenous labour market targets. They projected the employment growth (counting CDEP jobs as employment) that would be needed to maintain the current Indigenous employment-to-population ratio (requiring an extra 25 thousand Indigenous jobs by 2006), and match the employment-to-population ratio of non-Indigenous people as it was in 1996 (requiring an extra 77 thousand jobs). They predicted that, if the Howard government were to maintain policies as they were in 1998, the labour market status of Indigenous Australians by the 2001 and 2006 Censuses would be markedly worse than in the 1990s.

At the time of writing (early 2002) we have not yet seen the 2001 Census results, so we cannot compare the trends in Indigenous employment (1996–2001) with past intercensal trends. However, a number of conclusions about the long-term effects of the AEDP can be drawn from CAEPR research:

- All government efforts to increase Indigenous employment have faced an uphill battle in that the working-age Indigenous population has been growing very rapidly. It has been a case of 'running fast to stay in the same spot'.

- Where the AEDP appears to have made an improvement to Indigenous employment, the CDEP program can take most of the credit. This raises the question of whether participation in CDEP is to be counted as 'employment'.

- Even if we count CDEP as 'employment', it is clear that it is a form of employment with an income ceiling. Improvement in employment 'equity' via CDEP does not translate into improvement in income 'equity'.

- There are two kinds of markets for Indigenous labour: those in which CDEP is significant and those in which it is not. It is reasonable to adopt different expectations, strategies and criteria for success in these two different contexts. The evaluation of Indigenous well-being, if it is to be realistic about persistent structures of culture and political economy, must be regionally differentiated.

2
INDIGENOUS CULTURE AND INDIGENOUS CHOICE

If we take Indigenous choice seriously, the disappointing results of the AEDP are open to interpretation. Perhaps they are not so disappointing. Indigenous people's continuing inequality of labour market status could be understood as a reflection of their different 'aspirations', 'values' and choices. If the Indigenous rate of employment continued below the non-Indigenous rate, are we to conclude that the AEDP was *failing* to achieve employment equality? Or was it rather that the policy was *succeeding* in allowing a choice not to be employed?

In answering these questions, the problem is partly methodological. CAEPR has had plenty of data (Census and other) by which to gauge (in)equality of socio-economic outcome; but as I showed in my Introduction, there are no data that can tell us *precisely* the extent to which persistent inequalities reflect Indigenous choice. Yet CAEPR researchers have inferred that Indigenous choice contributes in some way to the pattern and rate of their employment and unemployment. These researchers have imagined what I call the 'choosing Indigenous subject'. This chapter will review the changing terms in which CAEPR researchers have constructed this figure.

WHAT DOES IT MEAN TO BE 'NOT IN THE LABOUR FORCE'?

Although CAEPR researchers have used the Census prolifically to measure the outcomes of the AEDP, they have not done so uncritically. In 1991 Diane Smith found good reasons to doubt the Census category 'not in the labour force'. On the one hand, it could *understate Indigenous unemployment*:

Evidence from surveys and case studies indicates that the unemployment level of Aboriginal people is likely, if anything, to be far higher than official data imply. In a number of cases census statistics appear to underestimate Aboriginal unemployment by as much as 30–40 per cent.[1]

On the other hand, the Census might *underestimate Indigenous employment*, Smith argued in a subsequent (1994) paper, because 'notions of work and employment are culturally specific …'.[2] Smith's 1994 critique of labour market statistics went further than her 1991 questioning of the empirical adequacy of Census data. Her concerns in 1994 were not only empirical but conceptual. In particular, Smith kept faith with a critical element of the Miller Report, in two related respects. First she sought to highlight the possibility of Indigenous 'choice'; second she designated an entity beyond 'the mainstream economy' which makes possible the choices of Indigenous Australians: the 'Aboriginal economy'.

The Census category 'not in the labour force' could disguise and therefore understate culturally specific forms of Indigenous 'employment', she pointed out. Were the Census to count as work all the activities which Indigenous Australians themselves conceive to be 'work', including subsistence activities, then the labour force participation (and 'employment') rates would be much higher than recorded in the Census. Census data could not be meaningful without contextual interpretation through study of ethnographic data. Ethnographic studies give a more dynamic account of regional economic factors than the Census' five-yearly snapshots can convey. As Smith pointed out, there are no Census questions about short-term entry to and exit from the labour force, nor about short-term movement from having a job to being 'unemployed'. Evoking 'distinctly Aboriginal mores' from these ethnographic accounts, she concluded that 'Aboriginal work rhythms and levels of participation in the mainstream labour market need to be considered within a context of kin-based resource networks and structures of reciprocity, as well as in relation to seasonal cycles and population mobility'.[3] She noted that Indigenous peoples' opportunistic engagement with the labour market was reinforced by the nature of labour demand in remote regions: 'predominantly part-time, short-term and in the community services sector'.[4] In the absence of relevant studies of urban and rural communities, she cautioned against attributing such patterns of engagement exclusively to remote Indigenous people.

Lamenting the 'gap between statistical representations and Aboriginal lived experience', Smith cast doubt on the value of Census-based evaluations of the AEDP.[5] To rely on official statistics — and in particular to put faith in that problematic category 'not in the labour force' — is to risk blindness to the possibility that some

Indigenous people *'have chosen a strategically casual attachment to the labour force'*.[6] The status of many Aborigines whom the Census seeks to sort into the three categories, 'employed', 'unemployed' and 'not in labour force', is perhaps better understood by recognising that *'their primary attachment is to the Aboriginal economy* and their access to cash is via welfare transfers and processes of cash redistribution operating in the Aboriginal kin network'.[7]

THE INDIGENOUS ECONOMY AS THE GROUND OF CHOICE

Other CAEPR writers have effectively substantiated the 'Aboriginal economy', in three ways.

First, in a number of papers that I will describe more fully later in this book, Altman and others have attempted to estimate the significance of Indigenous Australians' continuing subsistence activity.[8] Arthur has suggested that subsistence fishing and gardening remains an important source of wealth for Torres Strait Islanders.[9]

Second, Martin and Schwab have attempted to derive from ethnographies a cultural model of the intentions, motives and normative reasoning that are characteristic of exchanges of goods and services among Indigenous Australians. David Martin argues that there is a danger that policy-makers, while ready to acknowledge distinct features of Indigenous language, religion and art, will not recognise distinct '"economic" values and practices' — what he refers to as 'the internal Indigenous economy'.[10] Drawing on his ethnography of Cape York people, Martin argues that they reckon their relatedness to one another in an idiom of kinship and that the flows of goods, money and services between people are conditioned by people's explicit and implicit adherence to concepts of 'love, nurturance, respect and obligation'. Exchanges of food, consumer goods and cash:

> are encoded in the formal structures of kinship, in terms of the system of kin categories by which people are linked, and the associated normative rights and obligations between them. These structures are realised in mundane social life in the interactions and the flows of goods and services between kin. Simultaneously, kinship relations are themselves reproduced by the exchanges and distributions between people.[11]

He speculated that 'such beliefs and practices may well be incompatible with integration into the mainstream economy, through labour market participation or enterprise development ...'.[12] Schwab came to a similar conclusion after adducing from his survey of ethnographies six 'principles of Aboriginal reciprocity'.[13] Their combined implications he summarised as follows:

For many Indigenous Australians, the social and financial support of kin is a more predictable resource than the labour market, and training and job opportunities are often weighed up in terms of costs and benefits to the participant. Consideration of this support system would be important when attempting to understand patterns of mobility among Indigenous Australians; a job or training program which requires movement away (physically or culturally) from a network of kin is a high-risk economic proposition for many Indigenous people. Attractive salaries, travel and accommodation or guarantees of special support and promotion opportunities may not compensate for the loss of social support many Indigenous people feel when entering a mainstream labour market program.[14]

The third way that CAEPR has substantiated what Smith calls 'the Aboriginal economy' has been to pay attention to a finding of the 1994 National Aboriginal and Torres Strait Islander Survey (NATSIS) that Indigenous Australians do a lot of work outside the formal, monetary economy. Respondents were asked whether they did voluntary work, and how many hours per week they devoted to it. The survey nominated only six kinds of activity as 'voluntary work': 'caring for sick or aged people', 'community or sports', 'school or youth group', 'committee work', 'hunting, fishing and gathering', and 'other'. Notwithstanding this restricted definition, Smith and Roach were able to report the significance of 'voluntary work' in the allocation of Indigenous adults' time. They posed questions for research: is voluntary work 'a form of labour market training'? Do voluntary workers who are not employed find employment? Does voluntary work restrict people 'from pursuing paid employment in the mainstream'?[15] These questions, particularly the last, imply the possibility that much 'voluntary work' can be understood to be part of the 'Aboriginal economy' (I will prefer to use the term 'Indigenous economy'), an alternative site and focus of Indigenous working life.

THE OPTIMISING INDIGENOUS CHOOSER

Schwab referred to the 'costs and benefits' to individuals of transferring their efforts from 'the Aboriginal economy' to paid employment in the 'mainstream economy'. In this phrase he implied a notion of the choosing Indigenous subject as a utility optimiser. Other CAEPR writers have also evoked this figure, focusing on the monetary incentives and disincentives that such a person faces.

Daly has measured 'the replacement ratio' for Aboriginal women — that is, 'the extent to which income from welfare compensates for lack of income from employment' — and concluded that Aboriginal women in 1986 had less financial incentive than non-Aboriginal women to enter paid employment.[16] Hunter and Daly, while warning that monetary costs and benefits of employment are a less important explanation for Indigenous joblessness than whether there is a job actually available, have considered a richer variety of circumstances in which Indigenous people may be choosing between employment or welfare.[17] Hunter and Daly calculated costs and benefits according to whether people are single or married (*de facto* or *de jure*), and whether the work on offer was CDEP or non-CDEP. They also differentiated according to their numbers of dependants, and according to the individual's position in the life cycle. They calculated also the monetary disincentives of moving in the opposite direction — leaving or losing a job. In their conclusion they acknowledged 'many other reasons why Indigenous Australians have high unemployment rates, for example their geographical dispersion, any discrimination against them and *lifestyle preferences*'.[18] Their conception of what went on inside a choosing Indigenous subject thus combined 'lifestyle' choice and income maximising.

WELFARE DEPENDENCE

A lifestyle-choosing Indigenous subject is also the implied central figure in the syndrome known as 'welfare dependence'. However, the phrase 'welfare dependence' introduces researchers' doubts as to how wisely this figure chooses.

Altman and Sanders titled the first CAEPR Discussion Paper 'From exclusion to dependence: Aborigines and the welfare state in Australia'. They remarked that 'escaping from dependence on the welfare state is a legitimate and important goal both for Aboriginal people and for Aboriginal affairs policy'.[19] What did they mean by 'welfare dependence'? Altman and Smith queried the AEDP policy statement's definition: being in receipt of Unemployment Benefits.[20] They preferred a wider definition: receipt of any transfer payment from the Commonwealth government.

Whether one uses the CAEPR or the Commonwealth definition, the phrase 'welfare dependence', as Fraser and Gordon have pointed out, is heavy with socio-psychological connotations.[21] It points not only to source of income but also to a problematic subjectivity among the recipients of welfare and a social milieu ripe for some kind of remedial intervention. Accordingly, in the CAEPR literature, the phrase 'welfare dependence' co-exists uneasily with the notion of 'Aboriginal economy'. Some CAEPR commentaries have attempted to link these terms sympathetically, noting that welfare payments complement some Aboriginal people's subsistence activity. Altman and Smith suggest that 'in the face of fluctuating and recently decreasing employment opportunities in many parts of Australia, welfare may represent a source of more reliable income for many Aboriginal people and provide a degree of economic autonomy and security lacking in employment'.[22] The phrase 'welfare dependence' does not necessarily deny that Indigenous people on welfare may be involved in subsistence and voluntary work and in personally meaningful exchanges, both monetary and non-monetary, with other Indigenous Australians reckoned as 'kin'. However, the effect of the connotations of 'welfare dependence' is usually to push these positive possibilities into the background and to highlight the vulnerability of the Indigenous recipients. Thus Altman and Smith say that 'those relying on welfare are in a dependent situation vulnerable to changes in government policy' and that some income units are in a 'poverty trap'.[23] (It is not clear how many Indigenous Australians see such risks in their reliance on welfare. When reporting fieldwork in Kuranda and Yuendumu in 1999, Smith noted that no Indigenous person interviewed had identified as a problem their reliance on welfare income.[24])

Some CAEPR writings on 'welfare dependence', not taking up the question of its relationship with the Indigenous economy, have attempted to specify its constitutive features — what Daly and Hawke called 'the underlying sources of this welfare dependence'.[25] Regression analysis of Census data has been their characteristic method of investigation. Daly found from her regression analyses of 1986 Census data that, even when Aborigines were equal in education to non-Aborigines, they were less likely to have a job. Referring to this result as 'a strong negative Aboriginal effect', she speculated about its possible behavioural constituents:[26]

> [M]any Aborigines living traditional lifestyles may not be interested in entering the formal labour market. Alternatively, those in remote areas may have been discouraged by the absence of jobs in these regions and ceased to think of themselves as members of a formal labour market. This 'discouraged worker' effect may also apply in the more settled parts of Australia if employers discriminate against Aborigines and are unwilling to employ them at the award wages set by the Industrial Relations Commission.[27]

As she remarked, 'The social security system does not discriminate according to race but employers may do so'.[28]

By showing what Census-defined socio-economic characteristics were statistically associated with being in receipt of government transfer payments, regression analyses gave Daly a kind of social profile of 'welfare dependency'. There began to be fleshed out in CAEPR literature a bundle of social and cultural characteristics, understood by Daly to be the 'underlying factors' of 'welfare dependency'. As Daly acknowledged, her data and mode of analysis could not lead her to any conclusions about the significance of Indigenous people's *choices* as a determinant of their 'welfare dependency'. Her comments on 'welfare dependence' have allowed for the possible significance of Indigenous choices. For example, she remarked that Indigenous welfare recipients 'may not be interested in entering the formal labour market'.[29] Her work does not put forward a notion of the Indigenous subject as simply *determined* by the variables teased out in her regression analyses.

Because the 'welfare dependent' (whether 'unemployed' or not in the labour force) were much more likely to be 'poor' (using Henderson's definition of poverty) there was a convergence, in the CAEPR literature, between the characterisations of Indigenous 'welfare dependency' and of Indigenous 'poverty'.[30] However, CAEPR researchers have generally been more cautious in defining 'poverty' than in defining 'welfare dependency'. Such caution bespeaks their sensitivity to the ways that Indigenous values play a part in their choice of livelihood and in Indigenous evaluations of their own material conditions. 'Any discussion of changes in Indigenous poverty over time', warned Altman and Hunter, should recognise 'emerging Indigenous priorities, as increasingly articulated by Indigenous people themselves'.[31] That is, Indigenous people, in making choices about the way they live, contribute to their measured material well-being, or lack of it. Altman and Hunter gave examples of such choices. Some choices will stretch the Indigenous dollar further. Apparently 'poor' Indigenous people might be better off than they seem because research has difficulty quantifying the fruits of their hunting, fishing and gathering. As well, if people choose to live in large households, they might enjoy economies of scale in child-rearing. Other choices, such as preferring to live in a remote community where transported goods cost more, will diminish the purchasing power of their dollar.[32]

THE NATIONAL ABORIGINAL AND TORRES STRAIT ISLANDER SURVEY (NATSIS) AND THE DIMENSIONS OF INDIGENOUS POVERTY

Hunter has gone further than any other CAEPR researcher to determine by statistical analysis some of the characteristics of Indigenous poverty. However, some of the variables to which he has paid attention do not necessarily imply a picture of Indigenous people strategically regulating the degree of their engagement with the mainstream economy. Rather, many of the variables of interest to Hunter are better understood as indices of misfortune and social pathology. In 1996 he showed that urban Indigenous people were concentrated in suburbs that have fared poorly in the structural changes in the Australian economy. He speculated that residential concentration in poor parts of cities 'will increase the risk that the urban Indigenous population are either exposed to or involved in crime', leading to their reduced involvement in education, training and (licit) paid employment.[33] He speculated as well that there may be 'institutional or other impediments' to 'Indigenous people choosing freely where to live'.[34]

Hunter found in the 1994 NATSIS data a rich array of social variables whose relationship with employment outcomes he could analyse by statistical methods. He identified as significant such factors as: whether a person had been arrested, whether a person had voted in a recent election, whether they had a long-term health condition, whether a person had been removed from his/her family as a child. Though arrest emerged as the single most significant variable associated with employment, Hunter and Borland warned that their analysis did not determine 'the direction of causality between arrest and Indigenous employment'.[35] Notwithstanding the lack of a clear causal connection between variables, their study expanded the range of factors that could be considered as associated with Indigenous employment, with 'unemployment' and with not participating in the labour force. Whereas previous studies had considered those not in employment in terms of their 'educational attainment, employment history, number of dependent children, English-language ability, and location', it was now possible to add variables measured in the NATSIS such as 'whether the respondent speaks an Indigenous language, voted in any recent election, has a long-term health condition, spent time in hunting and gathering activities in the previous year, had ever drunk alcohol'.[36] The NATSIS, in Hunter's analysis, enriched the possibilities for describing 'the social environment in which individuals make decisions about labour supply and labour demand'. Indigenous Australians' high arrest rate was the outstanding feature of that social environment.[37]

In adding new dimensions to our picture of Indigenous deprivation, Hunter was not trying to identify the factors 'underlying' it. Rather he attempted to disturb received wisdom about what Indigenous poverty is; housing, health, justice and 'affinity with land' were, in his view, variables relevant to their well-being or their unhappiness. Noting poor outcomes in these non-monetary spheres, Hunter argued that even among the relatively well-off Indigenous households there was deprivation. It was therefore inappropriate to focus solely on income poverty. 'Inadequate housing, high arrest rates, poor health and a dislocation from traditional lands are a common experience in Indigenous households irrespective of their income.'[38] 'Simply increasing the financial resources available to the Indigenous poor may not be sufficient to alleviate their poverty.'[39] Nonetheless, income poverty had a special place in Hunter's account of Indigenous poverty. He found that labour force status was strongly associated with income poverty —

far stronger than the associations between Indigenous income and education, arrest rates, health and geographical variables. Arrest rates, however, were indirectly associated with income because of their strong association with poor labour force status and educational attainment.

Towards the end of this attempt to give a multi-dimensional account of Indigenous poverty, Hunter raised the question of Indigenous Australians' 'social alienation' — their possible lack of 'the desire to participate fully in Australian society' — as a factor helping to perpetuate their poverty.[40] In two subsequent papers (one devoted to the employed, the other to the unemployed) he has attempted empirically to specify 'alienation' and inclusion.

WORK AND SOCIAL INCLUSION

Using data from the 1995 Australian Workplace Industrial Relations Survey (AWIRS) of 2001 workplaces, Hunter and Hawke found significant differences between the 725 workplaces that did and the 1066 workplaces that did not include Indigenous Australian employees. Indigenous workers were more likely to be in the public sector, in government business enterprises, in charities, churches and non-governmental welfare bodies. The workplaces in which Indigenous employees were more likely to be found were more likely to be governed by written workplace agreements covering such matters as grievance procedures (for racial and sexual harassment), occupational health and safety, leave arrangements, training, and measures against racial and sexual discrimination. In short, they were 'qualitatively different from other workplaces' because they 'use industrial relations practices consistent with encouraging greater cultural diversity within the firm'.[41]

As I will show in the next chapter, CAEPR studies of Community Development Employment Project schemes have made it clear that Indigenous employees are sensitive to variations in the 'culture' of workplaces: they make employment choices partly according to their perceptions of work's social dimension. Work is one place where Indigenous people feel themselves to be at risk of racial vilification. Indigenous people's 'social inclusion' via the daily workplace depends partly on whether management is aware that workplace social dynamics may in some places invite and in others spurn the Indigenous worker.

Two points are worthy of emphasis. First, the choice facing Indigenous people is not merely job or no job. Within the option 'job' there may be a vast range of social experiences afforded by work. Some places of employment have a racist culture or simply allow Indigenous people to feel isolated from their own kind;

some places of employment make an effort (of one kind or another) to make the Indigenous person feel that they belong there. Second, an Indigenous person seeking a daily feeling of security may find it either in avoiding employment or in accepting only employment in a sympathetic workplace. To be jobless may *enhance* an Indigenous person's social 'inclusion' in his/her 'own group, if the alternative is to be employed in a place that one feels to be unwelcoming and hostile to one's cultural identity', as Hunter conceded in his paper on 'social capital'. He argued that unemployment may empower a person to build up their 'social capital', in the sense of their positive involvement with other Indigenous people.[42] In making this point, Hunter acknowledged the efforts by Smith and others to substantiate the 'Indigenous economy' in some early CAEPR papers (see above). However, Hunter's primary interest in his 2000 paper was to identify the 'social costs' of unemployment, and he effectively ignored, in the rest of his paper, the 'social benefits' that might come from not having a paid job.

Hunter suggested that we distinguish between the different kinds of Indigenous social solidarity. Some are 'useful' to the individual, others are detrimental. As he explained, 'the main problem stemming from low levels of social capital is not necessarily the lack of any network, but rather the lack of a "useful" network'.[43] He pointed to some ways in which it might be less than 'useful' for an Indigenous person to be socially integrated with networks of Indigenous people lacking employment:

> [A] downward levelling of norms and expectations about employment prospects may result from a lengthy period of discrimination and restricted labour market mobility. If Indigenous social networks are largely confined to the jobless, then such reductions in expectations can become a self-fulfilling prophecy whereby people fail to see the advantages in gaining further education. This, in turn, diminishes the skill acquisition that facilitates entry into the labour market. This downward levelling of norms is often associated with socially unacceptable codes of conduct.[44]

Here Hunter is evoking a choosing Indigenous subject. However, this figure's most important attribute is his/her diminishing quality of choice. The forces determining that decline are two: the objective features of the labour market, and the interpretive frames that are available to him/her to make sense of the frustration of job searching. The second factor ('downward levelling of norms') is the crucial one for Hunter in this paper, and it gives rise to his Appendix, an essay on the application of the concept 'social capital' to Indigenous culture, in which he lists 'positive' and 'negative' consequences of Indigenous 'social capital'.[45]

Hunter's positive consequences are 'bounded solidarity', 'enforceable trust', 'family support' (including distributions of 'collective resources'), and the possibility of securing 'network-mediated benefits beyond the immediate family'.[46] Negative consequences of Indigenous social capital are 'the exclusion of outsiders' (restricting access to resources which would benefit Indigenous people, such as 'education, employment, or financial resources' and health services), 'excessive' claims that Indigenous Australians make upon one another's resources, 'restrictions on the freedom of individuals', and the 'downward levelling of norms' which reinforces Indigenous Australians' 'failure to see the value of gaining further education'.[47]

In making these distinctions, Hunter cited Schwab. He could also have cited Martin and Smith, CAEPR authors who have attempted also to substantiate the notion 'Indigenous economy'.[48] Hunter has taken their notion of 'the Indigenous economy' and, reading it through the concept of 'social capital', drawn attention what he calls its 'dark side'.[49] (This was perhaps an unfortunate choice of words.)

CONCLUSION

Let me review the trajectory of the CAEPR construction of the choosing Indigenous subject. Recall that the Miller Report linked two objectives of government policy: the economic development and the self-determination of Indigenous Australians. The key move in the Miller Report was to argue that 'livelihood' remained a matter of Indigenous people's choice. Choice was doubly significant. On the one hand, to choose a 'livelihood' was to choose a 'lifestyle' and thus to make a crucial decision about the ways in which Indigenous forms of life were or were not to be socially reproduced. On the other hand, choosing a livelihood would have effects on the chooser's employment status and on his/her income levels.

I have discerned three phases in CAEPR writers' consideration of these 'livelihood' choices.

In the first phase, some CAEPR writers confidently referred to an Indigenous social order that remained distinguishable from the wider Australian society. In particular, it was argued that there was such a thing as an Indigenous economy, with its own norms and practices. Bearing in mind the continuing attractions of the Indigenous economy, it was possible to make sense of the presence or absence of Indigenous Australians within the officially defined labour market as the outcome of their choice between the lifestyles characteristic of paid employment (or the resolute search for paid employment) and the lifestyles made possible by giving priority, at least some of the time, to the claims made on one's time by other Indigenous Australians. Ethnography was the characteristic knowledge base for this way of imagining Indigenous options.

In the second phase, the fact that many Indigenous people were not employed and/or not even in the labour force was taken to be more problematic. Using Census data, researchers looked for factors associated with Indigenous people's entering the labour force and getting jobs, or not. One factor was found to be the financial disincentive to give up welfare payments, though researchers expressed reasonable uncertainty about the degree to which monetary considerations were salient for Indigenous people. Other factors associated with non-employment were education, region, marital status and responsibility for children. The phrase 'welfare dependency' was prominent in this phase of CAEPR writing, and the regression analyses of Census data seemed to flesh out 'welfare dependency' as a social syndrome of 'underlying factors' that might help to explain the failure of Indigenous people to move into paid employment.

In the third phase, the emphasis in CAEPR literature shifted from 'welfare dependency' to 'poverty'. 'Poverty' was a more inclusive notion in two senses. First, whether one's income came from employment or from welfare transfers was only one ingredient (though a powerful one) of poverty. It was possible to be waged and yet poor. Thus the phenomena of Indigenous 'welfare dependency' and Indigenous 'poverty' overlapped but were not synonymous. Second, it was argued that income is only one of the dimensions of Indigenous poverty that should attract the attention of governments. Hunter's efforts to develop a more socially grounded and multidimensional description of Indigenous poverty have been based on his exploration (more far-reaching than any other CAEPR researcher) of associations between variables in the NATSIS database. Indeed, the existence of the NATSIS made possible this third phase of CAEPR investigation of disadvantage. By adding a suite of 'social' variables whose association with employment status can be measured, the NATSIS has enabled Hunter, in particular, to rethink how to construct a policy-relevant definition of 'Indigenous culture'. He has selected some NATSIS variables to specify the concepts 'social capital' and 'social inclusion'.

Hunter's reading of the self-limiting possibilities of the 'Indigenous economy' in the context of Indigenous 'social capital' was innovative in its terminology, but not in its fundamental ambivalence about the cultural bases of Indigenous choice. For we can find that same ambivalence in one of the very earliest of CAEPR papers, Altman and Sanders' 1991 argument for AEDP 'policy realism'.

By drawing attention in this paper to the deep roots of employment inequality, Altman and Sanders questioned the 'realism' of making equality — in employment status and income — an objective of policy. They identified four deep factors militating against the achievement of such equality:

1   that the exclusion of Aborigines from beneficial government programs had only recently been terminated;

2   that the age structure of the Indigenous population was relatively young;

3   that many Aborigines lived far from where labour was in demand ('locational disadvantage'); and

4   the possible cultural inappropriateness of employment.[50]

Elaborating on this fourth factor, they explained that 'in the urban and rural areas, the question of the cultural appropriateness of employment ... may have as much to do with how regular employment fits with *a pervasive community culture of poverty and unemployment, as with a tradition-oriented culture*'.[51] In proposing this duality of Indigenous cultures — a culture of poverty and 'tradition-oriented' culture — Altman and Sanders made a space for researchers' discriminating judgment about the cultural bases of Indigenous people's detachment from the labour market. Perhaps some of that detachment reflected the Indigenous culture of poverty, they implied, rather than the cultural richness of the Indigenous way of life.

If in the Miller Report Indigenous lifestyle choice is implied to be instrinsically worthy of respect (so that Miller could even see it as the basis of a 'right' to choose lifestyles), in the CAEPR corpus there has long been another possibility: an Indigenous 'culture of poverty' from which bad choices might flow. Whereas Miller had postulated a sovereign adaptive Indigenous chooser of lifestyles, Altman and Sanders were concerned from as early as 1991 that some lifestyle choices could work against the economic development of the chooser. They thus rendered such choices problematic, as possibly being among the deepest roots of labour market injustice. CAEPR's subsequent work has entertained a number of different ways of describing the Indigenous cultures that ground Indigenous choice. The papers I have reviewed in this chapter have thus displayed the conceptual and ethical ambivalence of social policy intellectuals towards 'Indigenous culture'.

The significance of 'choice' in the Miller Report was not exceptional in the policy tradition relevant to CAEPR's work. ATSIC echoed and endorsed 'choice' in 1994 when reviewing the AEDP. The AEDP was intended to support self-determined economic development by:

- enabling Aboriginal and Torres Strait Islander people to *make effective choices* about the extent and nature of their participation in business and labour markets;

- enabling equitable participation in the general labour market *for those who seek it*;

- enabling maximum independence for Aboriginal and Torres Strait Islander communities through assistance to develop their local economies;

- enabling expansion of employment opportunities in both the general labour market and community-based employment to increase Aboriginal and Torres Strait Islanders employment to at least the national average; and

- ensuring program support is *relevant to, and consistent with*, Aboriginal and Torres Strait Islander *social, cultural and economic circumstances and values.*[52]

While policy continues to value choice in the way that Miller and ATSIC have done, policy evaluations and wider public debate will continue to be ambivalent in the characterisation of Indigenous orientations and motivations.

3
THE PROBLEM OF MOTIVATION IN EDUCATION, TRAINING AND EMPLOYMENT

Do we know what motivates Indigenous Australians to 'better' themselves? Are there clear and uncontested meanings of 'better'? These questions arise when we examine what CAEPR researchers have said about a number of themes concerned in the evaluation of the AEDP: the industrial and occupational distribution of Indigenous employees, and the involvement of Indigenous Australians in education and training.

THE INDIVIDUAL VALUE OF EDUCATION AND TRAINING

CAEPR researchers acknowledge that education, while important, is not the only determinant of Indigenous labour market outcomes. CAEPR's collective understanding of the significance of education by the mid-1990s can best be described as intelligently ambivalent.

On the one hand, CAEPR researchers have promoted the view that it would help Indigenous Australians if governments enabled them to get more education. Daly's research, for example, showed it was still well worth having a university education. A degree was strongly associated with getting higher incomes for Indigenous men and women.[1] Daly and Liu developed this point, distinguishing between the relatively low-income incentive to complete secondary school, with the relatively high incentive to get a post-secondary qualification. They offered the following explanations: for low rewards of secondary education, they identified 'the lesser attachment of Indigenous people to the labour force and many difficulties they face in retaining well-paid employment'; for high rewards of post-secondary education, that those who complete secondary school and get a post-secondary qualification 'are particularly highly motivated and able individuals' who are likely also to benefit from 'positive discrimination in favour of Indigenous Australians in both the public and the private sectors'.[2] Hunter used the NATSIS to find out the statistical relationships between education and employment, in the context of other variables not included in the Census, such as having poor health and being arrested. He found that education far exceeded other variables in its influence on whether or not an Indigenous person was employed.[3]

There is evidence of a strong rise in Indigenous participation in labour market training in the early 1990s. Using the DEET (Department of Employment, Education and Training) database for 1992–95 (in which time the number of participants doubled), Taylor and Hunter examined characteristics of Indigenous clients of labour market programs. They noted that the proportions of trainees in Indigenous-specific programs declined relative to those in mainstream programs. As well, 46 per cent of clients had more than one placement in the period 1990–95.[4] The NATSIS showed eight per cent of Indigenous persons aged 15+ had participated in training programs (of all kinds) in the previous 12 months. What were the rewards? Taylor and Hunter found that 'both males and females who had attended a training course in the 12 months prior to the survey were more likely to be in employment at the time of the survey than those who had not attended a training course. In addition, they were far more likely to be employed in non-CDEP jobs ... [T]raining was significantly associated with being employed even after controlling for other underlying factors such as age, educational attainment and location'.[5] This association was particularly strong for rural females.

Aware that non-Indigenous Australians were also benefiting from these training programs, Taylor and Hunter suggested that if Indigenous job-seekers were to be helped to compete with others, their prospects would have to be assessed region by region, since regions vary significantly in their labour supply and demand characteristics. 'To ensure that Indigenous job seekers are not left behind in a changing labour market there is need for regional estimation of likely areas of employment growth (and decline) and an attempt to focus training and work experience towards matching supply with anticipated demand.'[6] The main source of job growth in rural and remote regions was CDEP, they noted. CDEP's training function was important and required government support.

What returns were Indigenous people getting from their increasing participation in schooling and training between the 1986 and 1996 Censuses? Indigenous Australians were not turning their back on the economic opportunities that education offers. However, the anticipated economic rewards were diminished by the fact that non-Indigenous rates of participation in education also increased from 1986 to 1996. The 1994 AEDP review 'found it difficult to explain a gap between high levels of [training] program participation and a low net increase in employment outcomes between 1986 and 1991'.[7] One way to interpret this result is to understand 'human capital' in relative terms. Relative to non-Indigenous levels of education, Indigenous people did not become better endowed with human capital. Perhaps it is their relative, not their absolute, educational attainment which serves the employer as a predictor of Indigenous people's productivity, suggested Gray, Hunter and Schwab.[8] With an 'absolute improvement, but relative decline, in Indigenous education outcomes ... it is clear that the Indigenous people will fall further behind the non-Indigenous population's labour market outcomes and there may well be an absolute worsening of the Indigenous labour market position'.[9]

This *relative* decline of Indigenous human capital is an effect not only of choices made by Indigenous parents and students but also of the choices that non-Indigenous people have been making. The nexus, education-employment-income, is affected by structural changes in the Australian economy (in particular, movement to more knowledge-based industries that require specific credentials and experience in their work force, such as IT skills). The adaptive responses that the numerically dominant non-Indigenous people make to such structural change may have improved their job prospects relative to those of Indigenous job-seekers. Of course, this pattern of relative decline in the 'human capital' of Indigenous workers applies to the total populations of Indigenous and non-Indigenous Australians. It does not mean that it was futile or irrational for *individual* Indigenous people to 'make an investment' in their own education and training. The significance of the 'relational' notion of human capital suggested by Gray, Hunter and Schwab is rather that it gives policy-makers another explanation for the failure of total increases in Indigenous 'human capital' to give effect to higher Indigenous employment rates and incomes in the aggregate.

CAEPR AND INDIGENOUS MOTIVATION

In 1995 CAEPR researcher Jerry Schwab reviewed twenty years of policy-making about Indigenous education. The main problems to which policy has been addressed have been Indigenous people's lower rates of participation in the formal system of education and their lower levels of qualification. Should 'equity' in participation and outcome (with non-Indigenous Australians) be the aim of policy? he asked. 'Statistical equality in Indigenous education in the immediate future may remain elusive for the same reasons that economic equality has', he remarked.[10] To make a fetish of 'equality' between Indigenous and non-Indigenous Australians obscured important differences of need, he pointed out. Thus, he queried the aggregation of figures on Indigenous educational access, participation and outcomes 'without reference to what are sharply different contexts ...' of remote and urban areas. As well, he highlighted 'the very different lifestyle choices and beliefs about education of Indigenous people', arguing that they 'call into question simple blanket comparisons with other Australians. It cannot be assumed that choices, needs, and outcomes are constant either within or among Indigenous communities or between Indigenous and other Australian communities'.[11]

In a subsequent paper Schwab summarised what he saw as the three main orientations to education to be found among Indigenous Australians:

> ... for one community, education may be viewed as the avenue to equity in employment opportunity; for another, it is a means to increased facility with the tools and conventions of a second (the dominant) culture; for a third, education may be one of a series of mechanisms for ensuring the continuing vitality of Indigenous culture.[12]

Rather than assume that any one of these orientations could be the basis of Indigenous education policy, researchers and policy-makers should pay careful attention to the following issues: student motivations; what it means in practice to 'consult' Indigenous Australians; and the extent of the demand for Indigenous-controlled institutions.[13] The critical issues, he concluded 'are not the "what", "who" and "how" questions of education policy, but the "why" questions ... related to what Indigenous education is all about, what it promises, and what it ultimately can and cannot deliver to Indigenous people'.[14] In commending this open-minded, empirical approach to a consideration of Indigenous aims and motivations, Schwab particularly encouraged alternatives to 'a human capital model wherein education is seen to be an investment from which both the individual and ultimately the nation benefit'.[15]

In this chapter I will show that all of CAEPR's research on education can be understood as a more or less critical dialogue with 'human capital theory'.

EDUCATION AND EMPLOYMENT

In one of CAEPR's earliest considerations of the AEDP, Bruce Chapman stated what he saw as the essence of the human capital perspective: 'the treatment of skill acquisition as an investment process':

> Workers are seen to face choices concerning training, including education and on-the-job skill attainment, in that gaining skills entails costs, the most important of these being the foregone income associated with the training. The benefits for workers from the process are seen to accrue in the form of improved job opportunities, most obviously with regard to increased wages and reduced unemployment probabilities.[16]

Chapman acknowledged that there was much that the human capital approach could not explain. For example, the 'variations in the measurable human capital between men and women in Australia and the United States contribute almost nothing to an explanation of the large differences in the sex earnings ratios between the two countries'. On that basis he hypothesised that human capital differences may not be significant contributors to the difference between Aboriginal and non-Aboriginal labour market outcomes.[17] Chapman's analysis of 1986 Census data found that the human capital perspective 'falls a long way short of explaining average income differences between Aboriginal and non-Aboriginal males'.[18]

However, the educational attainments of Indigenous Australians were not irrelevant to their employment and income prospects. Subsequent cross-sectional analyses of Census data encouraged CAEPR researchers to highlight education's *possible* contribution to achieving income and employment 'equity'.[19]

Those researchers preoccupied with the labour market benefits of education were, like Schwab, concerned about the relationship between the Aboriginal Education Policy (AEP) and AEDP. Daly pointed out that the aims of Indigenous 'education' might be subordinated to the AEDP's striving for labour market and income 'equity'; specifically, Daly was worried about:

> a conflict between the incentives offered under AEDP employment programs (eg the CDEP scheme) and the AEP programs to promote school retention. The offer of part-time employment within the community under the CDEP scheme may discourage individuals from leaving home in pursuit of further education. While not wishing to under-estimate the wider social benefits which may arise from this choice, it may have important implications for an individual's future income potential.[20]

That is, one AEDP program (the CDEP) might dissuade some Indigenous Australians' 'investment' in education.

Thus Indigenous 'choice' again became a research theme. Just as CAEPR's writing on the category 'not in the labour force' provoked researchers to speculate about the Indigenous culture from which 'choice' was made (Chapter 2), so there has been a speculative model of Indigenous motivation running through CAEPR writing about education and the labour market. CAEPR researchers, while sometimes evoking the Indigenous person as an 'investor' responding to 'incentives', also found reasons to doubt that this was all there was to Indigenous motivations.

For example, when they considered the 'problem' of the occupational and industrial distribution of Indigenous employees, CAEPR researchers admitted that they were uncertain about what made Indigenous Australians who were employed prefer certain industries and occupations. Was it income, or something else?

EMPLOYMENT MOTIVATION AND THE INDIGENOUS SECTOR

In an early CAEPR paper, Taylor noted what he called 'an Aboriginal sector' in the labour market.[21] 'In many places, the main employers of Aboriginal people are Aboriginal organisations as well as the State and Commonwealth departments responsible for the delivery of services to the Aboriginal population.' CAEPR researchers were at first prompted by the AEDP's aims to see this concentration of Indigenous labour as a failure of policy. If Indigenous Australians are concentrated in certain jobs and in certain industries and if these jobs and industries suffer a downturn, or fail to grow quickly, then the consequent loss of demand for labour (even if it is only a relative loss) will be borne disproportionately by Indigenous Australians. Indigenous Australians would be better off, some CAEPR researchers suggested, if they were distributed over occupations and industries in the same proportions as all Australian employees. In CAEPR's exploration of this theme, researchers found themselves speculating about the motivations of Indigenous Australians.

John Taylor used Census data to measure the maldistribution — the 'over-representation' and 'under-representation' — of Indigenous Australians in certain industries and occupations. Analysing 1986 Census data, for example, he found Indigenous males (and to a lesser extent, females) to be over-represented in 'welfare' and in 'charitable services and community organisations', reflecting 'the crucial role played by Aboriginal and Islander organisations in providing a focus of local employment in many communities'.[22] Other significant employers were: alcohol rehabilitation centres, refuge operations, family welfare agencies and child-minding services. That is, Indigenous employers were 'over-represented' in the public sector 'whether funded directly by government or via a community organisation servicing the Aboriginal [or Torres Strait Islander] population'.[23] He worried that 'Aboriginal and Islander employment is dependent upon a very narrow industry base supported to a large extent by public expenditure'.[24] From the standpoint of the government's AEDP — aiming for 'statistical equality in employment distribution' — this was a problem.[25]

A related dimension of 'statistical equality in employment distribution' was the distribution of Indigenous employees between the private and public sectors. Here there arose a problem of definition. As Altman and Taylor pointed out in their analysis of 1986 and 1991 Census data, many employers of Indigenous Australians are 'private' in the sense of not being part of the three tiers of government, but 'public' in the sense of 'dependent entirely on public subsidy'. (It is this kind of difficulty that encourages me to put forward the term 'Indigenous Sector'.) They suggested a new, stricter definition of 'private': 'those economic activities that do not depend primarily on government funding for their existence'.[26] 'Indigenous people', they observed, 'are growing more reliant on employment that is dependent for its continuation on special government support'. They found this to be a worrying trend because 'experience in the United States shows that employment in the public sector, while safe and reliable (to a degree, given the recent experience of public sector downsizing), creates upper limits on rewards. The real gains to income are acquired through participation in private sector activity'.[27]

But was this pattern not a result of Indigenous choices? 'Whether rural- or urban-based, participation in publicly-funded community service activities may precisely reflect employment aspirations.' Altman and Taylor conceded that for many Indigenous Australians, maximising income might not be the overriding objective. If Indigenous Australians valued rewards other than high incomes, such as the social gratifications of working with and for their own people, was it plausible to model Indigenous Australians as 'investors' in education, as in 'human capital' theory?[28] How were we to understand and to measure the return on that 'investment'?

'Job segregation' and 'industry segregation' (the corollaries of 'over-' and 'under-representation') continued to intrigue John Taylor. He calculated indices of industry and occupational segregation for the Northern Territory, from 1986 and 1991 Census data, finding reinforcement of 'a distinctly Indigenous segment in the regional labour market': 'community services' tended towards being an Indigenous enclave, while 'manufacturing' was a non-Indigenous enclave.[29] The top five industry classes for employed Indigenous people in the Northern Territory in 1991 were: community services (not elsewhere classified), local government administration, community services undefined, Territory government administration, Commonwealth government administration.[30] However, he warned that 'community services n.e.c.' embraced a great variety of jobs (from stacking shelves in a remote community store to screen-printing Indigenous designed t-shirts). Taylor feared that investors in the Northern Territory were more likely to stimulate growth in industries and occupations in which Indigenous people were 'under-represented'. He recommended that Indigenous Australians be trained to take jobs in industries and occupations in which there was likely to be the highest job growth, though he did not attempt to predict what industries, jobs and skills these were. Unless Indigenous Australians spread into industries and occupations in which they were now under-represented, he warned, their low levels of income would be entrenched.[31]

Taylor and Liu were similarly disturbed by their Australia-wide analysis of changes in industrial and occupational distribution, 1986–1991.[32] Though 'community services' and 'public administration' were expected (in government projections) to grow by 2001, Taylor and Liu worried that Indigenous workers were 'potentially vulnerable to the vagaries of government spending'.[33] They acknowledged, however, that 'participation in a limited range of industries may be precisely in keeping with employment aspirations especially if this involves work in a more culturally-attuned situation', notwithstanding the characteristically lower incomes of such industries.[34] They noted that jobs in community organisations required not only skills 'used by public sector officers' but also 'other skills which are more culturally derived'.[35] 'Culturally derived' skills are not obtained by an investment in formal education, but through informal processes of Indigenous socialisation — another reason to question the relevance of 'human capital' theory. As well, Taylor and Liu speculated that the social honour associated with such occupations may be specific to Indigenous Australians' scale of values. Human capital theory, by contrast, has made money the universal unit for comparing the rewards of employment.

Taylor and Liu's analysis implied that a pattern of employment that compromised one government goal (Indigenous under-representation in jobs with high incomes) might arise in part from Indigenous choices. Taylor acknowledged that it was not only people's qualifications that determined their industry and occupation:

> On the surface, industries that under-employ Aborigines and Islanders appear to share high human capital requirements, such as medicine, education, accounting, and various trades-based industries. Equally, however, there are many examples, such as cafes and restaurants, department stores, and banks, where this is less likely to be the case and where factors such as discrimination or personal choice may be more responsible. In some industries, therefore, the general thrust of the Aboriginal Education Policy towards upgrading Aboriginal and Islander skills may be beneficial in bringing about greater equality in employment distribution. In other cases, however, attempts at raising the level of human capital may prove ineffective owing to Aboriginal and Islander preferences in the labour market.[36]

On the one hand, the continuing and deepening occupational and industrial segregation of Indigenous and non-Indigenous jobs, particularly outside urban areas, could be represented as a failure to realise the AEDP's goals of statistical equality of income, occupational distribution and industrial distribution. On the other hand, the goals of the policy of self-determination would seem to be realised in those same labour market patterns. Clearly, the CAEPR researchers were finding it necessary to investigate Indigenous motivation, rather than let 'human capital' theory provide them with a crude, ready-made model of the Indigenous subject.

Daly found it necessary to speculate about Indigenous aspirations after measuring the strength of association between Indigenous incomes and a number of 'human capital endowments', including level of formal education. She found that education was more strongly associated with non-Aboriginal men's than with Aboriginal men's incomes. A similar, less pronounced, difference was found for women. Why might it be that non-Indigenous people get more (income) from their education 'investment' than Indigenous people do? Perhaps Indigenous people suffer employers' discrimination, she speculated. Or, 'Aboriginal people may make employment choices which do not maximise their monetary income potential' — for example, the choice to live in a remote area, or a preference for casual work.[37]

CAEPR's research on occupational and industrial distribution and on the association between education and income can be read against the (AEDP) grain. This research pointed persistently to a phenomenon that it did not name. Those 'community organisations' in which Indigenous employees are 'over-represented' are part of what I have been calling the Indigenous Sector — which provides jobs where people already live and allows people to work with and for those with whom they have many strong ties of kinship, ceremony and other associations.

If we can read their work with the Indigenous Sector in mind, CAEPR researchers such as Taylor, Liu and Daly offer support for alternative plausible narratives about the distribution of Indigenous employees. One laid emphasis on Indigenous choice and implicitly questioned the assumption that Indigenous motivation was to maximise monetary return on the investment in education, training and job-seeking. In this narrative, Indigenous people were choosing to work in the Indigenous Sector because of its social rewards. The other story pointed not to Indigenous people's choice but to their vulnerability. They had the least pick of jobs because they had the least skills, and the Indigenous Sector loomed large among places of employment where Indigenous Australians felt comfortable, free of racism, social isolation and competitive interactions within people unfamiliar to them.

Choosing or put upon? Both stories are plausible.

THE 'COSTS' OF EDUCATION

So far in this chapter I have dwelled on the ways that the notion of 'human capital' can imply a misleadingly narrow model of Indigenous aspirations. Yet in the CAEPR literature there are studies that liken Indigenous people to 'investors' in education in order to illuminate the Indigenous perspective on education and training. CAEPR's researchers could adapt the notion of the individual 'investor' by attributing to the Indigenous 'investor' different ideas about what was 'costly' and what was 'rewarding' about the investment. 'The problem', wrote Schwab in 1997, 'is that many Indigenous Australians employ a cost benefit analysis for education that is quite different from the analysis of other Australians'.[38]

After examining the distribution of Indigenous tertiary enrolments by institution and field and level of study, Schwab concluded that 'most individuals are not making the sorts of decisions that would most benefit' their incomes.[39] To explain this pattern he suggested that there are some unrecognised costs to Indigenous people when they participate in higher education. That is, to be highly motivated to become educated may place at risk their integration into their community of origin. It is possible for students to hedge that risk by studying courses that would equip them when they graduate to help their community of origin, such as education, nursing or Aboriginal Studies, whatever the monetary rate of return to the individual. As they acquire more education, they 'face a range of new responsibilities and are often called upon to assist people back home and to sit on various committees'.[40] These are onerous demands making further study difficult and possibly unattractive.

Schwab presented the individual Indigenous person as a calculator 'employing a cultural cost-benefit analysis' — a calculator who is very much aware of the costs as well as the benefits of tertiary study.[41] It would be possible to reduce these costs, he argued, for example by modes of educational delivery that minimised students' social isolation.[42] It could also be made easier for them to enrol in courses beyond arts and education; and governments could support community-controlled education providers. He was not confident that governments would act on his recommendations of more culturally appropriate service delivery, however, 'since the attempts to make education more efficient challenge many of the educational desires of Indigenous people'. In particular, 'revised curricula with mandatory inclusion of Aboriginal studies, increases in the numbers of Indigenous teachers and classroom aides, support for special enclave programs, separate facilities within mainstream institutions and in some cases wholly autonomous institutions, including a national Indigenous university ... [and] increased community control of education' would all require 'decentralisation, customisation and diversity in service; all will push costs up and, presumably, efficiency down'.[43] An 'efficient' education system was less likely to produce service diversity and choice for consumers.

In these observations Schwab implied a deeper critique that questions mainstream Australian educational values from the point of view of Indigenous values and expectations. He referred to a tension between 'government economic imperatives and culturally-based Indigenous educational goals'.[44] One way to handle this tension is to subsidise more Indigenous community-controlled education providers. Another is to recognise that 'mainstream' education providers might, in some circumstances, be subject to informal renegotiation of their aims by their Indigenous clients. Schwab's work lends itself to a refocusing of attention — from the calculating individual (and his/her 'costs') to collectively held Indigenous values and their institutional expression.

Schwab has gone so far as to say of one community, Maningrida, that 'the notion of education as an investment is not intuitively obvious to many students or parents'.[45] Maningrida people do not subscribe to the education system's own view of itself as dedicated to the production of economically competent persons. Because Maningrida residents stand at the periphery of the world of paid employment they are able to retain their own ideas about what it is to be a competent person — in their world.

Schwab evoked four themes in the 'intentions, goals and desires' and in the 'choice, strategy and action' of Indigenous residents of Maningrida:[46]

- Maningrida people value the individual autonomy of their children and are reluctant to enforce their attendance at school, even though they think school is good for their children.

- Maningrida people find the social ambience of school strange, 'shaming' and even frightening. This is partly because it is a 'white' place and partly because the school concentrates, within a relatively small space, different categories of Indigenous people who by custom prefer to mingle only a little or not at all. Thus 'school is not merely an intellectual challenge, but a cultural one as well'.[47]

- They have their own ways of accounting for and regulating the flows of goods and money among themselves. They find at school a much-valued practice of food distribution, but they find also a rather different set of rules that govern such 'sharing'.

- They see themselves as being looked after by the school, and from this perspective they see limits to the school's ability to 'boss them around'. Their notions of legitimate school authority do not necessarily mesh with those of school staff.

Maningrida residents' interaction with their school enacts these four ideas. 'What they desire of education is quite different from what the Western institution expects.' They want their school to secure 'cultural competence, cultural maintenance, material resources and social resources'.[48] The co-existence of two such different sets of expectations of schooling (professional v. lay, non-Indigenous v. Indigenous) gives rise to tensions — not least a sense of failure on the part of non-Indigenous authorities. However, according to Schwab, it is possible for the people of Maningrida to find 'equity' in these permanently crossed purposes. He reported that they conceive their education 'as a fundamental right of Australian citizenship won in exchange for allowing non-Aboriginal people onto their traditional lands and into their world'.[49]

DIVERSITY AND CHOICE

In emphasising how sharply Indigenous perspectives *could* differ from those of official providers Schwab was not seeking to make Maningrida views the typical or essential instance of 'the Indigenous' point of view. Indeed, a theme of Schwab's work is the diversity of Indigenous orientations to education. As he has noted, the 1995 *Final Report of the National Review of Education for Aboriginal and Torres Strait Islander Peoples* (henceforth the Yunupingu Review, after its chair Mandawuy Yunupingu) came to the conclusion that among both Indigenous and non-Indigenous people there were three views on Indigenous education:

> According to the first view, equity for Indigenous students can best be achieved through their own adaptation to the 'mainstream'. Equity is ultimately the responsibility of individuals and will only result from individual effort. Underlying this view is the belief that Indigenous students must lift their performance to the level of other Australians. While most proponents of this view realise the need to address structural disadvantage and historical legacy in order to 'level the playing field' the onus is on the individual to take advantage of equal opportunities and — to continue the metaphor — 'lift their game'. Critics of this view claim the mainstream approach is simply assimilationist.[50]

The view evoked in this passage is compatible with the analytic framework of 'human capital' theory in which society is made up of individuals, each of whom determines the extent of his/her 'investment' in education and eventually reaps the reward of that decision. It would be wrong to assume that this view finds no adherents among Indigenous Australians. For example, Arthur and David-Petero sum up their analysis of a small survey (105 respondents) of Torres Strait youth (15–24 years old) with the words: 'As in human capital theory, young Islanders appear to value education and training as a form of investment that will allow them to further their careers'.[51] Young Torres Strait Islanders often spoke of staying at school to improve their prospects for further education, for training and for employment. As well, they said that they found their education 'interesting'. Some mentioned family obligations (including pregnancy) as reasons for leaving school before the end of Year 12, but it was important to them that, when older, they could complete their secondary education through TAFE.

The second perspective on education noted by the Yunupingu Review:

> holds that lower levels of educational performance are not simply an outcome of inadequate individual effort but are related to cultural factors that need to be taken into account in addressing inequity. For example, it may be that differences in Indigenous 'learning styles' affect performance and teachers need to develop appropriate teaching strategies for varied learning styles. Yet this perspective assumes that Indigenous students can and should attain the same educational outcomes as other Australians. According to this view, the existing educational system should promote increases in cultural awareness and sensitivity and should look for solutions which accommodate cultural differences in ways that will enhance the educational performance of Indigenous Australians.[52]

Much of Schwab's work has been within this second perspective, as I have pointed out above — looking for ways that 'the system' can adapt to meet particular circumstances and expectations of Indigenous people.

There is some evidence that Indigenous Australians have found some parts of the education system more adaptive than others. TAFE has turned out to be a 'key provider of post-compulsory education for Indigenous Australians'.[53] Data for one year only (1994 Graduate Outcomes Technical and Further Education 1995 survey) on labour force status of TAFE graduates is consistent with the hypothesis that 'Indigenous completion of a TAFE course not only increases the likelihood of employment, it decreases the likelihood of unemployment, a pattern that differs from that of the general population'.[54] Both Indigenous and non-Indigenous graduates said that the point of their TAFE study was to get a job. However, 'personal development' was nominated more frequently by Indigenous than non-Indigenous graduates, and a larger number of Indigenous than non-Indigenous graduates were taking a further course at time of interview. This is consistent with their over-representation in courses that give basic certificates. As Schwab comments, 'individuals undertake study for a wide range of reasons, and sometimes these reasons may not be propelled by economic considerations.

The educational interests and aspirations of Indigenous people are diverse ...'.[55]

Campbell has summarised research (including Schwab's) that seeks to explain the rapidly increasing Indigenous participation in vocational education and training (VET) in the 1990s. The factors include:

> the development of alternative pathways into vocational education and training, and improved articulation with institutions of adult education and higher education; increased government funding initiatives to assist Indigenous students in their pursuit of further education; the development of identified support centres within institutions to provide cultural, administrative, and academic support.

As 'an alternative pathway to education and training' VET is 'a kind of barometer of the failure of compulsory and secondary schooling to engage and retain Indigenous students'.[56] More positively, it can be said that Indigenous students have found the TAFE system (where nearly all Indigenous VET takes place) better adapted to features of their life course — early pregnancy, competing economic opportunities in the subsistence economy and in CDEP — that have made it comparatively difficult to finish secondary school.[57]

The third perspective on Indigenous education noted by the Yunupingu Review focuses not on the adaptation of the individual to the mainstream nor on the adaptation of the mainstream to the varieties of Indigenous life course. Rather it:

> explicitly questions the assumption that there is a single set of educational outcomes that are applicable or even desirable for all Australians. More specifically, it suggests that an individual's or community's performance can only be assessed against a set of particular educational outcomes if those outcomes are defined by the community. Thus, different outcomes are not only appropriate but the opportunity for Indigenous communities to define them as such is essential.[58]

This perspective takes us beyond the materials that I have been summarising in this chapter, as it raises the issue of the Indigenous Sector itself. That is my theme in the next chapter.

CONCLUSION

In considering the pattern of Indigenous employment and the options for Indigenous education policy, CAEPR researchers have had to consider the pertinence of human capital theory. They have found it possible to place their faith in that theory's model of the individual as rational 'investor' only if they could avoid the usual assumptions about what is rewarding about paid employment. They have tried to specify Indigenous notions about the ways that employment may be rewarding and about the costs associated with getting an education. In producing their Indigenous variations on the notion of the 'investor' in education, they have been careful not to postulate a unifying model of Indigenous orientations. Yunupingu's (and Schwab's) three-part schema of Indigenous orientations is an essential corrective to the delusion that there is a single 'Indigenous way' in matters educational, and the NATSIS survey data reinforce such scepticism about simple cultural models.

4
INDIGENOUS INSTITUTIONS AND THE LABOUR MARKET

In Chapters 2 and 3 I have reviewed CAEPR's commentaries on the failure of the AEDP that focused on individuals and their choices. In this chapter, my focus shifts to institutions. As I said in my Introduction, when we make 'Indigenous choice' a principle of public policy, we must be careful not to assume that the 'choosing subject' is necessarily an individual. There are 'collective subjects' of Indigenous choice as well. That is, under the self-determination policy, Indigenous Australians have formed organisations of various kinds and through those organisations they make some of their most important choices about how to adapt to the pressures of living in a settler-colonial society. Most of this chapter is about one type of institution that has flourished since 1977: the CDEP schemes. Towards the end of the chapter, I link CDEPs to the rest of the Indigenous Sector in order to suggest that, if we take the Indigenous Sector seriously, it will make a difference to the way that we think about Indigenous education and training.

CDEP

Community Development Employment Project (CDEP) schemes began in 1977 and were an established feature of Commonwealth policy at the time of the AEDP's commencement ten years later. A community that chooses CDEP chooses to place into a common fund all the payments made to 'the unemployed'. The community uses that fund to pay unemployed residents to do whatever the community considers to be worthwhile work.

From the moment of its formation in 1989, ATSIC was responsible for the program. One ATSIC officer described CDEP's aims to an early CAEPR conference:

> The CDEP scheme ... is a group employment based scheme; it is a reciprocal program whereby participants earn a wage for employment performed. Invariably the employment is considered to be part-time, and therefore the total wages paid are low. The scheme assists in developing skills in management, supervision and specific job-related areas. The CDEP scheme provides a stimulus for developing long-term social and cultural cohesion which provides the potential to lead to economic independence.[1]

At the same symposium, Altman and Sanders worried that perhaps CDEP made too great a concession to the 'intractability' of Indigenous employment problems. Noting that CDEP was now being embraced by 'Aboriginal communities in more settled areas of Australia', they warned:

> There is a fine line between, on the one hand, being realistic about the intractability of the economic problems of many Aboriginal people and the measures that can feasibly help overcome them and, on the other hand, reinforcing the low economic status of Aborigines through policies which are unwilling to move beyond the present situation.[2]

CAEPR writers have been treading this 'fine line' ever since.

DEFINING AND MEASURING CDEP OUTCOMES

In one of CAEPR's earliest studies of the local significance of CDEP, Arthur pointed out that in the Torres Strait the scheme was in some respects a 'development subsidy' of the region's commercial fishing industry and in other respects a barrier to participation in commercial fishing, so that it had become an unconditional prop to 'the very dependency which government policy proposes to remove'.[3] He concluded that the CDEP scheme was likely to be no more than an 'on-going remote-area income support or subsidy'. Perhaps this was the scheme's 'unstated intention', he speculated.[4] Altman and Sanders noted that CDEP was both a welfare and a workforce program. 'These different objectives push the scheme towards different funding and administrative arrangements and in different policy directions.'[5] Smith noted the problems this caused for program evaluation; she described CDEP's impact as the 'artificial expansion' of the demand for Indigenous labour; it would obscure, she suggested, the actual lack of demand for Indigenous labour.[6] Altman and Smith noted that CDEP sat awkwardly among the programs of the AEDP for two reasons. First, it made the measurement of 'welfare dependency' subject to a decision about whether CDEP payments were a 'form of welfare' or a wage attached to a job. Second, because CDEP funds were determined by the community's collective 'dole' entitlement, CDEP could help achieve the AEDP goal of employment equality only at the expense of the AEDP goal of income equality.[7]

In 1993, it seemed to Altman and Smith that it was better to acknowledge that CDEP had 'multiple objectives, including community infrastructure development, income support, employment creation, enterprise development, and social and cultural objectives'; they acknowledged, however, that since the introduction of the AEDP 'the scheme has been increasingly regarded [by government, they implied] as a labour market program'.[8] CAEPR authors distanced themselves from this official view by pointing out that, if CDEP was so attractive to Indigenous communities, there must be more to it than this. Thus Altman and Hawke referred non-specifically to the scheme's 'many social externalities'.[9] Addressing the trade union movement in June 1993, Altman and Hawke acknowledged that CDEP job conditions were in many respects inferior to those enjoyed by workers covered by industrial awards. They nonetheless warned that any union attempt 'to ensure full award coverage for CDEP scheme participants may result in its decline' and so 'jeopardise Indigenous aspirations to both participate in, and expand, the scheme'.[10] 'There is a clear tension', Altman and Smith pointed out, 'between local Indigenous management and nationally-established economic objectives, accountability and program evaluation'.[11]

Notwithstanding the many difficulties of defining the goals and evaluating the impacts of CDEP, the program has not only persisted but grown in geographical coverage and in the fullness of its funding. On-costs increased from 10 per cent to 20 per cent in the early 1980s, and in 1987 the Commonwealth added a capital support component equal to about 20 per cent.[12] Such changes were unlikely to make the scheme less attractive to Indigenous communities.

In a series of papers, Sanders has followed the political and administrative history of CDEP, making the point that CDEP's multiple rationales, while giving rise to a series of administrative and evaluation problems, have also ensured for the schemes a broad base of political support.[13] Because CDEP was about 'community-level Aboriginal self-determination and self-management' and because the Department of Finance allowed an open-ended budget for CDEP wages, the DAA and later ATSIC championed it against the scepticism of critics such as the Department of Social Security and invigilators such as the Australian National Audit Office.[14] Independent government inquiries (the Miller Committee 1985, the Royal Commission into Aboriginal Deaths in Custody 1991) endorsed CDEP. Aboriginal Community Councils liked CDEP because it empowered them in relation both to ATSIC and to other local

Indigenous authorities.[15] Since the AEDP was introduced in 1987, governments who wanted to say that they were doing something about Indigenous employment could point to CDEP.

Sanders concluded that a program such as CDEP could survive and grow despite its unsettled rationale and its unresolved administrative problems because a number of constituencies — bureaucratic, political and Indigenous — have benefited from its existence.[16] Those benefits are open to criticism, when CDEP-funded services become a cheap substitute for services not delivered by the usual government agencies. For example, Ray Madden has described how a Victorian CDEP, Worn Gundidj, expanded after Howard government budget cuts forced ATSIC to abandon some programs. Organisations previously supported by the deleted programs increased their reliance on CDEP wages 'in order to maintain previous levels of staff and services'.[17] Whatever the rights and wrongs of such 'substitutions', their effect has been further to entrench CDEP.

ARE CDEP JOBS REAL?

Let us for the moment adopt the narrow view that CDEP is fundamentally about creating jobs. This raises an important issue: are CDEP jobs 'real'? There is no 'correct' answer to that question. It depends on what is at issue.

In measuring changes in labour market status it became common practice at CAEPR to differentiate CDEP from non-CDEP employment, in the hope of identifying determinants of employment 'where direct government intervention through job creation schemes is absent'.[18] As the ABS (in collaboration with Hunter and Taylor) have pointed out:

> Any failure to distinguish CDEP scheme employment from jobs in the mainstream labour market leads to an overestimation of the impact of certain variables on employment in the scheme and an underestimation of their impact on other employment.[19]

That is, it is easy to get a CDEP job even if you lack formal education, speak little English and have had trouble with the police; but these factors have a strong negative effect on your chances of getting a non-CDEP job. Therefore, if the question is: what is the economic significance of Indigenous arrest rates? the answer 'a lot' applies to the probability of getting a 'mainstream' (non-CDEP) job. In his analysis of 1996 Census data, Taylor offered another reason for distinguishing 'employed in CDEP' from 'employed in non-CDEP'.[20] He wanted to compare Indigenous and non-Indigenous employment rates 'without the prop of program intervention in the labour market'.[21]

To see CDEP as among the 'props' of an 'artificial' rate of Indigenous employment would be consistent with a view (not necessarily held by Taylor) that capitalist economies are based fundamentally on market-based activity free of any public support or interference. In such a society what justifies 'props'? Public sector support for job creation is greater in the Indigenous case than for any other category of the Australian population. It is possible to see CDEP as a substantial *political* achievement — an ongoing concession to the very different social and economic needs of Indigenous Australians.

CAEPR authors have sometimes understood Commonwealth policy to be unsympathetic to such concessions. For example, Smith cited the Keating government manifesto 'Working Nation' as indicating that:

> Increasingly, the scheme is being constituted by both ATSIC and government as a labour market program that will develop 'a sustainable economy' for Indigenous communities, and facilitate the transition of individuals into full-time employment in the mainstream economy. Expectations of remote CDEP communities are beginning to be distinguished from those for urban participants who are seen to be more attached to the mainstream economy and, therefore, more readily able to establish access to urban labour markets.[22]

She cited, for example, the proposal by the House of Representatives Standing Committee on Aboriginal Affairs that a 'sunset clause' apply to urban CDEPs. Altman and Hunter suggested in 1996 that CDEP remained vulnerable in a 'political environment with an increasing emphasis on outcomes' (by which they meant graduation of participants into 'mainstream' jobs). ATSIC, they noted, had recently estimated that CDEP now cost 37 per cent more than welfare entitlements. What could be said to justify that cost?[23]

Arthur's work on Indigenous 'careers' in the Torres Strait revealed to him that some Indigenous elites may also question the long-term necessity of CDEP. Did young Islanders see CDEP employment as a 'career'? It was certainly possible to hold such a view, if you wished to participate partly in the monetary economy and partly in the subsistence economy. CDEP employment complemented seasonal or part-time work in commercial fishing. And some young people have grown up with parents who were CDEP participants. In the view of some Straits leaders, however, this habituation to CDEP was becoming a problem. One such person told Arthur 'that he would prefer to see the scheme removed and replaced with some other device which would be designed for local conditions and controlled locally'. Arthur commented that it was not clear 'what precise objections leaders might have to the CDEP scheme':

Possibly it is the negative connotation of welfare dependency inherent in the scheme. However, if, as suggested above, the scheme provides a platform from which people can exploit the commercial fisheries (which are subject to seasons and the climate) then the overall result could well be characterised as a form of welfare autonomy.[24]

Seeking a more rounded and complex evaluation of CDEP, CAEPR's researchers have looked at CDEP from more than one angle.

For example, they have asked what CDEP-induced improvements in Indigenous economic status could CAEPR point to? One study found that CDEP participation was not resulting in a greater measurable income (as measured by the 1991 Census) than in comparable communities without CDEP.[25] On the other hand, geographic analysis of CDEP showed its importance as a source of jobs where there were otherwise poor job prospects. Not only did CDEP cater for Indigenous workers in regions where there was little demand for labour, CDEP was also significant in regions where the employers' demand was for the kind of labour that Indigenous people were ill-suited to supply.[26]

CAEPR studies of CDEP's impact were limited by the failure of the Census, until 1996, to identify CDEP-employed participants. In 1996, the ABS's use of Special Indigenous Personal Forms produced data on CDEP employment in remote and rural communities and on some town camps. Altman and Gray concluded from their analysis of these data that CDEP was a significant source of employment in regions of relatively high Indigenous population and that the CDEP-employed received higher incomes than the unemployed. They remained aware that some possible effects of the CDEP remained unrecorded by the Census. Proper evaluation of CDEP would require data on 'a far wider range of variables, such as health status, arrest rates, and the flows between CDEP employment and the other labour force states'.[27] In an earlier paper Altman had noted a further deficiency of data: no systematic enumeration of 'participants that work' as distinct from 'non-working participants who are usually spouses of workers'.[28]

It is not only through analysis of Census and other data that CAEPR researchers have come to a complex understanding of CDEP. As well, their local studies have brought out the point that CDEP schemes have particular missions in particular places. To say that 'the scheme appears to suit the circumstances of many Indigenous Australians' is to invite attention to these particularities.[29]

Three studies of urban CDEPs, by Diane Smith, took seriously the communal benefits of CDEP and placed in a critical perspective the individual-centred, 'labour-market' understanding of CDEP.[30] Two points emerged strongly from her work.

First, Smith disputed the assumption that urban CDEPs, because of their proximity to large labour markets, differed from remote and rural CDEPS. The common 'urban' location of her three studies (Port Lincoln, Redfern, Newcastle) gave them only a superficial similarity; she found a range of social characteristics among the three urban CDEP client bases: 'The diversity is such that levels of socio-economic disadvantage in some urban populations are more like those in remote communities'.[31] She advised policy makers not to base their analysis of CDEP on the category of the 'urban' Indigenous Australian.

Second, Smith urged policy-makers to recall that Indigenous aspirations were not necessarily to find employment within the wider labour market. CDEP schemes gave participants a legitimate basis for choice:

> [T]he barriers to shifting CDEP participants into the non-Aboriginal labour market are not just structural. Nor are they solely associated with a lack of relevant skills or attitude to work. The social environment of the work gangs is fundamental to the attractions of the 'comfort zone', and some participants have been reluctant to move into non-Aboriginal employment as a result. Whilst this culturally-based proclivity might be seen as a barrier to participants leaving the scheme for full-time employment, it is also a major strength of the scheme.[32]

In her Redfern study, Smith underlined the social, as opposed to the economic, rationales of CDEP, from the point of view of participants:

> Simply put by one participant, people who work together on particular work gangs and programs *like* to work together because of friendships, long-term residential associations and kin connections; so that important cultural ties reinforce the stability of work gangs. In this way, CDEP employment becomes part of the Aboriginal community's social fabric.[33]

Her point raises the question: How to make that 'social fabric' as real to governments as the other CDEP effects — incomes levels, graduation to 'mainstream' jobs, commercial viability of CDEP enterprises — to which governments are attentive? According to Smith:

> The refinement of CDEP policy and program administration in this area would be facilitated by participating organisations themselves documenting such community and individual benefits.[34]

It is consistent with CDEP's 'community development' purposes that governments might take Smith's suggestion seriously — that is, to devolve to CDEP managers not only day to day administration and periodic financial acquittal but also much of the work of program evaluation. One CAEPR study of a CDEP has been co-authored by that scheme's ATSIC project officer while on secondment to CAEPR.[35]

The recent work of Arthur and David-Petero records some negative comments about CDEP from Torres Strait Islanders. They did not rate CDEP highly as a route to a job and many of them described CDEP work as 'boring':

> The element of boredom seems to take two forms. One was that the work done on CDEP was in itself uninteresting, hence people might say that CDEP is either picking up stones or sitting in the office doing nothing. People felt that they gained no skills and learnt nothing while doing this kind of work. The other form of boredom stemmed from the part-time nature of the work ... One person indicated that CDEP was not a real job and that he only joined it to be with his friends.[36]

The authors conclude that 'a challenge for policy makers and communities' is to create 'more, and more interesting, CDEP work and/or training positions'.[37] Badu Island's CDEP scheme, they found, was doing so in its apprenticeship program.[38]

CDEP AS AN INSTITUTION OF THE INDIGENOUS SECTOR

CDEPs make up an important component of the Indigenous Sector, and they typify that sector in that the criteria for evaluating them are contested and uncertain rather than clearly established. I want to suggest that we take this uncertainty as a clue to their relative autonomy. A CDEP scheme can be considered as a newly emergent form of Indigenous political authority.

Throughout the history of CDEP, it has been too easy to forget that each CDEP scheme cannot fail to be, among other things, a structure of political authority whose relationship with governmental authority is a matter for unending negotiation. The 'labour market' perspective underlying so much of the government effort to improve Indigenous welfare may obscure CDEPs' political dimensions. CDEPs are institutions whose aims include perpetuating and increasing their own empowerment. I suggest that we make it explicit that the so-called 'non-labour market outcomes', 'social externalities' and 'community development, social and cultural outcomes' of CDEP include the political empowerment of Indigenous participants in CDEPs.

A CDEP scheme is a form of Indigenous authority, in three ways.[39]

- CDEPs mediate between government and participants.
- CDEPs exercise authority over workers.
- CDEPs become players in the regional political field.

CDEPS AS MEDIATORS BETWEEN GOVERNMENT AND PARTICIPANTS

CDEP schemes derive authority from the fact that the Commonwealth government endows them with money and delegates to each scheme a great deal of discretion about how that money is to be spent. That discretion is not unlimited. The Commonwealth's grant of money is conditional on each CDEP scheme addressing certain policy objectives. However, these policy objectives are multiple, and it would be rather difficult to demonstrate that a CDEP scheme is not addressing *any* of the stated objectives of Commonwealth government policy. This means that although CDEP schemes derive their authority from the fact that the government gives them money, they have a high degree of autonomy.

One of the most important expressions of that autonomy is that CDEPs can define 'work'. For example, when ATSIC's Office of Evaluation and Audit examined the range of definitions of 'work' used in urban CDEPs, it found that about three out of every five CDEPs in their survey paid people for 'home duties'. Across 53 CDEP schemes, seven per cent of participants had their home duties recognised, and paid, as 'work'.[40]

However, CDEP managers' understanding of the long-term interests of participants may be subject to competing perspectives. I have mentioned above that some Islander leaders may be closer to the government view that CDEP participation is merely a stepping stone to 'real' jobs than to some Islanders' view that it is a valid part of a regional 'career'. And in their study of Maningrida's Bawinanga CDEP, Altman and Johnson point to a tension between CDEP scheme's accountability to ATSIC and to the perspectives of local 'stakeholders'.[41]

CDEPS' AUTHORITY OVER WORKERS

Once endowed with authority derived from the government, the CDEP scheme exercises its authority over the work-time of its participants. However, a CDEP scheme is unusual when compared with other 'bosses' who have authority over 'workers', because CDEP workers are, in some respects, like shareholders in the CDEP. Because CDEPs are community-based organisations, their managers are not only bosses over the participants, they are also, to some degree, the employees or servants of each scheme's participants. Diane Smith found that in Port Lincoln's CDEP, 'changes to work practices must be agreed upon by participants and the Board'.[42] Gray and Thacker describe Bungala CDEP as a kind of federation of different work cultures, each determined by the affiliated Aboriginal organisation in which it is based. Bungala thus constitutes an 'internal labour market' through which individuals may move as their needs and capacities change.[43]

It is possible to conceive this variation of work cultures within a CDEP to be a problem rather than as an intelligent adaptive response. At Maningrida the Bawinanga CDEP comprises two rather different domains of work: town, where 'work' is defined specifically and prescriptively, and 'country', where a more permissive and open-ended notion of work is applied. It is common for individuals to move between the two domains. Town workers who visit outstations are treated less permissively by the CDEP managers than outstation workers who visit town.[44]

CDEPS IN THE REGIONAL POLITICAL FIELD

By being able to direct the collective working capacity of participants towards certain ends, CDEP schemes become effective players in the local political scene. That is, a CDEP scheme forms relationships with other organisations — whether they be other Indigenous organisations in the region, or the local shire or municipal council, or State/Territory and Commonwealth agencies that have responsibilities in the area. Sometimes these relationships take the form of contracts for the CDEP scheme to deliver a service. However, not all the significant relationships between CDEP schemes and other regional players are contracts of service. A CDEP scheme may be a political player because its leaders (its governing Board or Council and its senior managers) include some of the most experienced and hard-working Indigenous leaders in that region. A CDEP scheme may be a power base for the emergence of a regional Indigenous leadership. For example, because Bungala (Port Augusta) CDEP's board members are elected CDEP participants:

> there are no representatives of other agencies or Aboriginal organisations on its board, although participants may of course be involved in other Aboriginal organisations. The lack of formal linkages between Bungala and other Aboriginal organisations may in fact work in Bungala's favour, by allowing it to operate more independently and to make decisions that are not necessarily popular with politically powerful individuals within the local Indigenous community.[45]

Within a region, the CDEP's relationship with other Indigenous organisations may change. Madden has described the way that the Worn Gundidj CDEP (Victoria) has contributed materially to the functioning of other Indigenous organisations of south-west Victoria whose government funding has fallen. It has been important for Worn Gundidj to respect the 'local autonomy' of these 'satellite' co-operatives, while exercising its command over Indigenous labour in such a way as to promote 'regional co-operation'.[46]

CDEP is attractive to governments, and to those dependent on government subsidy, as a 'substitute funding' mechanism. As I noted above, CAEPR researchers have long been conscious of the 'equity' objections to propping up poorly resourced public services with CDEP-funded labour.⁴⁷ However, such 'substitution' can also be viewed as a CDEP scheme's 'colonisation' of the regional or local public sector, bringing within the domain of the CDEP functions that were once controlled by others. At Maningrida, according to Altman and Johnson, 'CDEP scheme participants have penetrated all sections of the township labour market, a phenomenon also observed at other remote Indigenous communities'.⁴⁸ The situation in Ngukurr is similar.⁴⁹ The issue for local Indigenous leaders is not necessarily the inequity of such 'substitution' funding, but rather (as Madden points out) how to assure Indigenous 'satellite' organisations a degree of autonomy from the local CDEP, because that program contributes a greater proportion of the public funding of services. Altman and Johnson worry that the 'rivalry and tension' occasioned by Bawinanga's growing command over labour may inhibit a collaborative approach to developing the Maningrida region.⁵⁰

THE INDIGENOUS SECTOR AS AN 'INDUSTRY'

In this chapter I have focused on the principal institutional device through which a margin of Indigenous choice has been secured in labour market policies — CDEP. My theme has been CAEPR writers' appreciation of the ambiguous significance of CDEP in evaluation of programs of Indigenous economic advancement. Without claiming to eliminate altogether CDEP's ambiguity in this sense, I have argued that we can appreciate CDEP in terms other than those provided by the AEDP, that is, by seeing CDEP schemes as a vigorously growing institution of the Indigenous Sector. CDEP shares a characteristic with other institutions of the Indigenous Sector: they are all employers, and most of the labour they employ is Indigenous. In this sense, the Indigenous Sector is an 'industry' — an industry sustained largely by public funds, to be sure, but an industry nonetheless. If the Indigenous Sector is the industry in which a large proportion of Indigenous people are employed, how are we to think about education and training?

In Chapter 3 I argued that CAEPR's critical dialogue with 'human capital' assumptions about motivation rested, in part, on appreciating that many Indigenous Australians are training themselves for service within the Indigenous Sector. If reform of the institutions of Vocational Education and Training (VET) is to be consistent with Indigenous 'self-determination', the Indigenous Sector should be considered to be an 'industry' with its own training needs. Of course, in many respects, such as basic literacy and numeracy, the needs of the Indigenous Sector are no different from those of any other industry. However, to the extent that there is an Indigenous Sector dedicated to realising the many facets of Indigenous self-determination, the political and administrative experience of that Sector's employers should now be informing the design of training for Indigenous (and non-Indigenous) personnel.[51]

The notion that education and training are an investment in 'human capital' may be of persisting relevance to understanding the Indigenous Sector, even if it is questionable as a way to conceptualise individual choice. Rather we might ask: what kind of human capital does the Indigenous Sector need? To recognise the Indigenous Sector entails conceding that it collectively must consider the dynamics of its own reproduction: the training of personnel who can understand and sympathise with the tasks of Indigenous Sector organisations.

Schwab and Anderson have set out such a framework, considering VET as the pathway to higher education in health training, a substitute for secondary schooling. Their paper is about creating Indigenous person power as part of a strategy to build the health organisations of the Indigenous Sector.[52] In another paper, on Indigenous participation in health sciences education in 43 higher education institutions, Schwab and Anderson were concerned with the health service delivery industry as a whole. However, their interest in the formation of a policy intelligentsia is clear in their worried comment about a 'lack of depth in the current [1997] profile of students'. Will 'a cadre of indigenous public health and health sciences leaders and policy makers' emerge from those now training predominantly in 'health support' roles?[53]

There are very few schools and colleges directly under Indigenous management. Schwab summarised NATSIS and DEETYA data on independent community-controlled schools in 1994. In that year there were only 20 of them, and they taught only 1.6 per cent of Indigenous primary and secondary students. Though more than half the staff of these schools were Indigenous, more than four out every five of these staff were *not* teachers. Nonetheless, these schools were providing an alternative education, oriented to sustaining features of Indigenous culture. 'Indigenous students in independent schools are far more likely to learn about Indigenous culture and learn Indigenous languages than are their counterparts in other types of Australian schools; their chances of receiving that instruction from an Indigenous teacher are also much greater.'[54] In vocational education and training, in 1998, just under twenty per cent of Indigenous participants were outside TAFE, served by 'community education providers' and 'other registered training organisations', not all of which are Indigenous-controlled.

One message in these figures is clear. The Indigenous Sector plays only a small part in the flow of education and training services to Indigenous Australians. Indigenous Australians who go to school and who get vocational training do so, for the most part, in 'mainstream' institutions.

If institutions of the Indigenous Sector are not education and training providers, they could nonetheless be made more influential in determining what other providers do. Campbell has shown that in the 1990s reforms to VET were designed to empower employers. However, in these reforms, Indigenous institutions were not taken seriously as an employer interest. In the 'Policy for Training Packages', 'each industry was charged with the task of identifying a range of relevant occupational skills and the necessary competencies that make employment within the industry efficient and competitive'.[55] However, the Indigenous Sector was not among the 'industries' consulted. Accordingly, the resulting national-standard 'training packages', according to Campbell, 'are essentially based upon the identified needs of a mainstream, industry-driven training framework' so that 'Indigenous people have few, if any, avenues for influencing the design of training packages'.[56] It is the aim of VET policy reform to allow the 'customising' of training packages, but one must ask: who does the 'customising'?

Until those administering the reformed VET sector encourage the institutions of the Indigenous Sector to see themselves as 'employers' and as 'industries' that may 'customise' training packages, the needs of non-Indigenous employers will continue to mould the training of Indigenous Australians. CAEPR's research on the industrial and occupational distribution of Indigenous employees shows that the 'Indigenous Sector' exists; it should be a player — and a major one in some regions — in the 'customising' game. The potential influence of Indigenous Sector views on training is hardly realised by the forming of an Aboriginal and Torres Strait Islander Peoples Advisory Council in May 1996. The word 'advisory' signalled a clear departure from the principles of 'self-determination'. The defects of a policy that does not take the Indigenous Sector seriously as an industry can also be seen in the way that CDEP schemes have found it difficult to win recognition as providers of training. Only if Commonwealth policy starts to recognises a CDEP job as an 'employment outcome' will CDEP win recognition (and funding) as trainers.[57]

From the point of view of Indigenous VET 'customers', trained 'competency' is more than job skills. 'Competency' could be broadened to recognise Indigenous aspirations such as 'personal improvement through education, the maintenance of Indigenous culture, and the perceived role that education has in improving community life'.[58] Campbell concedes that there are some opportunities locally to modify training packages. She gives the example of the Maningrida service provider's ability to determine the contents, but not the funded time-frame, of such materials. The diverse needs of customers is also considered under the 'user choice' principle; this allows Indigenous trainees (like all VET participants) to select their training provider from a (theoretically) competitive array. Campbell wonders whether Indigenous communities will have the information and the resources for planning that would be required to take advantage of this choice. As well, she fears that the market for courses may constrain all providers, including Indigenous providers, to delete less popular courses, thus reducing choice. Independent Indigenous providers, she urges, need extra resources to develop training for their Indigenous clients. To assume that training is profitable will disadvantage those who have least to pay for training and those whose training is most expensive to deliver.

Whatever the disadvantages and/or advantages of the reformed VET sector for Indigenous people as trainers and trainees, 'it is hard to see how Indigenous Australians can significantly contribute to [the formation of a 'training culture' in Australia] given they have minimal industry or employer representation'.[59] Campbell recommends that 'Indigenous organisations, regionally based and with a specific focus on education and training, could provide the conduit through which local needs are identified, strategies designed, and information disseminated'.[60]

PART 2

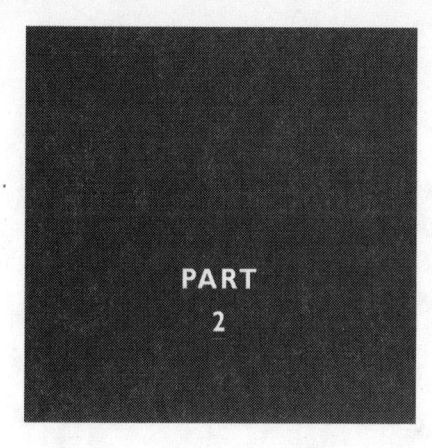

LAND, SEA AND ECONOMIC DEVELOPMENT

INTRODUCTION

By 2001, sixteen to eighteen per cent of Australia was under Indigenous ownership.[1] More is to come. Could land (and sea, where sea rights are granted) be the basis of Indigenous economic recovery?

The Miller Report concluded in 1985 that 'the fundamental historical factor that has ensured the continuing low economic status of Aboriginal and Torres Strait Islander people is their loss of ownership of natural resources'. It continued: 'the ownership of land and other sources is the first necessary step towards providing Aboriginal people with the means to improve their economic status'.[2] Miller qualified these assertions in two ways.

First, the economic potential of land is affected by many factors. Because of great distances from large markets, for example, long-term government support would be needed 'for productive activity in remote areas'.[3] Second, if any development project were to take place without the consent of local Aboriginal people and/or without their holding some equity in the project, they would be less likely to take up its job opportunities, Miller suggested.[4]

As Altman has noted in several publications, if land is a factor of economic development, then it is a very inequitably distributed factor, because of differences in the ways that States, Territories and the Commonwealth have approached Indigenous land tenure.[5] Because there is such political resistance to the expansion of the Indigenous land and sea base, it was difficult to project the future significance of these 'factors' to Indigenous Australians.[6]

Even where Indigenous tenure is strong and the lands are extensive, we cannot assume that owners value their land for its potential to generate an income (whether by equity participation in development projects, by royalty entitlements, or by employment). Indigenous people may reject proposed new ways to use their land, notwithstanding associated prospects of higher incomes, because they value the way of life that is embedded in their existing land uses. David Trigger has given us an instance of Indigenous Australians debating this issue — the Waanyi discussion of Century mine and its associated pipeline in the mid-1990s:

> From the perspective of those who stress the value of what appear to be promises of substantial economic benefits (employment, training for young people, funds for new business operations) it is pointless and wrong-headed to ignore the opportunities that the mine presents.[7]

However, other Waanyi argued that were the government equitably to provide their citizenship entitlements, they would not have to embrace the mine. 'Why should we have to sell our souls for a house?' he heard one person ask.[8]

As Diane Smith has pointed out, even when Indigenous Australians do achieve consensus on these issues within a defined political community, the succeeding generation may not feel bound. Consent to the Jabiluka mine in Kakadu National Park was reopened to debate in the mid-1990s. '[A]pparently workable and agreed solutions may become unworkable when they are seen to take away from subsequent generations the right to speak for country …'[9]

The Indigenous interest in land is not necessarily a straightforward desire to maximise the monetary returns from it. Just as the economic potential of land is conditioned by many factors, so the Indigenous interest in land may vary according to their circumstances and to their judgments about the alternative scenarios they face. According to Finlayson, one of the formative documents in recent Indigenous affairs policy was sensitive to possible variation in the Indigenous outlook. When Justice Woodward outlined the terms of what became the *Aboriginal Land Rights (Northern Territory) Act* he tried to allow for change in the nature of Aboriginal land interest. His intention was not to favour any particular way that Aborigines might view their land's significance but to assure legislatively that there would be 'consultation, informed consent, and autonomy for Aboriginal communities in decision-making and choices about their "manner of living"'.[10] Not only did Woodward outline a royalties payment regime, he also took seriously the possibility that Aboriginal land-owners might prefer to forego such incomes, in order to preserve established land uses.

Robert Levitus has suggested that if the goal of 'development' is to enhance 'people's ability to do and be what they have reason to value', then we should broaden our questions about the integration of 'remote-area Aboriginal life' into the wider economy. He gave examples of issues raised by a properly open sense of 'development':

> What is the relationship between welfare payments and the maintenance of personal autonomy free from the demands of waged work, and how can that conception of personal autonomy fit with a policy concept of communal self-determination? What mapping of networks over what geographical area do we need to have done to understand the sociology of sport and ceremony across the Aboriginal Northern Territory, and how should that affect our assessment of the health and vitality of regional societies? What role are Aboriginal people in bush camps and on pastoral stations playing in the contemporary environmental history of those areas, where they are the sole human agents? And what significance, if any, does traditionally based land ownership have for the sustenance of all these socio-environmental systems?[11]

These are unusual questions to pose in Australian public policy discussion. As my quotations from Miller demonstrate, there is a tendency for policy discourse to imagine that the primary Indigenous interest in land is that it is a source of increased wealth, a factor in 'economic development'. Thus, in a characteristic clarification, Altman and Allen wrote: 'Aboriginal hunting, fishing and gathering activities have important social, cultural and economic benefits to participating Aboriginal people', but 'the emphasis in this paper is on the economic aspects of subsistence'.[12] To the extent that the 'economic aspects of subsistence' can be isolated, subsistence then becomes comparable with other kinds of production system in terms of its returns to land-owners. Thus may the options of land use be compared.

CAEPR authors have adopted the working hypothesis that land as 'property' is, or could be, a factor of production from which Indigenous people will try to realise a monetary income. Altman even gave this emphasis on the 'economic' an epistemological basis when he declared that 'it is important that an ideological commitment to land rights for a range of social, cultural and political reasons is not confused with economic reality'.[13] However, as CAEPR authors have noted, their effort to identify a distinctly 'economic' dimension of land-use has been frustrated — in the case of subsistence — by a paucity of data on the inputs (labour time, capital goods) and outputs (imputed monetary value of hunted and gathered materials) of the subsistence 'economy'. The 'economic' was too embedded in the pre-capitalist, kin-based society of Indigenous Australians to be observable as a distinct realm of behaviour. To disembed it is to make an enormous change to Indigenous social life. To isolate the 'economic' dimension of land requires not a lifting of the fog of 'ideology' to reveal 'reality', as Altman might put it. Rather, there must be actual social transformation to enable a new apparatus of data definition, collection and accountancy. These changes make 'the economy' possible and available as an observable thing. To constitute 'the economic' as an object of knowledge is an intellectual innovation with social conditions of existence.[14] The isolation of the 'economic' as a dimension of life is an emergent effect of the institutional order under which Indigenous land is now to be owned and used.

CAEPR's effort to identify the 'economic' value of the Indigenous land base has been tempered by recognition that the value of Indigenous land may be realised in a variety of ways and that each of these ways has 'lifestyle' or socio-cultural implications. This point is consistent with some CAEPR authors' complex appreciation of 'welfare dependency'. As Altman and Smith remarked in 1992: 'In the face of fluctuating and recently decreasing employment opportunities in many parts of Australia, welfare may represent a source of more reliable income for many Aboriginal people and provide a degree of economic autonomy and security lacking in employment.'[15] Applying this reasoning to land-use decisions, it is clear that with uncertain markets for commodities produced from the land, and given the lifestyle changes that some changes in land-use would require, Indigenous Australians might think carefully before abandoning subsistence production (subsidised by welfare). CAEPR writings thus postulate a margin of Indigenous choice about how they could use their land and sea 'property'.

In the next three chapters I will show that in CAEPR's research on the value of Indigenous land we find a persistent tension between 'monetary' and 'lifestyle' senses of 'value'. In Chapter 5 my focus is tourism and national parks. In Chapter 6 I look at the issues posed by the royalties regime of the Northern Territory Land Rights Act. In Chapter 7 I examine the terms in which CAEPR authors have considered the incidents of 'native title'. In Chapter 8 I consider the challenge that land and sea ownership pose for Indigenous political development.

5
HUNTING, GATHERING AND TOURISM

Taylor, examining the dispersion of the Indigenous population of the Northern Territory into hundreds of tiny outstations, considered how the nation might calculate the costs and benefits of that decentralised pattern of settlement. The costs to government of providing services to these people were plain enough, but were not outstations also a 'resource with national benefits'?:

> Apart from obvious spin-offs in areas such as defence and coastal surveillance, the most cogent example is provided by the ecological benefits inherent in traditional Aboriginal land management practices. These are increasingly relevant in the context of debate on sustainable development and need to be considered in an accounting framework which sets the cost of supporting remote area settlement against the environmental well-being of the nation. Other more social benefits may also accrue from the establishment of more appropriately-scaled cultural environments away from the alienating influence of large polyglot townships in which some Aboriginal people are inevitably marginalised.[16]

In this perspective, Indigenous hunting and gathering — the main form of resource exploitation for outstation residents — is of value to the nation, not just to the hunters and gatherers themselves. However, Taylor's perspective in this passage is uncharacteristic of CAEPR research. In most of CAEPR's consideration of subsistence use of land and sea, the imagined point of view is that of Indigenous owners and residents, rather than of the 'nation'.

Altman and Allen have suggested that Indigenous peoples' commitment to hunting and gathering is a product of three factors: tradition, land tenure and the availability of alternative modes of productive activity. Not only are people influenced by 'strong continuities with pre-contact lifestyles', but a combination of 'land rights and resource rights' may be a 'catalyst to resurrect apparently defunct foraging economies'. Such people may also find that they have 'few economic options in the mainstream labour market'.[17] Summarising available studies of Aboriginal subsistence, they comment that, in some places (possibly including some national parks), Aboriginal people devote much more of their time to this form of 'employment' than official labour market statistics measure. Altman and Allen complained that despite the 'lip service' paid to '"traditional" activities, the issue of subsistence is generally marginalised in policy debate and the comparative economic advantages that Aboriginal people in remote areas enjoy in such activities are either ignored or tolerated, but are rarely encouraged'.[18] Elsewhere, noting 'the market mentality of most policy-makers and academics', they argued for a 'broadening of the standard definition of employment and income'.[19] In a later publication, CAEPR authors broadened their conception of the significance of subsistence production, adducing evidence that it could be valued as much for its nutritional benefit as for its imputed monetary value.[20] (They could also have added that the physical exercise would benefit a people whose Type 2 diabetes prevalence is very high.)

In order to promote consideration of Indigenous subsistence on one type of Indigenous land, national parks, Altman and Allen discussed the main factors influencing hunting and gathering by the Aboriginal people who live on them: the type of Indigenous legal tenure and the degree of Indigenous political influence over park management; tourist pressure on natural resources; government demands on welfare recipients that they orient themselves to paid employment; conservation-based park management rules; changes in the distribution of species that may be hunted and gathered; changes in technology; and the incentive to switch from subsistence to commercial production. Park management regimes, particularly those over which Indigenous Australians have control, must consider each of these factors if they wish to maximise the economic benefit of Indigenous subsistence practices.

Concluding their survey of the possible economic significance of additions to the Indigenous land base through native title and through Indigenous Land Fund purchases, Altman, Bek and Roach made the plea:

> ... that the choices of Indigenous Australians remain open, allowing new possibilities to expand subsistence activities in these changing circumstances without limiting Indigenous people in the long term by tying them irrevocably into a production system predicated on the availability of wildlife.[21]

In these words, the authors in fact entertained the possibility of two changes: from subsistence to commercial use of 'wildlife', and from a 'production system predicated on the availability of wildlife' to one that was not so predicated.

Three CAEPR authors in 1997 discussed the first of these possibilities: commercial harvesting of wildlife. They cited survey evidence of Indigenous Australians favouring commercialisation of wildlife resources, in order to create jobs and make 'wild foods' more readily available.[22] However, they issued two cautions: that Indigenous interests not be edged out by non-Indigenous investment, and that biodiversity be respected. Although there are scientific data on some wildlife species, 'there is little overall understanding about impacts on biodiversity and the Australian environment from commercial utilisation', they warned.[23] Conceding the need to regulate wildlife harvesting, the authors urged that Indigenous Australians be given a say in the design and enforcement of regulatory regimes. One legal issue for any such regime was whether native title legislation might provide for recognition of 'Indigenous property rights in species'. The value of such rights could be realised either by their sale to a commercial harvester or by joint venturing between Indigenous and non-Indigenous parties. Whether or not such rights were recognised, it would be unwise, they suggested, to prejudge whether subsistence or commercial use of wildlife was more highly valued by Indigenous people themselves.

VARIETIES OF ECONOMIC POTENTIAL: FISHERIES

In the Torres Strait, Indigenous Australians have access to the natural resources of both sea and land. Since the 1970s, they have successfully opposed the development of sea-bed exploration for oil. For them the sea's bounty is realised primarily through fishing, both commercial and non-commercial (subsistence). The Torres Strait Treaty between Australia and New Guinea (signed in 1978 and ratified in 1985) recognised customary, and limited commercial, Indigenous rights in marine resources in the Torres Strait. As Arthur saw it in 1991, given the limits of marine organisms' reproduction, there were two alternative scenarios of economic development through fishing: 'a small number of unsubsidised commercial fishers wholly dependent on fishing for their livelihood, or a larger number of fishers, most of whom receive income support as an indirect subsidy'.[24]

In 1994, the Torres Strait Regional Authority (TSRA) was formed. Among its stated ambitions was the commercial development of Straits fisheries. Although there were no data to tell such economic planners of the extent of the Indigenous involvement in commercial fishing, nor whether it was rising or falling, Altman,

Arthur and Bek were able to establish that there was no Islander involvement in commercial exploitation of prawn and of cultured pearls and very little in commercial mackerel fishing.[25] They explained the uneven pattern of Indigenous commercial participation in fisheries in terms of high capital costs, low skills in the use of certain technologies, and different profit margins. They discussed whether Torres Strait Islanders could participate (or participate more) in these three sectors of the fishing industry, either by resource rental (after enhancement of their property rights) or as commercial fishers themselves.

Davis's study of the 'outer' island of Saibai over eighteen months from March 1992 to July 1994 produced a cameo of the difficulties that the TSRA faced in promoting the shift from subsistence to commercial production. Davis developed a point that Arthur had made in 1991: that CDEP was central to the maintenance of the Torres Strait's non-commercial economy. CDEP on Saibai employed most men. The ratio of dependants to employed was high, even by comparison with all Indigenous Australians. The population was mobile, travelling to and from mainland Australia and the nearby coastal villages of Papua New Guinea, with whom there are long-standing relationships of exchange. Cash incomes were low compared with other islands in the region and with Indigenous Australia as a whole. Davis did not attempt to impute the monetary value of the subsistence economy — most importantly fishing, but also including gardening — but he insisted that it was 'central to the reproduction of social relations'. His account of the sources of cash income showed how the CDEP scheme upheld the subsistence economy, and so allowed cultural continuity.

Cash income on Saibai was derived from employment and from social security entitlement. If CDEP is 'employment', then employment accounted for about 65 per cent of cash income. Alternatively, if CDEP is counted as a welfare payment, then Saibai households were getting almost 70 per cent of their income from 'welfare'. We have already encountered (in Chapter 4) this ambiguity in CDEP. From the point of view of 'the reproduction of social relations' on Saibai, the important question was not so much whether islanders' incomes came from 'welfare' or 'employment' but into which activities CDEP, households and individuals put cash. CDEP paid for activities traditionally gendered 'masculine', such as providing basic community services, ceremonial dancing and the manufacture and repair of dancing accessories. Participation in 'large church-related occasions and funeral preparations' was also credited to CDEP. On Saibai, CDEP tended not to provide training for jobs in the mainstream labour market, nor was it a platform for enterprise development.

Though fishing had the potential to be a cash-based and even commercially organised activity, Saibai people (with some exceptions) preferred to fish for household subsistence and non-monetary exchanges. The preferred technologies of subsistence food-gathering also favoured sustainable use of natural resources. Although cash could substitute for culturally valued goods, the pursuit of cash incomes seemed to Davis to be subordinate to the perpetuation of older ways of getting and distributing the necessities of life. These priorities gave the CDEP scheme its local logic.

These features of Saibai culture could be represented either as obstacles to economic development or as an adaptive autonomy underwritten by 'citizen entitlement' income in a region of low employment potential. Davis implied support for the latter view. He saw looming challenges to that autonomy: the review of a moratorium on seabed mining in the Torres Strait Protected Zone, and the stated economic development ambition of the Torres Strait Regional Authority. Where Altman, Arthur and Bek had speculated on the possibility of enhancing Indigenous property rights over marine resources, Davis showed Saibai Islanders satisfying themselves from a combination of subsistence fishing (to which they were already customarily entitled) and citizenship entitlements (welfare income). Thus, 'the economic development rhetoric of the TSRA's Corporate Plan is to a large extent countermanded by the example of Saibai Islanders, who maintain an economic strategy which balances traditional subsistence practices with government transfers to retain a desired standard of living'.[26]

VARIETIES OF ECONOMIC POTENTIAL: TOURISM

Aboriginal land and people figured prominently in the Australian government's interest in tourism development in the early 1990s.[27] Though Indigenous Australians may participate in the tourism industry whether or not they have a land base, a secure land base may make their participation more attractive and sustainable. Aboriginal land may be of great aesthetic interest to tourists, and Aboriginal people living on their own country may produce artefacts marketable for their Indigenous authenticity; and land tenure establishes a margin of choice about how Indigenous Australians 'host' tourism.

In a 1992 literature review Altman and Finlayson listed the following as 'prerequisites for successful and sustainable Aboriginal participation in tourism ...: *Aboriginal control*, market realism for Aboriginal participants, appropriate corporate structures, appropriate scale of enterprise, *accommodation of cultural and social factors*, educating the industry, and realistic subvention'.[28] They illustrated 'Aboriginal control' by referring to situations where, as an effect of land rights, tourism was not an imposed but an invited industry. The accommodation of cultural and social factors, they pointed out, might include restricting visitors' access to certain areas.[29] However, they warned that 'Aboriginal landownership is no guarantee of substantial financial returns from commercial enterprises'.[30] Indeed, they anticipated that tourism would be a small and culturally conservative path of Indigenous economic development: 'the sustainability of Aboriginal cultural tourism will be largely dependent on an appropriately slow rate of development'.[31]

In cautioning those who sought to intensify Aboriginal involvement in the tourism industry, Altman argued that 'from an Aboriginal perspective, cultural impacts can rarely be neatly separated from economic, social and environmental impacts'.[32] He illustrated his point by reference to Anangu use of their land in and around Uluru National Park. The Aboriginal desire to limit strangers' access to their land meant that 'in the immediate future a great deal of Aboriginal involvement in tourism will occur via the sale of arts and crafts; it will be indirect, part-time or occasional, and will only supplement existing sources of income'.[33]

While land title is not essential to Indigenous people's participation in tourism, because that participation may include a proud declaration of distinct cultural features it may stimulate among participants a greater awareness of their traditions of land ownership. Finlayson's study of the Tjapukai Dance Theatre of Kuranda (Qld) showed not only that it 'has undoubtedly expanded employment options for Aboriginal people in Kuranda and improved income levels', but also that this commercial success contributed to Djabugay [Tjakupai] people's identity and thus to their more confident 'participation in current debates about land and commercial development throughout the Cairns region'.[34] For example, 'a native title claim over the Barron Falls National Park was lodged by a member of the Djabugay Aboriginal Tribal Corporation in May 1994'.[35] Non-Indigenous investors were thus made aware that they had rival interests to consider when planning tourism development. Indigenous commercial interest in tourism thus developed into an Indigenous political interest in regional land use planning. Native title legislation has given the Djabugay people hope that their participation in tourism will eventually be based not only on the attractiveness of their culture to tourists but also on their title to land that the tourism industry requires.

Indigenous claimants to land are sometimes rivalled by other Indigenous interests. The prospects of tourism might quicken such rivalries. Finlayson noted that the Tjapukai Dance Company was but one Indigenous interest to have emerged in the Kuranda region. In similar vein, Altman found that when the leaders of Cape York's Seisia community sought to develop their town's tourism infrastructure, they aspired also to assert the claims of its Torres Strait Islander residents to land title. In and around Seisia, Aboriginal land claims on customary grounds are also strong. In Seisia, a town 'locationally advantaged with respect to tourism', the residents were developing tourism infrastructure 'as a strategic means of asserting [their] historic association with the land'.[36] It was not that Seisia people aspired to *jobs* servicing tourists. On the contrary, it seemed to Altman that such jobs were unlikely to be more attractive than what was already available: CDEP employment and subsistence.

Altman went on to point out that, whichever Indigenous groups were successful in their title bid, economic development through tourism could lead to a reconsideration of the forms of land ownership. 'Property rights in the region's main tourist attractions, namely the Cape itself, recreational fishing and the environment *are poorly defined and/or held in common*', he observed.[37] Clearly, he was referring to property rights in the commercial sense; he made that judgment from the point of view of a consultant hired to clarify the obstacles and opportunities for tourism development. He acknowledged that the people of Seisia were not uniformly involved in the ambition of the 'community leadership ... to become economically independent of government, on the basis of tourism, by the year 2000'. The 'limited participation of Seisia residents in tourism-related enterprises or employment' suggested that many people had other goals.[38] He doubted that there was sufficient entrepreneurial ambition among the Seisians to sustain the small businesses that a more developed tourism industry might bring into existence. Here again, he questioned 'the nature of land tenure'. Combined with 'the public sector's role in development', it had 'not assisted the creation of a competitive entrepreneurial business environment, a scenario that is all too common for Indigenous community-owned enterprises in remote regions'.[39] Three features of land ownership militated against entrepreneurial initiative: land's inalienability, the land-leasing policy of the Seisia Island Council, and the current uncertainty about who would ending up owning what land once the recent State (1991) and Commonwealth (1993) land laws were brought into local effect. The Seisia leaders' aspirations to benefit from tourism would require their attention to each of these problems.

CAEPR's writings on tourism as a possible path of Indigenous economic development lead us to an important conclusion about the changing content of Indigenous customs. Indigenous land-owners may or may not consider tourism to be a threat that they can best respond to through judicious exercise of their title. However, it would seem that the economic opportunities of tourism have emerged as a potent stimulus to the political and legal expression of the Indigenous land interest. In that process, the Indigenous land interest is not only reproduced but redefined.

6
MINING INCOMES

When it comes to mining as a possible realisation of the wealth of Indigenous land, the Indigenous 'interest' is not only to 'achieve benefits' but to 'avoid outcomes they regard as undesirable'.[1] Altman and Pollack suggest that a tension between these two desires is built into the Northern Territory Land Rights Act — 'between the policy intent and statutory provision of a right to veto development on Aboriginal land and the politically expedient desire to provide an incentive structure that will encourage traditional owners to trade away this veto'.[2] CAEPR writings have tended to emphasise the opportunities, rather than the disadvantages, of Indigenous owners negotiating to allow mining on their lands. Nearly all the work published by CAEPR on the economic significance of mining to Aboriginal land-owners has considered the Northern Territory case.

In this chapter I will trace three Northern Territory themes: How do Aboriginal land-owners negotiate royalties, rentals and other benefits? How does the Aboriginal Benefits Account (ABA, formerly the Aboriginal Benefits Trust Account (ABTA), and the Aboriginal Benefits Reserve (ABR)) allocate the 'statutory royalty equivalents'? How do Aboriginal royalty associations — receiving both statutory and negotiated royalties — use those funds?

NEGOTIATION

The *Aboriginal Land Rights (Northern Territory) Act 1976* (henceforth the Land Rights Act) makes it necessary for mining companies to obtain the consent of traditional owners before exploring for minerals on their land. In return for giving consent, traditional owners have negotiated royalties and other benefits.

Reviewing five agreements in the Northern Territory and Queensland signed between 1992 and 1994 Ciaran O'Faircheallaigh concluded that 'the wide variety of approaches being utilised by Aboriginal communities and organisations shows very clearly their willingness to find ways of facilitating mineral development, while at the same time seeking to benefit from it'.[3] His comparative approach found significance in the government's role in negotiations, in two ways. First, the legislative requirement of Indigenous consent made a difference to the initial distribution of bargaining power. Second, governments may increase the possibility of agreement by committing public funds to meeting some of the aspirations expressed by Indigenous negotiators. 'Where consent must be sought, agreements tend to incorporate substantial benefits for Aboriginal communities, especially in the key areas of royalty and other forms of economic benefit and of control over environmental and heritage issues. Most if not all of those benefits are funded by the developer, not by government.'[4] He expressed reservations about governments providing benefits as a 'sweetener'. Government commitments were not necessarily contractually bound, and government policies were subject to change. In any case, governments have responsibilities to provide essential services for Indigenous citizens; their discharge of those responsibilities should not be a negotiable item in a government strategy to facilitate mining.

How do Indigenous land-owners come to have a negotiable position on a mining proposal? Trigger's study of the Century Mine process illustrates the possibility that people may find it difficult to come to a common view as to their interests.[5] O'Faircheallaigh, having observed the negotiation of two mining agreements with Cape York communities, Hope Vale and Old and New Mapoons/Napranum, suggested a number of factors that seemed to affect their mobilisation of a negotiating position. To establish the communities' goals, Economic and Social Impact Assessments (ESIAs) may be useful. Not only do such studies make informed predictions about mining's effects, but the process of producing them, combining research and consultation, may itself assist people to explore possible negotiating positions. O'Faircheallaigh pointed to remediable inequities in negotiators' access to information about each other and in access to other resources such as legal and research expertise. He criticised jurisdictions such as Queensland for conferring negotiating rights while failing to resource Aboriginal negotiating capacity. Regional land councils can be an ongoing source of such expertise, he suggested. However, good working relationships between Indigenous people and their technical advisers cannot be assumed; they must be nurtured. O'Faircheallaigh also noted features of well-conducted meetings, including child-care and a series of short sessions punctuated by breaks. Even the best meetings must be supplemented by other processes, he urged, such as one-to-one and small group discussion, 'since certain categories of people (for example women, the aged, young people) are less likely to attend such meetings or to voice their opinions if they do attend'.[6] Finally, O'Faircheallaigh gave instances from his Northern Territory research of mining agreements not being honoured by governments and mining companies. Agreements should include protocols for monitoring their implementation.[7]

Although Northern Territory Aboriginal land-owners do not own the minerals on their lands, from the point of view of a mining company, they enjoy a 'property' right by virtue of being able to negotiate with the mining company its conditions of access to the land to be explored. Until 1987, exploration and mining were subject to separate negotiation. As a consequence of a 1987 amendment to the Land Rights Act, once Aborigines have consented to exploration, they may not deny the mining of the explored land. Their effective property right — negotiated consent — is thus exercised at an early stage in the total mining process. John Quiggin has suggested that both Aboriginal and mining interests are inhibited from committing themselves to co-operation because the government, as owner of the minerals and as legislator of the negotiating right and of the disposal of statutory royalties, is open to political pressure from the other party to change the incentives confronting the two parties. Both sides have an incentive to create delays. Quiggin suggests that 'if the policy goal in establishing a mining rights regime is to improve the welfare of Aboriginal land owners as efficiently and equitably as possible, the optimal policy is to attach outright ownership of minerals to ownership of land under the Land Rights Act'. Miners and Aborigines would then have 'a joint interest in the successful implementation of mining projects whenever the expected benefits of those projects exceeded costs'.[8]

DISTRIBUTING ROYALTIES

Under the Land Rights Act, the Commonwealth must pay to the ABTA/ABR an amount equivalent to the statutory royalties it gets from mining companies operating on Aboriginal land. To a large extent the Act ties the ABTA/ABR's hands. The ABR must give no less than 40 per cent to the Land Councils for operating costs. It must give 30 per cent to Land Councils for their distribution to Aboriginal corporations representing the interests of Aborigines living in 'areas affected' by mining. What is left must be given to other applicant Northern Territory Aborigines.

Until the mid-1990s, the ABTA's expenditure had particularly favoured the Land Councils (which got 52.5 per cent of ABTA disbursements up to 1996–97). The ABTA placed no pressure on other recipients to invest their money in income-generating assets. Altman judged that it had been worth spending a lot of money on the land claims process (effected by the Land Councils) because that had resulted in a massive expansion of the Indigenous land base in the Territory.[9] However, by the mid-1990s, with the end of the claims process in sight, it was time to reconsider how to convert into productive capital the monetary returns from mining on Aboriginal land, so that the purpose of the institutions of land rights might change from 'land claim to land management'.[10]

But who is to determine that purpose? Altman has noted that 'one of the continual tensions that has influenced the ABTA's granting operations is that between the policy of self-determination, which emphasises that granting activity should be according to Aboriginal prerogatives and which has resulted in high expenditure, and the economic rationality of accumulation' — with the latter perspective favoured by governments.[11] Favouring a 'radical recasting of the financial provisions', Altman has discussed a number of possible reforms to the Land Rights Act.[12]

First, he has raised the issue of whether the Land Councils should be funded directly by the Commonwealth. That would free a large proportion of statutory royalty equivalents to be invested in economic development.

Second, Altman has noted a point made by the mining industry and by the Industries Commission, that the three-way division of statutory royalty equivalents has possibly reduced the monetary incentive for groups of Aboriginal owners to consent to mining. That is, the wider distribution of statutory royalty equivalents demanded by the Act has vitiated the clarity of the property right of discrete groups of traditional owners.[13] A related problem was that:

> the payment of royalty equivalents to incorporated bodies in areas affected by mining will often result in excessive regional politicking for these mining moneys, with a concomitant lack of attention to longer-term economic opportunities and an inability to accumulate venture capital for investment.[14]

However, though Altman has found appealing the theoretical view that clearer property rights reduce transaction costs and increase owners' incentives to negotiate a deal with resource developers, he has not endorsed the Industries Commission recommendation that full ownership of minerals be vested in Aboriginal traditional owners and that 70 per cent of statutory royalties (as well as all negotiated royalties) should be paid to the traditional owners of the land on which the mine is located.[15] Quiggin has pointed out two reasons for finding that proposal worrying: it would be inequitable, in relation to other Australian land-owners, and 'the greater the value of rights granted to successful Aboriginal land claimants, the greater will be the political resistance to land claims'.[16]

There is an additional reason to reject the Industries Commission proposal to concentrate the rewards of mining in the hands of the traditional owners. If part of the point of that reform were that it made investment of that money more likely, then there is possibly another way to achieve this effect. Thus the third of the possible reforms to the Land Rights Act discussed by Altman was that royalty associations and the ABTA/ABR could be compelled to invest a proportion of their receipts in income-generating assets.

The Commonwealth's commissioned review of the Land Rights Act in 1997–98 (by John Reeves QC) provided the opportunity to develop these ideas. Before summarising the views expressed by CAEPR authors in the debate on the Reeves Report, however, it is necessary to examine more closely what CAEPR researchers have said about Aborigines' use of royalties from mining.

ROYALTY ASSOCIATIONS

Among the many institutions of the Indigenous Sector, royalty associations are possibly the least likely to be recognised as political institutions. It is tempting to see them as mere legal devices created by the Land Councils so that they may distance themselves from the inevitably messy and contentious business of deciding who gets how much royalties. I will argue that CAEPR's studies of royalty associations give us reasons to see royalty associations as 'political', in the sense that they mediate between competing understandings of what is prudent and just in the distribution of royalties.

In 1984, Altman reviewed the Aboriginal Benefits Trust Account (ABTA). He found a significant divergence in understandings of Indigenous rights and responsibilities as receivers of statutory royalties. In one view, statutory royalties were 'public' money, and Aboriginal recipients were publicly accountable in their use of it. In the opposed view, Aboriginal people received statutory royalties in virtue of their ownership of their land, and they were no more accountable in their use of that income than were any other owners of property whose use or degradation had a market value. This 'public/private' ambiguity resonates through the discussion of an appropriate royalty regime because it raises the question of the *accountability* of Indigenous Sector institutions (the ABTA/ABR, the Land Councils and the royalty associations).

Altman and Pollack have discussed one way out of this 'public/private' definitional issue: to class as 'private' the proportion of mining income 'negotiated with the resource developer direct as agreement payments', and to class *all* statutory royalties as 'public'. However, they have little confidence in this solution because 'in assessing the financial performance of so-called "royalty associations" it is usually impossible to differentiate between these two types of money'.[17] Another solution would follow from the Industries Commission's proposed clarification of traditional owners' property rights. To vest most or all of the benefits of mining in the traditional owners would be to favour the understanding that communities' use of statutory and negotiated royalties was their own 'private' concern. Yet another possibility would be to argue that the decisions made by Aboriginal royalty receivers are so crucial in the economic development of their regions that, in their spending and investment decisions, they have a high degree of accountability to the government and their own people. Against the background of this unresolved philosophical issue we can appreciate the importance of CAEPR's studies of royalty associations.

In 1993 Altman and Smith examined the ways that the Nabarlek Traditional Owners Association (NTOA), a body formed in 1988, had used income derived from the operation of the Queensland Mines Limited uranium mine in Western Arnhem Land. They were conscious of the 'lack of clarity with regard to Aboriginal property rights in minerals'.[18] This same lack of clarity maintained a political space within which researchers could pertinently pose questions about Aborigines' use of this income. In the view of Altman and Smith, Aborigines would be prudent to save and invest as much of their mining royalty income, whether negotiated or statutory, as they could. Although Aboriginal people could be investors, in theory, as individuals, as households, as lineages or as corporate bodies, the assumption of this 'prudential' perspective has been that royalties are more likely to be invested — and invested productively — if they are not distributed to individuals and households, but amassed in some kind of community corporate account.

Altman and Smith reviewed the political risks that would have faced the Northern Land Council if it had tried to promote a policy of withholding and investing in the early years of the Nabarlek's operation, 1979–82.[19] In this period, and in subsequent years, most royalties were paid out in cash and in the form of consumer goods to families and to individuals. Disputes among Aborigines about who was entitled to what were endemic to this process. The portion that was invested (by the NTOA's predecessor, the Kunwinjku Association) did not yield dividends. In forming the NTOA in 1988, the Northern Land Council and the Department of Aboriginal Affairs hoped to deal with these problems, largely by narrowing the definition of 'beneficiary'. However, it had proved difficult for the NTOA to break with the Kunwinjku Association's pattern of favouring distribution over investment. The NTOA could have spent only its investment income for a few years in order to build up a capital base, but it had not done so. Why not? they asked.

Altman and Smith offer an instructive case study of the 'political, organisational and cultural factors that reinforced the almost exclusive emphasis on expenditure'.[20] The objectives of the NTOA reflected those of the people it tried to serve: 'short-term and oriented to consumer goods [especially motor vehicle purchase and maintenance] and cash distribution'.[21] The NTOA's investment portfolio was 'conservative' (trading bank accounts), it aimed at short-term returns, and it was vulnerable to expenditure proposals by NTOA members. Altman and Smith acknowledged 'the right of individuals and the Association to determine the nature of their expenditure', but they questioned the wisdom of devoting such sums to motor vehicles.[22] The NTOA needed an investment strategy and a set of priorities for infrastructure development. Not only did such strategies have to be sound in financial terms; they had also to find acceptance, in the eyes of NTOA members, as alternatives to consumption goods. To give the NTOA the strength to resist members' demands for consumption expenditure, should it be obliged by law to invest and to spend with an eye to the future? Altman and Smith withheld their support for statutory oversight of royalty associations, out of respect for the policy of self-determination. However, they urged the Northern Land Council to be more active in advising such bodies as the NTOA, and they suggested that a federation of royalty associations could be formed as the institutional base for advocating a more far-sighted approach to royalty incomes.

It is clear from Altman's study of another royalty association in the same region, the Gagudju Association, that there is no endemic 'Aboriginal' tendency to favour consumption over infrastructure investment and commercial investment. He and others agree that Gagudju has been a 'success' in that it has: 'invested heavily in the regional economy ..., actively supported outstation development and other regional community development goals ..., managed to make conservative distributions of cash to its adult members ... while ... holding equal shares in trust for juvenile members'.[23] Nonetheless, escalating rivalry between groups within the Gagudju Association provoked the Northern Land Council to review it in 1996. The NLC engaged Altman for part of that task. Among his conclusions were that the Land Rights Act should be amended to enhance the Land Councils' powers of oversight of royalty associations. He also regretted that the Act did not 'stipulate the purpose for which mining moneys are allocated' and that there remained 'an acute tension between Indigenous and bureaucratic perceptions about how the use of these resources should be monitored and acquitted'.[24] He did not spell out the terms he favoured for a new legislative regime guiding or binding the use of statutory royalties. However, he suggested that what was at stake was the very principle of paying statutory royalties:

> The payment of mining moneys to Aboriginal groups has been predicated, implicitly if not explicitly, on an assumption that these financial resources will be utilised to either ameliorate the negative socioeconomic impacts of resource development projects or to provide access to scarce capital to facilitate economic development. If the payment of mining moneys causes excessive disputation, a negative impact, or does not result in positive economic outcomes, then government may justifiably argue that such payments, a net cost to the Australian public and mining companies, should be reduced or cease.[25]

It was Altman's view that the performance of royalty associations was becoming central to the political survival of the Land Rights Act.

Royalty associations, like the Land Councils themselves, are new political institutions made necessary by the recognition of Aboriginal land rights. Their emergence is an important part of the story of the rise of the Indigenous Sector. What kind of political institutions are they? Altman and Smith ventured some answers to this question in their study of another royalty association, the Ngurratjuta Aboriginal Corporation (NgAC), in Central Australia.

Founded in 1985, the NgAC has developed two basic policies on royalties distribution. First, payments are to community and outstation trust accounts, not to individuals, for stipulated 'community purposes'. Altman and Smith described this as 'best practice'.[26] Second, half the money available for distribution after covering administration costs is to be invested, not distributed. Managing the consequences of an ill-judged investment preoccupied the NgAC in the 1990s. Altman and Smith suggest that this illustrates the prudence of spreading, rather than concentrating, investments. The NgAC has also developed a suite of services for member communities: outstation support (subsidised by ATSIC), an airline and aircraft maintenance service, and an accounting service. For NgAC, the issue has always been to find a balance between its 'social' and its commercial activities. In this it is typical of Indigenous royalty associations. As Altman and Smith generalised:

> in performing their primary function of receiving, managing and distributing moneys, royalty associations have become multi-dimensional financial organisations offering flexible membership and organisational frameworks, and delivering a wide range of social, economic, cultural and political services ... [They are] critically situated at the point of interaction between the Australian Indigenous and mainstream economic systems. They are required to operate in both and hence are constrained by a 'two-way' accountability ... on the one hand ... by an 'internal' accountability to its membership for the

delivery of services and representation ... on the other hand ... by accountability to an external constituency within the mainstream economy; in particular to the private and public sectors that place significant demands upon them for financial and commercial accountability.[27]

Royalty associations should establish, in the minds of all the constituencies to which they are accountable, the limits on what they can do. In Altman and Smith's view they:

> will not be able to create economic self-sufficiency within regions or even single communities; should not be substituting for the delivery of essential services that government and ATSIC should be providing; and will not be able to create sustainable regional employment on a significant scale.[28]

In 1996 Altman suggested that governments would be justified in assessing the contribution of royalty associations to the economic well-being of their members and regions. His later position, post-Reeves, was to urge caution in such evaluation and to emphasise that royalty associations were, inevitably and properly, accountable to more than one constituency.

REEVES' ROYALTY PROPOSALS

In 1999, with Robert Levitus and David Pollack, Altman debated the argument of John Reeves that land rights had not materially benefited Northern Territory Aborigines. It is possible to see how Reeves could have come to that conclusion. As Altman had pointed out in 1996, 'social indicators derived from the five-yearly census' showed that 'there has been little change in the overall economic status of Aboriginal people in the Northern Territory'. That stasis might be merely the impression given by flawed statistics, he was quick to point out. 'Land might be used for unorthodox commercial activities, like wildlife harvesting, or non-market activities, like hunting and gathering, activities that 'improve people's standards of living, but are not measured by official statistics'. Altman remained confident that, in the long term, with investment, education and entrepreneurship, land could be the basis of Aborigines' improved living standards as measured by Census-based 'social indicators'. The Land Rights Act, he reminded readers, did not oblige traditional owners to pursue 'economic betterment' in that sense.[29]

Reeves' critique of the Land Rights Act assumed that statutory mining royalties (and even negotiated royalties) were effectively 'public' money for whose expenditure Aborigines were accountable in public policy terms.[30] Economic and social betterment was now the primary goal that the financial provisions of the Act should serve. In the opinion of Robert Levitus, Reeves' 'intention to press all significant monetary flows from mining on Aboriginal land into the service of a uniform social engineering agenda is a substantial departure from the principles underlying the Woodward Report and the present Act'.[31] Reeves proposed a new way to apportion statutory royalty equivalents, allocating 29 per cent to cover the costs of land councils (and their peak body, the proposed Northern Territory Aboriginal Council, NTAC); 20 per cent for investment by the Aboriginal Benefits Reserve and the remaining 51 per cent to be spent on proposed NTAC programs of economic and social improvement. There would be no place for royalty associations in this scheme.

Altman and Pollack countered Reeves with an alternative reform scheme. Acknowledging the importance of 'economic betterment', they nonetheless attempted to respect the principle that statutory royalties should be at the disposal of institutions that were more accountable to Territory Aborigines than Reeves' NTAC, a body that would be composed, initially, of government-appointed 'representatives' of the Aboriginal people. They thus argued for the retention of the ABR, the existing Land Councils and the royalty associations. Altman and Levitus have devoted a paper to discussing the terms of the possible reformed relationships between these three levels of the Land Rights Act's financial apparatus.[32]

In matters financial, Altman and his co-authors have argued, these bodies should henceforth work according to a clearer statutory charter. That is, the Act should 'clarify the purpose' of statutory royalty equivalents. 'The purpose would include that the moneys are to ameliorate impacts of resource development projects by providing opportunities for enhanced community development, greater participation in regional economic development, and the creation of opportunity for future generations.'[33] Royalty Associations would be made more accountable — 'to the relevant Registrar, the land council, or the ABR, but ultimately to the Minister' — in the pursuit of 'a clear mission/vision'. What mission would be appropriate? Altman and Pollack implied their answer by remarking that 'some royalty associations are multi-million dollar organisations operating as community development organisations rather than business houses'. They called for a clear separation of the 'commercial' from the 'social' activities of royalty associations; and they wanted the law to discourage individual payments and to encourage investment.[34]

THE ACCOUNTABILITY OF GOVERNMENTS

For such reforms to be effective, Aboriginal agencies would not be the only bodies to need a forward-looking charter when making decisions about mining income. Governments also would have to reconsider their responsibilities in regions where Aborigines receive, in one form or another, statutory royalty equivalents. 'Substitution', the reduction of government funding, has been the price that one such region has paid for hosting mining, according to the Kakadu Region Social Impact Study. As Altman and Pollack put it, 'there may be no net financial benefit from mining ...', for Aboriginal owners 'may have unstrategically used compensation payments to finance services that government would have provided anyway or governments may have used mining as an excuse not to meet their obligation'.[35] Altman and Levitus suggest the following ways to ensure that statutory royalty equivalents are a *net addition* to traditional owners' wealth, and not a subsidy (in effect) to government:

> The possibility could be explored of tying ATSIC or the Northern Territory Government into dollar-for-dollar arrangements with affected group associations over common areas of concern. Conversely, royalty associations expenditure could be directed to projects outside the purview of official funding agencies. A major increase in the percentage of MREs [mining royalty equivalents] going to affected groups would reduce the need for official funding. A reduction in that percentage would make it apparent to external funding agencies that royalty income could not substitute for other sources. Similarly, a geographically broad definition of affected groups would spread royalties thinly, and remove the perception of independent wealth that motivates the psychology of substitution.[36]

CAEPR is continuing to research the impact of large-scale resource projects in remote regions with high Indigenous populations.

7
NATIVE TITLE

In 1993, the Australian government responded to the High Court's 1992 Mabo judgment by legislating 'native title'. The *Native Title Act* has the potential to add considerably to the Australian Indigenous land base, by recognition of customary ownership. As well, complementary legislation created the Indigenous Land Corporation (ILC) to buy land.

'Native title' is a new land tenure, and its economic potential is not easy to predict. David Martin and Christos Mantziaris point out why 'native title' might in practice be different in content to 'land rights' as defined in numerous State and Commonwealth statutes:

> Every instance of native title is different. A title might confer exclusive occupation and use of land, or more limited rights of occupation and use. It might include the right to occupy, maintain and manage an area of land, the right to hunt, fish and gather, the right to access the land, the right to make decisions about access to land, the right to preserve sites of significance, the right to engage in trade, and the right to conserve and safeguard the natural resources of an area. Furthermore, the identity of native title group members, and the manner in which they may exercise their native title rights and interests, may be defined in different ways.[1]

Similarly, Hal Wootten has urged anthropologists to make sure that native title is not restrictively codified. Lawyers will be the immediate proponents of codification, he predicted, adding that lawyers only express the deep and highly evolved tendency of western capitalist societies to ensure 'certainty' and uniformity:

> Where rights in land are concerned, several centuries of capitalism and industrialism have worked to bring title to an individualised, alienable

and recorded form so that it can be dealt with in a certain fashion as a security and a commodity. This entails certainty as to the exact scope of the rights of clearly identifiable individuals at any given point, and certainty as to how that allocation of rights may be changed, including a clear definition of who may change them and how, and what will happen to those rights on the demise of one or more or all of the individuals. Those are the kinds of things that lawyers recognise as rights ...[2]

Because customary law is a living and evolving tradition, native title is also evolving, Wootten continued. Just as freehold title gets its content from being part of an evolving system of law, so the content of native title should be understood as subject to the ongoing influence of the customary tradition of which it is part. 'Every determination of rights and interests under native title should, as part of the description of the rights and interests, refer to the system of customary law under which they exist and which defines them, and under which they may evolve.'[3]

I suggest that the uncertainty and variability in the way that Australian legal institutions are realising 'native title' in practice parallel the uncertainty and variability of Indigenous land-owners' perspectives on their land and their seas as 'assets'. Mantziaris and Martin seem to me to make this parallel explicit when they look at the 'openness' of native title from the point of view of the Indigenous entities which give effect to it. After reviewing extant judicial opinion about how 'native title' is to be defined, they conclude that:

> the lack of clarity in the law creates some uncertainty as to whether native title corporations ought to orient themselves towards a management of 'traditional' rights and interests, or to seek out commercial opportunities which flow from the exercise of these rights and interests. It also creates uncertainty as to the way in which the corporation is to engage with the evolutionary process ...[4]

It is against these depictions of the *emerging* nature of 'native title' that CAEPR's writings on the economic significance of native title should be read.

The *Native Title Act 1993* (NTA) did not give owners a veto over minerals exploration, but a 'right to negotiate'. As Smith described the NTA up to 1998:

> the right to negotiate is not a right of veto for native title parties. It is a right for them to be asked, and even to demand a veto. But there is no right to enforce a veto. The entire negotiation process is based on the legal fact that it is a right to agree. At most, it is a right to propose and agree to conditions about the doing of a future act and to seek compensation and other benefits for the potential impairment of native title; at the least, it is a right to *agree* to disagree. The stage at which a decision can be made to veto a future act is when exercised by the NNTT [National Native Title Tribunal] in arbitration. Finally, that

arbitral determination - whether it be a clearance or a veto of the future act — *can* subsequently be overridden by the relevant State, Territory or Commonwealth Minister.[5]

For Altman, the right to negotiate 'is a form of property because it can be traded away, much like a futures option'.[6]

Altman is sensitive to the ways that features of legislation and of the political environment could influence Indigenous conceptions of their 'interest' in land. Many of his comments about the rights conferred by native title have been based on the assumption that, more often than not, Aborigines want to do a deal and that both Aboriginal and developer interests would be served by minimising 'transaction costs'.[7] Although Altman adopted what he called an 'economics framework' in which 'Indigenous parties are rent maximisers', he acknowledged that 'in some cases Indigenous interests will be maximised by stopping development'.[8] It remains unclear to what extent such indisposition to 'development' is an effect of features of the NTA that could be changed. Sceptical responses to development may have other bases, such as well-entrenched alternative perspectives on land use that have nothing to do with the characteristics of the NTA. Without trivialising the latter 'cultural' factors, Altman has explored the possibility that changes in the law could influence Indigenous land-owners' willingness to negotiate with developers.

Was the NTA structured so as to encourage or discourage Indigenous negotiation? In Altman's view, the NTA created incentives for both miners and land-owners to negotiate compensation for the disturbance of the latter's land and lifestyle. Because the NTA did not provide for owners to receive statutory royalties, the owners were more likely, under the NTA, to negotiate compensation in the form of equity, employment and other economic benefits, thus stimulating Indigenous thinking about regional economic strategies.[9] Some features of the NTA militated against the emergence of native title holders' 'pro-development' tendencies, he suggested. Many Indigenous Australians did not yet know whether they would be allowed to exercise 'native title' rights. Their 'right to negotiate' (within specified time frames) was a relatively unclear property right. And the representative capacity of Native Title Representative Bodies was in doubt.

The transactional efficiency of the NTA was also Siobhan McKenna's theme. She argued that the processes of negotiation between miners and Aborigines were likely to be less expensive under the NTA than under the Land Rights Act (LRA). Her argument here implied some scepticism about the work of the existing land councils of the Northern Territory. Land Councils' powers under the LRA have sometimes lacked legitimacy among some

Aboriginal groups, she suggested. Under the NTA landowners' corporations would have more scope to choose a process of negotiation with miners which is not mediated by the Land Councils. As well, she judged the composition of the owning group to be more transparent under the NTA, making the extended anthropological research of Land Councils less necessary. McKenna thought that the NTA avoided spreading the benefits of a mining agreement too widely. Payments made by miners could go to the native title holders only, without having to be diluted among many Aboriginal people from 'areas affected' as under the Land Rights Act.[10]

One of the most intriguing differences between the Native Title Act and the Land Rights Act is that the former lacks (or is not encumbered by) a statutory royalty regime that delivers payments to Aboriginal people other than the negotiating group and to representative Land Councils. Was this a good or a bad innovation? Altman could see different points of view. On the one hand, lack of access to statutory royalty payments meant that there was less reason for native title holders generally to be well-disposed to mining.[11] Statutory royalties more widely spread their benefits. Distribution of such royalties may give recognition to the regional dimensions of Indigenous politics.[12] On the other hand, after analysing the Mt Todd agreement of 1993, Altman conjectured that because the NTA did not provide for any Aborigines (whether owners or other groups) to receive statutory royalties, the owners were less likely, under the NTA, to rely on 'economic rent' (income derived from ownership of assets). They would negotiate compensation in the form of equity, employment and other economic benefits.[13] On the whole, Altman's view of 'rent' as the form of Indigenous financial return has been more favourable than unfavourable. When considering the Howard government's proposed amendments to the NTA in 1996, he argued that the Commonwealth, by sharing its 'rent' with Indigenous interests, could help persuade native title holders to facilitate petroleum exploration and production.[14]

The consistent thrust of Altman's comments on the NTA has been to emphasise the importance of creating income incentives for native title holders to strike a deal with developers. His opinion about the best forms for such incentives has not been so settled. Thus, when he detected a 'growing recognition among Indigenous interests that the potential financial returns from NTA in terms of rent sharing' are less than under the Land Rights Act, he was noting a defect and building a case for reform of the NTA.[15] He implied the same view of the 'Indigenous interest' when he remarked in 1996 that 'the current framework is hardly working optimally for Indigenous interests'.[16] Unlike McKenna, Altman thought that the NTA was less effective than the Land Rights Act in encouraging

Indigenous Australians to the negotiating table.[17] If there were to be any reforms of the NTA, they should aim to increase Indigenous people's capacities and willingness to negotiate with mining companies, he concluded. His principles of reform were:

- Rights to returns from mining, rather than rights to negotiate exploration, should be the object of negotiators' considerations.
- To add statutory royalties to the returns from agreements would more widely spread their benefits and risks, and give realistic recognition to the regional dimensions of Indigenous politics.
- Native Title Representative Bodies were so integral to the native title process that they deserved statutory formulation of their roles and responsibilities.[18]

These principles underpinned his advice to the Australian Petroleum, Production and Exploration Association.[19] When addressing the policy issues of 'native title' as a property right Altman saw much value in the complex way that Justice Woodward had configured the Indigenous property right in 1973 and 1974.

In pointing to the benefits of statutory mining royalty equivalents, Altman was sensitive to the ways that Indigenous Australians make sense of their social life partly in regional terms — as networks of people and networks of land portions that they live on and control. Patrick Sullivan set out the implications of a regional conception of native title in the Kimberley. There Aboriginal people wanted to use their land in a number of ways: for residence, for hunting, for ceremony, for conservation, for mining, new forms of pastoralism and non-Indigenous tourism. It would require regional planning and a regional agreement, he pointed out, to allocate the available Indigenous lands to these various uses. In this way of seeing the problem, it was not a matter of Aborigines being for or against 'development'. He questioned 'the current orthodoxy that Aboriginal alternative land values and commercially efficient enterprises do not mix'.[20] It depends on the scale of the land portion(s), he argued.

That is, Sullivan suggested, it was possible to satisfy a range of Indigenous interests that may or may not be compatible in respect of any one portion of land, but were certainly compatible so long as land use within the region were considered as a whole, with different portions being valued and used in different ways. To consider issues of land ownership and use on a regional basis could thus make it easier to leave the content of 'native title' more open to 'evolution', as advocated by Wootten. One of the challenges to anyone advocating such a region-wide approach is to effect region-wide alliances among the Indigenous groups. I discuss Sullivan's presentation of this issue in Chapter 13.

In 1996, the Howard government proposed amendments to the NTA. Because the government did not command a majority in the Senate, there were differences between what was proposed and what, eventually, was enacted in 1998. CAEPR has not published an evaluation of this legislative result, but two CAEPR papers surveyed the Howard government's proposals. In Smith's view, their most significant effect would be to 'facilitate resource and other developments on Aboriginal lands ... by reducing the time taken for the negotiation process ...; by transforming the right of negotiation to a right of consultation in some cases; by enabling certain activities to be removed entirely from its coverage'; and by making it harder for aspiring native title holders to register their claim.[21] Smith also noted that these amendments displayed one of the codifying tendencies against which Wootten warned: equating 'native title' with an existing tenure. Appealing to a principle of 'equality' between non-Indigenous and Indigenous Australians, public policy could make that existing tenure a politically enforceable model for 'native title'. If 'the overall effect of the amendment package is potentially to favour a freehold equivalence reading of native title', Smith conjectured, then 'native title' was more likely to be realised in different ways in different States, for it is the systems of State legislation that effectively define 'freehold'.[22] (And it is the States that determine the conditions of mining tenures.) In Jenny Clarke's opinion, the proposed native title amendments would have made it 'less than freehold'.[23]

We should not underestimate the cultural stress that the native title regime has created. Previewing the 1998 amendments to the ways that native title holders can negotiate Indigenous Land Use Agreements (ILUAs), Smith noted the pressure on native title holders 'to explain, systematise and perhaps compromise their native title rights and identity to an unprecedented degree ...'.[24] In similar vein, Altman and Pollack describe negotiations as a 'a very fraught area where [native title holders] may be required not only to translate their culture to courts, lawyers, mining companies and governments, but also to place a value on loss or damage to this culture'.[25]

NATIVE TITLE AND THE INDIGENOUS SECTOR

Whatever codification of native title emerges from legislation, arbitration and negotiation, this new tenure requires a suite of Indigenous political institutions if it is to be practically effective. As more and more land falls under native title, governments must review their resourcing of Indigenous negotiators. Previewing the 1998 changes to the Native Title Act, Diane Smith commented that they made necessary additional ATSIC funding to cover the expanded workload of NTRBs:

> The wider cross-section of Indigenous persons able to participate as parties in [Indigenous Land Use Agreements] (such as common law holders of native title, Prescribed Bodies Corporate, NTRBs, traditional owners and other categories of Indigenous land owners defined under State legislation) will mean ATSIC will be faced with a broader range of requests for funding assistance ...[26]

Perhaps governments should set up State Negotiating Funds, funded from licence and lease fees and royalties from resource development and matched by Commonwealth money.[27]

Native Title Representative Bodies are not the only political institutions to be spawned by 'native title'. To hold title, there will be Prescribed Bodies Corporate. Mantziaris and Martin have devoted a substantial book to the issues that must be considered in designing these Bodies. I will not try to digest in a few paragraphs a work of such erudition, subtlety and good sense. Rather, I see their book as complementary to this, another effort to survey systematically the 'governance' issues of the emerging Indigenous Sector.[28] There is another body derived from the NTA that I will note here: the Indigenous Land Corporation. The ILC is set to become the single most important economic institution of the Indigenous Sector.

By 2004, the ILC will possess a fund of about 1.1 billion dollars; investment returns from that fund will purchase land — forever, if the fund is prudently managed — for Indigenous Australians. The ILC will also help the owners to manage that land. Indeed, the ILC has become responsible for advising all Indigenous landholders on land management, whether or not it played a part in the acquisition of the property. How will the ILC involve itself in the large issue I have discussed in this chapter (promoting, resisting and planning the transformation of Indigenous land into a factor of 'economic development')? According to Altman and Pollack, although the ILC does not see itself as 'a major player in the economic development arena', it does aspire to be a 'partner in the move toward greater economic well-being for Indigenous peoples'.[29] Accordingly, its purchases are based on 'cultural' rather than commercial considerations; however, where purchased land has commercial prospects the ILC can form subsidiaries. Thus, 'a land management subsidiary could sub-lease land from traditional owners for commercial operations'.[30]

The ILC has created a wholly owned subsidiary, Land Enterprise Australia, to handle all commercial land management projects. Altman and Pollack hope that it will 'mentor' Indigenous land-based enterprises:

> Land Enterprise Australia will facilitate the negotiation of joint ventures on Indigenous land, particularly in pastoral and agricultural businesses and permit a more clearly defined commercial focus than is presently possible for the ILC. Furthermore, by isolating its commercial risk,

ILC assets are protected ... A nationally focused service of this type is overdue in Indigenous land management.[31]

In the opinion of Altman and Pollack, the ILC cannot undertake on its own the task of land management of the Indigenous estate (16–18 per cent of Australia in 2000). 'Other Indigenous agencies such as ATSIC, land councils, NTRBs and the ABR in the Northern Territory will also be key players in Indigenous land management and development.'[32] One thing is clear: over the next few decades, the ILC's land purchases will provide the Indigenous Sector with a large territorial base and responsibility.

8
REPRESENTING THE LAND-OWNER INTEREST

There are four Northern Territory Land Councils. CAEPR's attention has been dominated by the work of the two larger Councils: the Northern (NLC) and the Central Land Councils (CLC). Both bodies were set up upon the recommendation of Justice Woodward, the Royal Commissioner whose 1973 and 1974 reports formed the basis of the Whitlam and Fraser governments' Northern Territory land rights legislation passed in 1976. In her retrospective on Woodward, the Act and its implementation, Finlayson pointed out that 'Woodward sought to encapsulate and translate into legislation indigenous concepts of consultation, authority, and decision-making operative in traditional land tenure systems'.[1] The principal representative mechanism, in Woodward's recommendations and in subsequent legislation, was that the traditional owners of any portion of land would be represented by a wider regional land council which would be obliged to ask their consent before approving any use of that land proposed by a non-owner. 'Land rights' legislation thus concerns not only land tenure, but the design of effective forms of Indigenous political authority over that land. The Land Councils, with their statutory obligations to traditional owners, were the Land Rights Act's most significant *political* innovation.

Finlayson quoted a 1988 comment by Altman and Dillon (1988) on the contested expectations of the Land Councils:

> [B]oth Territory and Federal Governments ... continue to emphasise that the land councils' statutory roles are to merely act as agents for traditional owners of land. However, land councils are operating increasingly as guardians of Aboriginal interests and representatives of Aboriginal people's views and aspirations. This is partly a consequence

of the inability of Australian political institutions to meet the specific needs of Aboriginal people. There is little scope for Aboriginal interests to be recognised and satisfied within the NT political system (based on political parties, formal elections and so forth) because this majoritarian system invariably leads to outcomes favoured by the mainstream ...[2]

This comment reflected, in particular, an enduring political polarity in Northern Territory politics over the place of Aboriginal interests in the Territory's 'development'. The long-term political agenda of the Northern Territory government has been to attain Statehood for the Northern Territory. Territory leaders until 2001 have presented as a glaring and correctable anomaly the Commonwealth's continuing responsibility for Aboriginal land rights in the Northern Territory.[3]

To save the Land Rights Act from being 'emasculated' by the Territory government's series of proposed legislative amendments in the 1980s and 1990s, the Land Councils became 'locked into a series of ideological and political battles with the Northern Territory Government'.[4] Stead speculated on the cost of this troubled political conjuncture:

> [P]olitical negotiation of a total land claim settlement package may have been a more effective and strategic tactic. Some initial loss of rights may have occurred. The immediate gain of Aboriginal control over a large portion of the Northern Territory and the associated political, economic and social benefits would have offset this.

He conjectured that 'Aboriginal monies' could then have been spent not on land claims and on political lobbying but on such activities as 'control over mining, social impact monitoring, ... land management and development issues ...'.[5] In other words, the road not taken would have broadened the governance functions of Land Councils. Rather than becoming the negotiators of a wholesale redistribution of Northern Territory lands, the Land Councils had to direct their resources to winning back land on a case-by-case basis, through submissions to the Aboriginal Land Commissioner.

This mode of Land Council work — forced on the Land Councils by a series of Northern Territory governments that were hostile to land rights — created two sources of tension between the Land Councils and their Indigenous constituents. First, land claims have to be prioritised, and second, within any land claim, the Land Council has had to decide between competing accounts of who, by Aboriginal custom, really owns the land in question. In managing tensions between constituents and between itself and dissatisfied constituents, a Land Council cannot merely 'reflect' Indigenous wishes. It has no choice but to try to intervene constructively in the manner of expression of those wishes. Conducting themselves in these difficult circumstances, the Land Councils have tended to increase the formality of their operations. When some dissatisfied constituents took action against the Northern Land Council in the Federal Court, Justice Olney in his 1991 judgment (in the matter of *Majar*) clarified the procedural obligations of Land Councils to enable 'disputing native title claimants equitable access to their services and to funding for the preparation and conduct of claims over the same land'.[6] 'Objectivity', 'transparency', 'formality' and 'representativeness' were keys to Land Council legitimacy.

LAND COUNCILS AND INDIGENOUS RIVALRIES

The anthropologist John Morton has reflected, largely in positive terms, on the Land Councils' formalising trajectory. Drawing on his experience as a consultant anthropologist preparing land claims for the Central Land Council, Morton declared that Land Councils, as bureaucracies, 'are places of "order" in which open disputation may seem "uncivilised"'.[7] Land Councils bridged a series of parallel antinomies: 'Aboriginal people remain simultaneously "unique" and "part of the nation"'. Their culture is both exotic and comprehensible within common civil codes. Land Councils depend 'at once on assertions of local autonomy and identity *and* on a network of legal, economic and political ties that are transnational'. Any consideration of the Land Councils' 'representation' and 'accountability' must come to terms with Morton's conclusion that 'land rights, with anthropology acting as its adjunct, is largely in the business of practically "refining" Aboriginality'.[8] To be responsive to one's constituents, while constructively intervening in the forms and idioms of their political mobilisation, has challenged Land Councils' legitimacy.

Competition between Land Councils and other Aboriginal interests for finance has been another challenge. The money to run the Northern Territory Land Councils comes from mining on Aboriginal land. That is, the Commonwealth pays into the Aboriginal Benefits Account an amount equivalent to the royalties received by the Commonwealth and Northern Territory governments from mining on Aboriginal land. The money is then disbursed according to a formula set out in the *Aboriginal Land Rights (Northern Territory) Act 1976*. At least 40 per cent goes to the Land Councils, whose budgets must be approved by the Minister for Aboriginal Affairs. The Minister has often exercised his discretion (conferred by a 1979 amendment to the Act) to approve the Land Councils getting in excess of the 40 per cent of ABTA moneys set out in the legislated formula. With 30 per cent of funds going to 'areas affected' by mining, if Land Councils get more than 40 per cent, other categories of Northern Territory Aboriginal beneficiary get less than the balancing 30 per cent. This sets up a competition between Land Councils and other categories of Indigenous beneficiary (who are also the constituents of the Land Councils). The Act's financial regime thus challenges the Land Councils to justify — to the Minister, to ATSIC and to the Indigenous constituency — the growing expense of their operations.

The Land Councils' resulting problems of legitimation have been of great interest to the Northern Territory Government and to policy intellectuals sharing that government's perspective. In 1998, John Reeves QC's commissioned review of the Land Rights Act criticised the Land Councils' performance in representing Indigenous interests. Reeves wanted to replace four Territory Land Councils with 18 Regional Land Councils and to make them all responsible to a new 'Northern Territory Aboriginal Council'. He argued that the two biggest Land Councils were too large and that they were obliged to reflect the wishes only of 'traditional owners' of Aboriginal land rather than of all residents on that land. His proposed Regional Councils would include all the region's residents as controlling members of the Council. (However, he did not prescribe any particular representative structure for the Regional Land Councils.) The Regional Land Councils would assume each Land Trust's title-holding function.[9]

Reeves' reforms would have dethroned the 'traditional owner' and made all residents equally responsible for Regional Land Council decisions. He argued that his proposal *to combine land ownership and land control in one regional representative body* was more consistent with Aboriginal custom than Woodward's separation of the two functions of land *ownership* (vested in the Land Trust) and traditional owner *representation* (the Land Council's obligations to consult traditional owners). One of CAEPR's research themes in 1999 was to reflect on Reeves' proposals for Land Council reform. Though Galligan found fault with the 'integrity and adequacy' of Reeves' evidence for the large Land Councils' failure and for the small Land Councils' success (Tiwi and Anindilyakwa — both based on islands), it remains an uncomfortable fact that the Tiwi and Anindilyakwa Land Councils owe their existence to the articulate dissidence of the Tiwi and the Anindilyakwa — breakaways respectively from the Northern and Central Land Councils.[10] Even without formal evaluation of their work, they stand as institutional expressions of the localised scope of Indigenous solidarities. Their very existence puts in question the size of the Northern and Central Land Councils, whose regional coverage owes more to non-Indigenous ideas of administrative efficiency than to Aboriginal notions of localised polities.

To debate Reeves it was thus necessary to face two issues. First, in what terms could such large representative bodies as the major

Land Councils defend their legitimacy? Second, how effective could Reeves' proposed Regional Land Councils be expected to be? CAEPR researchers, and those attracted to a conference on Reeves, co-sponsored by CAEPR, had much to say about both issues.

TRADITIONAL OWNERSHIP AS POLITICAL STATUS

Nic Peterson recalled that in 1973–74 Woodward had considered, then rejected, the idea that regional community structures, with all residents as members, should hold the title to Aboriginal land.[11] Peterson and Peter Sutton argued that it would be impractical and/or unjust to ignore the Indigenous perception that some people are 'owners' by virtue of attributes (such as genealogy and possession of knowledge) whose weight, in Indigenous opinion, far exceeds the shifting circumstances of residence.[12] Woodward had been right, they argued, to vest ownership in one entity (the Land Trust) and political representation in another (the Land Council), and the Act was also sound in stipulating that Land Councils defer to traditional owners' wishes about the uses of their land. 'Aboriginal tradition usually makes a clear and quite profound distinction between traditional affiliations to countries and residential associations with settlements or districts.'[13] In seeking to undermine the pre-eminence of the traditional owners in the Land Councils' political processes, they pointed out, Reeves was making an assault on the customary foundations of the Land Councils' legitimacy.

Martin spelled out the underlying logic of these observations:

> It should be accepted that the pressures towards increased autonomy at local and regional levels have legitimate origins, in part at least, within the Aboriginal polity itself. Centralised organisations such as the existing land councils will always be viewed with suspicion in a society whose imperatives lie so firmly at the local level. At the same time it must also be recognised that organisations such as land councils of necessity must operate in the ambiguous and fraught zone between the two political systems, the indigenous one and that of the wider society. In this interstitial arena the fundamental questions of effectiveness, legitimacy, representativeness and accountability are constantly contested in terms of the often incommensurable principles of the two political domains.[14]

He defended Woodward's institutional legacy in terms of this distinction of 'political domains':

> The Land Rights Act attempts to establish structures and processes whereby these incommensurabilities are addressed in terms of the principles of each political domain. In essence, effectiveness, legitimacy, representativeness and accountability within the wider political system are established by setting up an organisation with the resources, including funding, to undertake its statutory roles in a professional

manner, under the general direction of a council which is broadly 'representative' in at least regional terms. Effectiveness, legitimacy and accountability within the Aboriginal domain are established essentially by means of the 'informed consent' provisions of the Act.[15]

If there were to be regional land councils in the Northern Territory, they would be legitimate to the extent that their design honoured the different standards of both the political traditions that they served.

THE PROBLEMS OF SMALLER LAND COUNCILS

Second, commentary on Reeves considered whether Regional Land Councils could legitimise themselves through their effective delivery of services to Aboriginal land-owners. That is, CAEPR research considered some practical difficulties in Reeves' Regional Council proposal. David Pollack estimated the likely costs of the 18 new councils.[16] Assuming minimal staffing for effective service of their regional populations, Pollack estimated that an adequate budget for the new bodies would be almost three times the amount projected by Reeves. The budget for the body supervising the 18 new councils, the Northern Territory Aboriginal Council (NTAC), would also probably exceed Reeves' estimates. If NTAC and the 18 councils were funded to be effective, Pollack estimated, they would use up all the money likely to be received by the ABR, compared with the Land Councils' consumption of just over half of ABR funds since 1977 (as calculated by Altman).[17] Reeves' recommendation thus presented the government with a 'Hobson's choice' between a less cost-effective but adequately funded new Land Council apparatus, or a retinue of new Land Councils which was inexpensive but inadequate to its tasks.

In the CAEPR contribution to critical discussion of the Reeves proposals, there has been no presumption that the current Land Councils are beyond improvement. Whatever the flaws of the Reeves Report's proposed regionalisation of ownership and representation, his question was apt: could the Land Councils be improved as structures of Indigenous representation by some devolution of their functions to regional bodies? Levitus, Martin and Pollack considered both the customary and the financial basis of possible regionalisation policies. Contrasting regionalisation as a Land Council initiative with regionalisation as a constituents' initiative, they saw merit in both scenarios. They outlined several criteria that the Minister for Aboriginal and Torres Strait Islander Affairs should apply before granting the wishes of 'breakaways'. They also suggested that regionalisation, however it was initiated, could save on costs by retaining a core of centralised staff in Darwin and Alice Springs which would serve all regional bodies.[18]

There was a risk, however, in devolving decision-making. The Land Rights Act as it stands reserves decisions about land use to land-owners, they pointed out. Traditional owners' informed consent to changes in land-use must be demonstrated to the Land Council before it can approve any land-use agreement. Regional devolution risked compromising this principle. To the extent that a regional subset of the Land Council was made up of some of that region's 'traditional owners', there was a danger that traditional owners' deliberations would be conflated with those of the regional land council. The authors argued that a regional land council should be constituted as a body which *received*, but did not *make*, the decisions of traditional owners. To maintain the distinct prerogatives of traditional owners would therefore set limits to regionalisation. 'The closer these councils are to the level of local land management, the more dense will be the representation of local interests in their memberships, and the greater will be the tendency to blur the distinction between decision-making and decision-taking ...'[19] Traditional owners' informed consent remained essential to the Indigenous legitimacy of Land Councils, whatever their structure. This argument invites us to see a distinction between Indigenous and non-Indigenous rationales for the widely endorsed push to 'regionalise' Woodward's main political innovation, the Northern and Central Land Councils. The Indigenous rationale presumes that 'traditional owners' remain pre-eminent political actors in the Indigenous domain; the non-Indigenous (Reeves) rationale considers 'traditional ownership' to be an anachronism, an offence to a democratic model that levels traditional owners' political eminence down to 'residential' rights.

NATIVE TITLE REPRESENTATIVE BODIES (NTRBS)

Diane Smith has commented that if 'the High Court decision in *Mabo v Queensland no. 2* and the passage of the NTA [Native Title Act] have fundamentally changed the nature of the relationships between Indigenous peoples and the Australian government, then the progressive establishment of a nation-wide framework of NTRBs constitutes a similar, potentially fundamental development in Aboriginal political organisation'.[20]

Some NTRBs have been set up wholly in the wake of the Native Title Act; others have been constituted by adding NTRB functions to pre-existing organisations, such as legal services and land councils. Section 202(1) of the Native Title Act spelled out the functions of NTRBs: to supervise the preparation of land claims to be lodged under the Act; to mediate disputes among Indigenous claimants; and to represent the claimants in the native title process. The

Minister must be satisfied with an aspiring NTRB's representativeness before he/she declares it to be an NTRB.

At the Commonwealth government's request, Altman and Smith assessed the needs of these fledgling bodies in 1995. Their report was to be a touchstone for all subsequent CAEPR commentary on NTRBs. They recommended that the NTRBs' representative status, within each region, be more clearly defined and mandated by government. They found that NTRBs aspired to serve Indigenous land-owners broadly, consistent with the political purposes conceived by Justice Woodward in 1974 for the Northern Territory Land Councils. Smith noted that State and Territory governments and the mining industry were already recognising 'the importance to economic development prospects of having credible, professionally run representative organisations on the ground, which can ensure thorough, but relatively speedy consultations and negotiations with the correct native title parties'.[21] As NTRBs acquired legitimacy as effective representatives of Indigenous interests, they would become 'influential regional voices' within the Indigenous domain. They would thus help to crystallise emergent regional Indigenous political leadership. 'Their managers help constitute the regional and national Aboriginal leadership, and many are linked to networks of Indigenous stakeholders and to key individuals in government agencies. Almost all have focused their operations at a regional level minimally matching that of an ATSIC regional council, or to a series of major cultural blocs ... Relationships with regional councils will be critical.'[22]

Where NTRBs have been established 'on the back' of an already existing organisation, the momentum and credibility of that organisation may favour the legitimation of the NTRB. The Cape York Land Council (CYLC), for example, became the NTRB for that region. Even before the Native Title Act, the CYLC had 'been actively involved in negotiations over Aboriginal control and co-management of lands and seas in the region with a variety of State and Commonwealth agencies and commercial interests' such as 'the Great Barrier Reef Marine Park Authority, ... the State government over the proposed eastern Cape York conservation zone, ... mining companies over compensation and other issues in western Cape York, and in the development of CYPLUS and the Cape York Peninsula Heads of Agreement'.[23] The CYLC's policy and community development interests are broad enough to place its NTRB work within a wider regional strategy. For example, the CYLC has had a hand in setting up a regional health service and an economic development corporation. These developments have encouraged Noel Pearson to argue that regional organisations should be partners with governments in welfare reform.

A number of writers have pointed out that, without the statutory monopoly enjoyed by the Northern Territory Land Councils, NTRBs will have to struggle to become the sole voice of native title interests in their region. CAEPR devoted Research Monograph 12 to a number of papers on the theme 'fighting over country'. One contributor, David Trigger, pointed to the difficulty, in at least one region, of establishing the authority of a Native Title Representative Body. The Carpentaria Land Council found in the mid-1990s that it was not yet able to 'play an arbitrating role' in respect of conflicting Indigenous views of a proposed large mining project. He pointed to an irony that 'it can often be precisely because key people in the local representative bodies are so fully engaged within the field of regional Aboriginal politics that the organisation they work in is not seen as independent or neutral with respect to intra-Aboriginal disputes ... [A] representative body may itself be involved substantially in disputes with other Indigenous organisations and groups'.[24]

Another contributor, Julia Munster, discussed the weakness of NTRBs: 'NTRBs are unable to control the actions and representations of external parties, particularly governments, which may create and/or exacerbate disputes ... NTRBs are also unable to control the responses of their constituents to the actions and representations of external parties ... Unlike the ALRA, the NTA does not establish a statutory scheme requiring that all land-use proposals be directed through NTRBs'.[25] Altman adduced a case where the weak statutory underpinning of a NTRB frustrated a petroleum company, Tenneco Gas International, in its efforts to negotiate a pipeline agreement in south-west Queensland. In 1996, the NTRB, the Goolburri Land Council, found itself in dispute with one of its constituent land-owning groups, resulting in a delay to the pipeline's completion. The incident:

> demonstrates the risks for the industry of dealing with NTRBs that do not currently have mandatory statutory functions to identify all potential native title claimants to a future act (in this case the pipeline easement) nor the statutory requirement to sign off an agreement. It demonstrates that the pivotal role of NTRBs was not clearly understood when the NTA was originally passed. Resistance by both industry and State governments to their establishment as statutory bodies charged with ensuring an orderly claims and R[ight] T[o] N[egotiate] process have contributed to current difficulties, especially in situations of multiple claims.[26]

Altman noted however that at least one NTRB, the New South Wales Land Council, did not want a mandatory role and was currently encouraging industry and native title parties to negotiate directly.[27]

It could be argued that it is not only a matter of strengthening NTRBs legally, in their dealings with their constituents and with outside interests. The legitimacy of NTRBs can be cultivated also through each NTRB's strategies of staff and organisational development. Munster outlined several steps that would help NTRBs to persuade their disputing clientele that the NTRB was acting impartially.[28] She recommended also that the staff of NTRBs find ways to learn from each NTRB's experiences of conflict resolution and legitimation. One of Munster's recommendations — to 'facilitate discussions between disputing groups and provide them with opportunities for compromise and cooperation' — has been exemplified in the practice of two Western Australian NTRBs.[29]

In Kalgoorlie, the Goldfields Land Council in April 1996 began to establish a series of 'Working Groups' as arenas for rival claimant groups. 'Each Group comprises two representatives from each of the claimant groups in the region and operates under a set of cooperative principles which may differ from area to area.'[30] In Broome, the region's NTRB, the Kimberley Land Council, convened a Rubibi Working Group to co-ordinate the Broome area's many native title claims. 'With native title claims over all the vacant Crown land in the town and environs, over much of the sea and some leasehold land, and with potentially explosive heritage issues over the rest, the Working Group found itself inundated with requests for their involvement in consultations and negotiations even before many of the claims were accepted and mediated' by the National Native Title Tribunal (NNTT).[31] Thus empowered by multiple and pragmatically motivated non-Indigenous recognitions, as well as by its own internal processes of representation and conflict resolution, the resulting 'Rubibi Land Heritage and Development Council' was soon to become a 'prescribed body corporate' under the Native Title Act.[32] Non-Indigenous investor recognition looked like being important in confirming the status of the Working Groups in the Goldfields as well.[33]

In 1996, the Howard government circulated amendments to the Native Title Act, and in 1998 Parliament passed a version of these amendments. Among the changes was a stiffening of the legislative basis of the NTRBs, requiring them 'to undertake a range of activities including acting as a conduit for native title claims to the NNTT, as a mediator of conflict between competing native title interests and as a negotiator on behalf of appropriate native title interests with respect to future acts ...'. If they were adequately resourced, NTRBs could rejoice in these changes, Altman suggested.[34] Finlayson, however, suggested that the effect of the Howard government's amendments would be to increase the accountability of NTRBs without the 'balance' (or compensation) of greater powers.[35] She drew the implications of this policy emphasis: NTRBs would have to develop 'policy and procedural mechanisms for transparent decision-making; processes for accountability of claims prioritisation and review; contracts for out-sourcing of legal and anthropological work; mediation and dispute resolution mechanisms; staff and management accountability to regional land owners and board management duty statements and codes of conduct'.[36] She saw much for NTRBs to gain from this formalisation, as 'an NTRB is not fundamentally a grass-roots community organisation. It is a new creature which must operate according to statutory functions'.[37] Indigenous Australians with experience in other incorporated bodies would have to adjust to the NTRBs' more demanding and formal organisational culture. 'The transition from old ways of operating organisations to new and different models will not be easy', she predicted.[38]

Prime Minister Howard's 1998 Native Title Act amendments included provision for Indigenous Land Use Agreements; the amendments created a range of pathways for arriving at them. Smith's thorough description of these provisions illustrates the variety of possible roles for NTRBs in the negotiation of ILUAs 'ranging from representation and certification through to direct negotiation'.[39] Smith was concerned that the uncertainty of the NTRBs' status would not be resolved by Howard's 1998 amendments. Like Finlayson she judged that 'while the Bill proposes substantial accountability requirements ..., it fails to provide [NTRBs] with the mandatory functions necessary to reinforce their jurisdictional legitimacy and credibility'.[40] When an NTRB is called upon to 'certify' an Area Agreement, it is poorly positioned to do so unless it has been involved intimately in negotiation, yet the amendments did not make it *necessary* for the NTRB to be so involved. She cited Northern Land Council experience to illustrate the huge effort that would be required before an NTRB could confidently certify an Area Agreement. The NTRBs, she concluded, would be poorly served by Howard's amendments if they did not give NTRBs: 'a statutory mandate to facilitate all types of agreement'; a monopoly representative responsibility under the NTA in each region'; 'sole responsibility for funding native title claims and negotiations'; and 'full accountability to all native title holders and claimants within their jurisdictions'.[41]

In 1998 Finlayson reported uneven development in NTRBs' capacities. Some were not effective, some were not accepted by their region's Indigenous people as the best vehicle for native title claims and negotiations. Can NTRBs be made effective? she asked. Finlayson argued that the lessons and recommendations of ATSIC's 1995 review of NTRBs had not been absorbed with sufficient care. Finlayson did not say directly whether this was a failing of ATSIC or of the Commonwealth government; however, she argued that

ATSIC's performance was adversely affected by the climate of accountability in which it had worked. She wondered whether ATSIC 'can simultaneously deal with the external political pressures from government for repeated performance and financial auditing, and the internal question of bench marking best practice in NTRB performance and management, standardising administrative procedures and requiring responsible self-determination'.[42] As well, she pointed to the demands that publicly accountable self-determination placed on Indigenous notions of their accountability to one another. She assigned to ATSIC and to the National Native Title Tribunal the responsibility to reform the dysfunctional organisational cultures of NTRBs, by service agreements, 'national benchmarks' and the prioritisation of claims.[43]

CONCLUSION

CAEPR's writings on Northern Territory Land Councils and on Native Title Representative Bodies illustrate the many problems that they have faced in establishing themselves as effective mediators of the interests of Indigenous land-owners. To some extent the difficulties arise from the fact that many Australian political and economic interests have been slow to concede Indigenous land and native title rights. Thus, the Northern Territory Land Councils' first twenty years were dominated by the Territory government's determination to contest land claims. This has exacerbated the Land Councils' problems with their constituents, while also giving Land Council leaders a chance to present themselves in an heroic light. Yet because Australia's landed interests also desire an orderly system of land tenure, they have reasons to value the emergence of stable and effective representatives of Indigenous title-holders. Indigenous land-owners have also had things to learn: how to settle rivalries among themselves, and how to countenance representation of their land interests by non-kin who work in offices hundreds of kilometres distant.

Perhaps the most important and enduring innovation of the Land Councils has been to show that the customary eminence of the 'traditional owner' need not yield to the introduced political norm that renders all 'citizens' or residents juridically equal whatever their 'ownership' status. Now that native title holders are beginning to devise lasting institutions through which to exercise their entitlements, they too will find themselves considering the rival merits of two political traditions.

The Land Rights Act has helped to give legitimacy, in the Northern Territory, to the Indigenous tradition of privileging 'owners' over mere residents in the politics of determining land-use. However, the Native Title Act does not provide claimants or determined title holders with a right to negotiate, and in some regions where 'native title' is the effective land statute 'residence' has become more of a status to reckon with. As Chapter 13 will argue, there is no nationwide 'Indigenous' cultural principle for designing territorially based Indigenous institutions.

PART 3

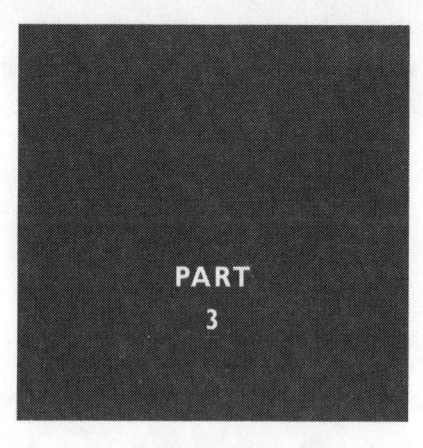

DOMESTIC CHOICES:
CHILDREN,
GENDER AND
IDENTITY

INTRODUCTION

While it has been government policy to develop the formal institutions of the Indigenous Sector, policy-makers have also had to take into account the basic units of Indigenous sociality — the patterns of behaviour determined by customs of kinship and family. In contributing to governmental thinking about Indigenous domesticity, CAEPR studies have drawn on ethnographies of kinship, household formation and sharing. They have been preoccupied in particular with the issue of whether terms such as 'family', 'sole parent' and 'household' make sense in the Indigenous context.[1] Although the research I review in Chapter 9 would lead one to distrust each of these terms — or to use them with great caution — they nonetheless remain in use, as if policy-oriented researchers cannot do without some vocabulary denoting basic units of Indigenous social life. The appeal of such terms is that they imply (but do not necessarily deliver) a grasp of some of the domestic dynamics of Indigenous poverty. Using terms such as 'family', 'sole parent' and 'household', the CAEPR researchers have attempted to connect Indigenous studies with the terms and the concepts employed in the wider Australian social policy literature.

To understand how the state (or any other responsible authority) could relieve poverty it is necessary to have a model of the relationship between those who receive no income and those who receive some. How are those with no income — for the most part, but not exclusively, children — able to access some of the money or goods of those who have some income? To answer this question is to build a model of the 'income units' typical of the governed population. No matter how great may be the difficulties of developing such a model, some notion of 'income unit' has usually been assumed to be essential. Without it, *all* children (and *all* non-recipients of income) would have to be understood to be poor, and the state would be expected to assume total responsibility for the maintenance of such people. To have some notion of 'income unit' is useful, in two ways.

First, a notion of income unit allows the state to distinguish between poor and non-poor dependents. That is, it allows a distinction between those non-recipients of income who benefit sufficiently from a relationship with an income recipient (such as children who are in a relationship with parents/carers of adequate income) and those non-recipients who are not in such a relationship. The latter group are among those whom the state should be helping — either by removing the dependants to a better provided environment (foster family, adoptive family or institution), or by transferring money and goods to that income unit.

Second, a notion of income unit allows the state to identify as *responsible agents* those to whom it supplies welfare incomes (or goods in kind, such as public housing). These responsible agents — adults, with or without children or other dependants — are understood to have a duty to use part of what they receive from the state to provide for the well-being of those within their income unit who have no income. Henry and Daly report that some residents of Kuranda judge the welfare payment program according to their conviction that 'the people who actually do the "looking after" of children (by feeding, clothing and sheltering them) should be the ones who receive the payments'.[2] To adopt the terms used by Finlayson and Auld, there is no doubt that 'an instrumental connection between program delivery and mundane practices exists ...'.[3] The 'mundane practice' is that people live within domestic groups that the state, encouraged by social scientists, tends to treat as 'income units'.

One of the things that makes social policies 'social' is that they make assumptions about the internal dynamics of such domestic groups (income units). As well, social policy is 'social' in the sense that state agencies and those groups/units will influence one another's actions. Chapters 9 and 10 synthesise what CAEPR research has to tell us about Indigenous domestic order. My work of synthesis is different in each chapter. Chapter 9 is about a highly self-conscious research program within CAEPR, a deliberated effort to mobilise the notions of 'household' and 'family' in order to identify a line of responsibility that could run between the welfare state and Indigenous domestic processes, through key adult carers. Chapter 10 is about a research theme, gender relations, that lies latent and untheorised within CAEPR's body of work.

Finally, in Chapter 11, I have drawn attention to one circumscribed but hugely important way in which the Indigenous household has emerged as a palpable locus of Indigenous self-determination. The enumeration of the 'Indigenous population' of Australia is effected through a highly standardised interaction between the Commonwealth government and every 'household' in Australia: the administration of the Census at five-year intervals. The Indigenous population has recently grown so quickly as to puzzle demographers and to trouble social scientists who use Census data. By summarising CAEPR's publications on these problems, I argue that the Census empowers the 'household' in the determination of 'identity', and thus that the household plays a crucial part in the construction of the Indigenous 'population'.

9
FAMILIES AND WELFARE

CAEPR research into Indigenous poverty has been strongly tempted to postulate some model(s) of Indigenous domestic groups as income and expenditure units. Researchers have attempted to answer the question that Smith formulated: 'What might be the central social arrangements of Indigenous family life that are relevant to formulating suitable policy and service delivery?'[4]

CAEPR researchers began to refer to the 'Aboriginal household' quite early in CAEPR's history. When Smith reviewed research on Aboriginal expenditure, she assumed that the 'spender' could be understood to be a household. The Australian government periodically collects data on the expenditure of a large sample of Australian households (the Household Expenditure Survey), so would it not be useful to compare Indigenous with non-Indigenous households' expenditure?[5] On the basis of the possible interest of that comparison, Smith used the phrase 'Aboriginal household' in these two 1991 papers.[6] The notion of 'Aboriginal household' entered the CAEPR literature by a process of imitation and repetition. It was then a category awaiting empirical content.

Demographic projection occasioned another early use of the notion 'household' in CAEPR literature. The Census enumerates Australians as members of 'households', so when Gray and Tesfaghiorghis projected population growth, their unit was not only individuals but also 'families' ('the most basic of social institutions') and Indigenous 'households' ('in which the so-called "reference person" [on the Census form] is Aboriginal or a Torres Strait Islander').[7] Adopting these terms enabled them to derive from their population projection a projection of the increase in demand for houses. As well, Jones' research on the need for housing postulated the household as an income unit. He calculated, for different regions, 'financial housing stress' (the ratio of housing costs to household income) and 'after-housing poverty' (household disposable income after housing expenditure).[8]

The category 'single-parent family' (or 'sole-parent family') also appeared early in the CAEPR research program. In 1991, Gray and Tesfaghiorghis analysed 1986 Census data and found that in about one-third of the 'households' in which the 'reference person' was Indigenous, there was a single father or a single mother.[9] Altman and Smith cited this figure in 1992 and made the point that 'one parent Aboriginal families had the lowest family incomes' and a very high rate of joblessness. They also cited research comparing the poverty of Aboriginal and non-Aboriginal 'sole parents'.[10]

While CAEPR researchers have adopted these terms for referring to Indigenous domestic life, they have also questioned their descriptive adequacy. Indeed, Altman and Smith sowed the seeds of doubt. In 1991, Smith wrote that because of the flows of people, money and goods between 'households', the 'assessments of the impact of incomes on household expenditure capacities, made on the basis of combining all household earnings and welfare payments, can be extremely misleading'.[11] In 1992 Altman and Smith remarked that ethnographies 'highlight the operation of an Aboriginal "welfare network", a system of social and economic relations within and between Aboriginal households whereby persons and families with negligible personal income are financially supported by recipients of social security payments ... Social security payments have, in effect, a wider "income catchment" as a result of the redistributive mechanisms operating within Aboriginal society'.[12] They did not then pursue the implication of these remarks — that in their getting and using of money, Indigenous Australians do not necessarily form 'households' or 'families' in the usual (Census or social policy) sense of those words.

ETHNOGRAPHY AND THE ABS

In a series of papers, Daly and Smith have examined the utility of Australian Bureau of Statistics data in constructing an empirically informed model of Indigenous income units. In particular, they have considered whether the terms 'household' and 'family' — widely used in the collection and analysis of statistics and in ethnographies — were of any help in coming to an understanding of the 'central social arrangements of Indigenous family life'.

Smith noted that in its Household Expenditure Survey the Australian Bureau of Statistics (ABS) defined a 'household' as:

a group of people who live together in a single dwelling as a single unit in the sense that they have common housekeeping arrangements, i.e. they have some common provision for food and other essentials of living.[13]

A 'household' could consist of one person, and there could be more than one 'household' in a dwelling. Smith further observed that the ABS definition tended to exclude from a 'household' those who were not residentially stable participants: a 'range of transient residents, whether they consider themselves members, visitors, lodgers or boarders'.[14] Would this ABS-defined 'household' — enabling an analytic distinction between 'household' and residents of a dwelling — serve as an approximate model of the Indigenous income unit?

Smith did not explicitly answer that question in her 1991 paper, though she made clear her reservations about the ABS definition. However, in reporting data from the 1986 Census, her use of the terms 'multi-family household' and 'family household' implied a second analytic distinction — between 'family' and 'household'. Smith's paper thus produced three distinguishable categories: residents of a *dwelling*, members of a household, and members of a family. That is, it would be possible to have a dwelling consisting of more than one household and to have within any household more than one family. However, we can find other usages in Smith's paper. When she referred to 'household size' and to numbers of people in a dwelling, she implied that they are one and the same.[15] Her paper effectively offered the reader a choice between two possible conceptual schemes: that there are three social units (dwelling, household, family) or that there are two (dwelling/household, family).

Smith did not favour the equation of 'dwelling' with 'household': 'Aboriginal households are not necessarily demarcated by the physical boundary of a dwelling'.[16] However, having said what an Aboriginal household is not, she declined to postulate what an Aboriginal household *is*, referring to their 'porous social boundaries reflecting highly dynamic life cycles'.[17] By way of illustration, she referred to John Taylor's research on the mobility of Aboriginal people around Katherine. Taylor, it should be noted, was sufficiently confident in a definition of Aboriginal 'household' to count 201 of them and to differentiate 'visitors' from others. Taylor's Katherine research is thus more suited to illustrating the point that a large number of Aboriginal people are 'visitors' to households than the point that the boundaries of Aboriginal households are 'porous' or difficult to discern.[18] The category 'visitor' is arguably predicated on a definition of 'household' membership, and a boundary is no less a boundary for being 'porous'. Smith's references to other studies of household visitation seemed to confirm rather than undermine the possibility of seeing Aboriginal social life in terms of 'households'.[19]

She generalised that Aboriginal households are often composed of 'a stable core with a highly mobile fringe of transient members'. If there were any referent for the term 'Aboriginal household' (a term used over and over in Smith's paper), it was based on that 'stable core'. Smith did not dismiss the category 'household' but differentiated its members according to residential stability.

Other researchers agreed that any user of the Census 'snapshot' of household composition should not assume constancy of numbers and composition of co-residents of a dwelling. Martin and Taylor, in a paper addressed primarily to problems of enumeration, declared that they had no use for the category 'household' because of 'the high level of day-to-day inter-household visitation. This is just one manifestation of the importance placed on sociality in many indigenous societies. Commonly ... such visiting takes place within kin or clan groupings whose members are dispersed across many households. In conducting surveys, it is common to find that there are no individuals present at some houses, while at others there may be large gatherings comprising both residents and visitors. In such circumstances, the compilation of lists of household residents is clearly rendered problematic'.[20] Careful not to overstate this point, they conceded that 'often' Aboriginal households have 'a more or less stable core'.[21]

Having raised doubts about 'household', some CAEPR researchers explored the pertinence of the category 'family'. As we shall see, this term also proved to be difficult to endorse and yet hard to do without.

In a 1995 paper, Daly and Smith referred to 'family' as 'the elementary structure of mother, father and their children'. It 'is commonly reported to be the central ordering principle within Aboriginal society'. They distinguished 'family' from 'household' in two ways. First, by giving the word 'family' a wide and open-ended meaning: '... the nuclear or elementary family is not the most common residential form, as each individual's investment in family relationships is widely distributed within a complex kinship system that emphasises classificatory and consanguineal relatedness, and is used to familiarise strangers'.[22] I will refer to this as the 'ethnographic' sense of 'family'. Second, they recognised a very restricted meaning for 'family', when they remarked that 'the households in which individuals live are often multi-family'.[23] This recalls the ABS notion of 'family'.

The result of these two definitional moves was that in distinguishing 'household' from 'family', Daly and Smith invoked two senses of 'family': either a very small group (so well-defined that one could count the number of families residing within one 'household') or a very large one (linking people residing in more than one dwelling) whose boundaries are so difficult to ascertain that such 'families' are also conceivable as 'networks'. Daly and Smith did not express a preference for one definition over another, finding them both useful.

In much of their subsequent research, Daly and Smith followed the ABS and reported Census data as if all residents of a dwelling could be considered a 'household'. Within any one dwelling/household there could be one, two or three families. That is, they used the very small group notion of 'family'. The ABS recognises 'four main elementary family types': two parents residing with dependants and/or offspring, the couple not residing with 'offspring', the one-parent family (residing with offspring and/or dependants), and co-resident and related persons. (If one-parent families are differentiated as male-headed/female-headed, then the ABS typology is fivefold.) The ABS recognises five possible relationships between adults and 'dependent offspring'. Four of the possible relationships are within a family (and thus within a household, as defined by the ABS): natural/adopted child of both parents or sole parent; stepchild of male parent; stepchild of female parent; foster child. The fifth possible adult/child relationship, 'child in a secondary family', acknowledges those situations in which a household includes two or three families.

In 1996, Daly and Smith pointed out that this set of categories limits the ability of the Census to describe Aboriginal domestic life. However, in making this critique they continued to be unable to stabilise the meaning of their key term 'family'.

First, they suggested that Aboriginal people, unlike the ABS, do not necessarily attach social significance to the physical reality of the dwelling. People who live in a number of associated dwellings may see themselves as 'one family' or as an extended 'household'. 'Aboriginal households are not necessarily demarcated by the physical boundary of a dwelling.'[24] The Census does not allow for the possibility that a household extends across more than one dwelling; it understands a 'household' to be the same thing as the co-residents of a dwelling. Moreover, the Census can code as a 'family' only people who co-reside within one dwelling (while allowing that within a dwelling/household, there may be up to three families). Aboriginal people might use the word 'family' to refer to people living in several dwellings. Daly and Smith insisted that, whatever the ABS might say, the extended notion of 'family' and of 'household' was of great significance in the ways that Aboriginal people understand their responsibilities towards each other, particularly the responsibilities of adults for children.

Second, they pointed out that the Census data, being a five-yearly snapshot, obscures the short-term mobility of visitors. 'It is not possible, from Census data, to examine the impact of short-term and frequent mobility on family structure and economic wellbeing.'[25] This comment may serve as an example of Daly and Smith switching from one notion of 'family' to another. They could not have been invoking the extended notion of 'family' when they made this complaint about the Census. From the point of view of the extended family network, 'short-term and frequent mobility' is of little if any consequence.[26] The extended network of kin is not a 'structure' whose composition or shape is altered by 'short-term and frequent mobility'. On the contrary, such mobility is an essential feature of that family network: as individuals move around within it, making claims in the idiom of kinship (consanguineal or classificatory), they *enact* that broader sense of 'family'. When Daly and Smith called attention to 'the impact of short-term and frequent mobility on family structure and economic wellbeing' they must have been invoking the more restricted ABS sense of 'family' — that unit which is coextensive with, or smaller than, a household.

Third, the Census tends to 'allocate people who have no "usual place of residence" with one; namely the place of enumeration on census night'.[27] Accordingly (and this follows from the previous point), the Census is likely to underestimate the proportion of Aboriginal people who are only weakly attached to any one household or 'family'. (Again in the restricted sense, since it is impossible, by definition, for an Aboriginal person to be peripheral, transient or a visitor from the point of view of the extended family network: he/she is simply mobile *within* that network.) The Census thus 'sees' far less of the residential mobility of 'visitors' and 'transients' than other kinds of survey might do.

Notwithstanding these defects of the Census, Daly and Smith made use of it. Reporting 1991 Census data, they replicated the Census notion of 'family', presenting five possible Indigenous 'family' types: female sole parent, male sole parent, couple, two-parent and 'other'. For each type of Indigenous family, the Census can tell us how commonly they occur, where they occur, and their age, labour force, educational and income characteristics. Daly and Smith also reported some of the characteristics of those Aboriginal 'households' in which there are two or three families. About half of co-resident families were related as mother's/father's family to son's/daughter's family; and a quarter of co-resident families were related within the same generational level (brother's/sister's family). Finally, they were able to show that one in four dependent offspring in 1991 was present within a family by virtue of some kind of 'fostering' relationship. They concluded that 'Indigenous families are more likely [than non-Indigenous families] to be sole-parent families and have on average a larger number of children. The adults are younger, have lower levels of education and are less likely to be in employment than other Australians'.[28]

In the 1995 paper from which I quote, the authors were continuing to understand 'Aboriginal family' in two different senses. On the one hand they deployed the five-part typology used by the ABS; on the other hand, they acknowledged that many Aborigines understand 'family' to refer to an open-ended network of mutual obligation whose solidarities are enunciated by its actors in an idiom of kinship — this network possibly (and perhaps usually?) extends across more than one household/dwelling and possibly (usually?) encompasses all five types of 'family' unit recognised by the ABS. While the authors urged policy-makers to keep in mind both senses of family, they acknowledged that it was possible to operationalise statistically only those notions of 'household' and 'family' which are given in the Census.

UNSUCCESSFUL SYNTHESIS

Why did Daly and Smith bother with the 'ethnographic' sense of 'family' at all then? I see two reasons. First, in keeping with the policy of self-determination, and true to the anthropological training of several of the CAEPR researchers, there was a presumption of the intrinsic worth of the Indigenous point of view. Second, CAEPR researchers were sensitive to policy-makers' need to identify the responsible agents within Indigenous domestic life. Ethnographic accounts of Indigenous domesticity were more likely than Census definitions of 'households' and 'families' to let us know which adults, in practice, took responsibility. These two reasons converge in a point that Finlayson made in 1995. 'Service delivery and objectives' must have regard to what she called 'cultural parameters' and 'on-ground conditions and experiences; otherwise, 'social policy for Aboriginal families will fail to move beyond statistically-based descriptions of systemic poverty'.[29] Adhering to this view, CAEPR researchers have attempted to read aggregate data, such as the Census gives, against the background of ethnographic accounts of Indigenous domestic forms. Ethnographic research, it has been assumed at CAEPR, grounds policy that is more sensitive to Indigenous ways and interests; policy so grounded is more likely to be effective.

In my reading, CAEPR's research has demonstrated the difficulty of producing a culturally informed understanding of the Indigenous 'income unit' from analysis of Census data. In the remainder of this part I will argue that a consistent, policy-relevant answer to the question 'What is the basic income unit among Indigenous Australians?' has not emerged from CAEPR's work. I do not intend this judgment to discredit the CAEPR researchers. They pursued an important question to the point where it became clear that they could not answer it. My intention is to make explicit that non-answer.

In 1996 Smith and Daly made two suggestions about how Census data should be read in the light of the realities revealed by ethnography. In effect, they proposed that the ABS category 'household' be taken as the best available approximation of 'family' as Aborigines understand that term. First, it would be useful to set aside the distinction between core and non-core household members: 'a more useful definition of household ... would be to include all visitors as members'.[30] 'To exclude them means omitting persons who in fact contribute significantly to (or deplete) the "usual" membership structure and economic wellbeing of a household.'[31] Secondly:

> household income is a more reliable measure of Indigenous income and status than family income, given that the census concept of household at least has the potential to capture extended kin formations via the multi-family type, than does the discrete 'family' concept.[32]

(Note that here Smith and Daly are using 'family' in the restricted, ABS sense, not in the extended ethnographic sense.)

This approach, taking the ABS 'household' (plus 'visitors') as the best approximation of the characteristic Aboriginal domestic unit, enabled Daly and Smith to compare Indigenous and other Australian households in respect to their size and their median incomes, broken down by section of State, and their dwelling tenure status. They concluded their paper by posing two questions for further research. First, it would be useful to disaggregate Aboriginal households according to the composition of different kinds of income. Second, it would be useful to know how many members of households were nett depleters of household welfare (by consuming household goods to greater value than their monetary contribution to household income). In both these lines of research, Daly and Smith began to identify features of Indigenous sociality that they thought might be exacerbating Indigenous poverty. I will start with the second: visitor predation.

VISITORS' PREDATION

When Daly and Smith referred to the depletion of household resources by certain members, they had in mind not only children but adults with neither employment nor welfare incomes. Some of them could be among those adults who were only loosely attached to the household — 'visitors'. They evoked in negative terms the impacts of such visitors:

> High visitation rates are likely to lead to greater and faster deterioration in the condition of the housing stock; exacerbate environmental health problems associated with overcrowding; and create

'visitor-induced' stress on the expenditure capacity of core household members and their potential to save cash and other resources.[33]

In this evocation Smith and Daly were departing from Smith's earlier treatment of the relative openness of Indigenous household membership. In her 1991 literature review Smith questioned the assumption 'that the income of all household members is contributed to, and shared within, the household'. Ethnographic research 'indicates that this is by no means the case. When sharing of resources and distribution of cash does occur, it may well be only within a particular economic unit in a household, or directed to specific individuals in other households. The evidence suggests that low-income Aboriginal households *remain viable because of financial support from members of other linked households*, rather than primarily from the financial contributions of their own members'.[34] A year later, Smith suggested that Indigenous reciprocity effectively levelled the incomes of households within a community:

> One of the economic variations within communities noted by researchers is the great difference in levels of household income and expenditure, which is not directly reflected in household living standards. The explanation for this lies in the process of sharing and demanding access to the cash and resources of others. Such cash redistribution does not occur indiscriminately as a result of some generalised ethic of reciprocity. Kinship and a range of historical ties are key idioms used to negotiate access to dollars and other goods and services. This redistributive mechanism is *sufficient to ameliorate considerable income disparities and associated differences in expenditure capacity between households*, especially those with low or intermittent incomes. Aboriginal economic well-being is, in this manner, supported by a fallback system; an informal network of personal borrowings and repayments used to fulfil obligations and promote economic survival.[35]

In these two passages the ethnographic record is understood to show that flows of goods, money and people between households have a levelling effect. By 1996 however, Daly and Smith were conceding a different possibility: that some households were left worse off by visitors' free access to their resources. Some visitors brought no resources; some took out more than they put in. The theme 'visitor predation' was beginning to challenge a theme of levelling through reciprocity.

SOLE-PARENT FAMILIES

In paying attention to the types of income that Indigenous households received, Daly and Smith became interested in the growing prominence within the Commonwealth welfare budget of 'sole-parent' payments to Indigenous Australians. How many sole-parent families were there? The Census could answer this question. Daly and Smith drew on the ABS five-part typology of Australian 'families'. Of the five types, they focused on two: male-headed sole-parent families and female-headed sole-parent families.

The Census told them that most Indigenous sole-parent families are female-headed. All sole-parent families, by definition, include dependent offspring, and in about a quarter of Indigenous sole-parent families the 1991 Census showed these dependants to be 'foster' children. Some sole-parent families included another related adult, such as the sole parent's sibling, mother or father. The proportion of 'sole-parent' Indigenous families has been rising. Daly and Smith reported the regional, age, marital, income and employment characteristics of Indigenous sole parents in 1991. They also reported the median incomes of the households of which sole-parent families were part, showing that, in terms of income per person, it was neither an advantage nor a disadvantage in 1991 for a sole-parent family to be part of a wider household.[36]

Given the very strong support that Daly and Smith had previously given to the notion of the Indigenous 'household', it was strange that they did not report what proportion of Indigenous sole-parent families were residing in households larger than the sole-parent family itself. And they were unable to test, with Census data, their hypothesis that when other adults co-reside with a sole-parent family they are more often a financial burden on that family than a help. If 'households' (ABS definition) are the best approximation of the Indigenous income unit, then it is hard to know how to interpret data on any Indigenous family type without knowing about its co-residence with (or its exclusion from) households comprising two or three family units. As they acknowledged, 'one must question the extent to which Indigenous sole parents are in fact "sole" in respect to parenting'.[37] Daly and Smith's paper showed how little we know about the social context in which Indigenous sole-parent families operate. We know nothing about 'the extent to which Indigenous sole parenthood is a transitory or recycling life-cycle state, the social distribution of parenting, and the degree of support a sole parent receives from the non-custodial parent and any subsequent partners'.[38]

If so little could be said with confidence about the domestic dynamics of the Indigenous 'sole-parent family', why make it an object of inquiry? The answer would appear to be that the government was becoming interested in the growing popularity of the 'Sole Parent Payment' (SPP). Daly and Smith acknowledged that there were no data confirming the inference that a high proportion of Indigenous sole parents were on the SPP.[39] Nonetheless, the Indigenous 'sole-parent family' became a phenomenon of interest because of an assumed overlap between the categories 'Indigenous sole-parent family' and 'SPP-recipient'. So the age, gender, educational qualifications of Indigenous sole parents and the numbers, ages and mobility characteristics of their children became data to ponder. Any data (from the Census) about these characteristics might help the government to design better services for Indigenous SPP-recipients. Daly and Smith suggested some possibilities. Adults other than the SPP-recipient might be substantially involved in the care of that person's children. Should they get financial support? Do Indigenous female SPP-recipients find it relatively difficult to get maintenance payments from the father of their children? Could vocational training programs be better designed so as to suit the needs of Indigenous sole parents? Do the eligibility rules for SPP inhibit SPP-recipients from accessing the CDEP program?[40]

This attempt to substantiate the category 'Indigenous sole-parent family' was always at risk of confusing administrative with sociological reasoning. While Indigenous SPP-recipients are undoubtedly a discrete client category, about which data can be collected for the government's consideration, it does not follow that 'the Indigenous sole-parent family' is a sociologically coherent category. That is, there is no identifiable type of domestic group to which we can give the label 'Indigenous sole-parent family'. Daly and Smith did not repudiate their argument that the 'household' is the best approximation of the Indigenous domestic unit, nor did they distance themselves from Smith's early emphasis on significance of the flows of money and goods between households. (Indeed, by drawing attention to the mobility of children between adult carers in their 1997 paper Daly and Smith gave a powerful example of those inter-household connections.) Reading the work of Daly and Smith persuades me that it is not possible to draw any conclusions about a social entity called 'the Indigenous sole-parent family'.

It is therefore surprising that Smith and Daly claimed in 1997 that 'the children of Indigenous sole parents are at great risk from the low economic status of their parent'.[41] That statement implied that we knew something specifically about the income and expenditure of 'Indigenous sole parents'. No less surprising was this claim:

> Sole-parent families are generally reported as being amongst the most economically vulnerable and impoverished families in Australia. This research shows that Indigenous sole-parent families are even more disadvantaged than other sole-parent families.[42]

Here the authors overlooked the importance of factors that they have underlined in other publications: that families (ABS definition) are parts of 'households' and that households are units within communities and networks. These facts make it impossible to specify and to compare the income (and expenditure) characteristics of particular ABS family types. (There is an additional reason for being sceptical of this claim. We now have reason to think the Census may seriously understate Indigenous incomes. A recent CAEPR study of the Katherine region questioned 'the quality of census-reported income data' when 'the income reported by those unemployed, or not in the labour force, is set against estimates of annual welfare payments derived from Centrelink administrative data'.[43])

Nonetheless, Daly and Smith persisted in their study of the Indigenous sole-parent family as if it were an identifiable unit of Indigenous income and expenditure. Thus they claimed in 1998 that 'Indigenous sole parent families have a distinct set of socioeconomic and culturally-based characteristics'.[44] However, 'distinct' was used here in the sense of different from non-Indigenous sole-parent families. Using 1996 Census data Daly and Smith showed that, in respect of certain characteristics (age, marital status, number of children, education and labour force status, levels of income) Indigenous female sole parents and their families had a different profile from non-Indigenous female sole parents and their families. However, they did not show that, compared with other Indigenous family types, Indigenous sole-parent families are better or worse off. Rather, they were at pains to point out how little we know about the way Indigenous sole-parent families fit into (or create problems for) the wider Indigenous society. They noted the high proportion of female sole parents who have never been married, commenting that little is known about how Indigenous sole-parent families are formed. And they pointed out how little we also know about 'the nature of their domestic cycles and household economies; the nature and impact of their immediate social environment; and the role which males and other kin play in sole parent family economies' and 'the actual domestic and socioeconomic circumstances of children in these families'.[45]

Daly and Smith wrote as if the phenomenon of the Indigenous sole-parent family was a matter for urgent policy concern. However, there was nothing in their paper to support their claim that Indigenous children dependent on sole parents were at greater risk of poverty, ill-health or any other evil than other categories of Indigenous children.

In 1999, Daly and Smith returned to the 'household'-based analysis of Census data, while continuing, in one section of their paper, to devote particular attention to the 'sole-parent family'. Their aim was to deploy both the ethnographic and the ABS senses of 'household' and to draw a conclusion about the difference between the data they revealed.

Indigenous households, according to ethnographic research:

commonly consist of extended families whose members may live together in a single dwelling (whether these be houses of improvised camps), but *more often than not*, will reside across several nearby dwellings. Typically, a household consists of a small, multi-family, multi-generational core of kin with a highly mobile fringe of transient members.[46]

As well, 'adult members of households do not necessarily share resources, nor do they all contribute to common domestic costs within a particular household'.[47] There is nonetheless much co-operation among the members of households: 'cooperative efforts for subsistence production, food purchases and capital accumulation, ... shared ownership and use of consumer durables, and shared child-care arrangements'.[48] The ABS definition of household and Census data collection methods tended to leave out much of this reality by equating households with co-residents of a dwelling, Daly and Smith reminded readers. The ABS definition allows that there might sometimes be more than one household in a dwelling, but it overlooks the extension of the Indigenous household *beyond* the dwelling. Daly and Smith also found implausibly low the 1996 Census count of visitors (only ten per cent of Indigenous households, compared with six per cent of non-Indigenous households, included visitors on Census night).

Nonetheless, having issued the familiar caveats about Census data, the remainder of their paper reported Census data, using the restricted (that is, household equals usual residents of a dwelling) notion of the Indigenous household. Those data showed that more than seven per cent of Indigenous family units in 1996 were 'second' or 'third' families, that is, that they live in multi-family households, and fifteen per cent of Indigenous households had six or more residents. About three in every ten Indigenous families were 'sole-parent families', but their analysis did not answer the question: what proportion of this type of Indigenous family lived within a multi-family household? Nor could their paper answer the question: what proportion of Indigenous sole-parent families benefit from (or suffer from) being embedded within a multi-dwelling network of kin? Without answers to these questions, one could only speculate about whether those counted within the family type 'sole-parent' were better off or worse off than Indigenous people counted within other types of Indigenous family.

Unable, again, to substantiate the category 'Indigenous sole-parent family' as a unit of Indigenous sociality, Daly and Smith were on surer ground when treating it simply as a statistical category — making Indigenous/non-Indigenous comparisons of the labour force and income characteristics. They also compared Indigenous and non-Indigenous household incomes and house tenures. In summary, according to the 1996 Census:

Indigenous households are more likely [than non-Indigenous households] to be multi-family, increasing in size progressively from capital cities to urban, rural and remote areas in terms of the average number of families, persons, adults and dependants per household. Overall, the adults are younger, have lower levels of education and are less likely to be in employment than non-Indigenous Australians. They are twice as likely to contain sole parent families and less likely to contain couple families.[49]

The question raised by these comparisons of Indigenous and non-Indigenous statistical categories is this: if Indigenous households have lower median incomes (per household and per household member) than non-Indigenous households, can this be explained simply as an effect of these households' comparatively lower levels of education and of employment, or do features of the domestic dynamics of these households also contribute to their greater poverty?[50]

In their frankly speculative answer to this question, Daly and Smith drew on ethnographic evidence:

> Given the prevalence ... of extended family formations, kin-based demand sharing, erratic sources of wage income, patterns of recycling unemployment, high mobility and visitor rates, *we can only surmise* that the real economic burden experienced by low-income Indigenous households is more substantial than the census depicts ... Mobility and related high visitation rates are likely to lead to the:
>
> - greater and faster deterioration in the condition of housing stock;
> - exacerbation of environmental health problems associated with overcrowding; and
> - creation of 'visitor-induced' economic stress on the expenditure capacity of core household members and their potential to save.
>
> These impacts reinforce poverty entrapments for low income households.[51]

In not being able to register these domestic dynamics, they added, the Census probably understates the economic burden that they impose on Indigenous households. Policy-makers should be particularly concerned about those multi-family Indigenous households that include sole-parent families, they emphasised.

Daly and Smith seemed determined to promote the 'sole-parent family' as a specific problem for Indigenous social policy. However, three features of their argument should give us pause:

- Notwithstanding the special attention given in their 1999 paper to the sole-parent type of family unit, their conclusion was about types of Indigenous households, rather than about any type of family unit.

- Although the conclusion was comparative, the comparisons drawn in this paper were not between different kinds of Indigenous household. All the comparisons in Daly and Smith's 1999 paper were between Indigenous and non-Indigenous statistical categories. So a conclusion comparing the different domestic circumstances to be found among Indigenous people is purely speculative.

- In adducing ethnographic accounts of Indigenous domestic life, Daly and Smith again emphasised the negative potentials of flows of money, people and goods among Indigenous households — the reinforcement of certain households' poverty entrapment. This emphasis contrasted with Smith's more positive summary in 1992 of what ethnographies say about Indigenous exchanges, that they effect a levelling of households' economic well-being.[52] This shift in interpretive emphasis was not driven by new data but by a more pessimistic (or realistic?) reading of the literature cited.

CHILD WELFARE IN YUENDUMU AND KURANDA

In their most recent work on the Indigenous household, Daly and Smith sought to investigate: 'the household and family organisational structures and composition ..., the nature of the household welfare economy based on the sources of incomes of the individual members ..., the key cultural parameters of child care ..., the patterns of mobility of children and their parents ..., the impact of that mobility on child care and the delivery of welfare payments for the care of children ...'[53] They hoped to discover 'the central social arrangements of Indigenous family life that are relevant to formulating suitable policy and service delivery'.[54] As they pointed out, not all of 'the factors influencing the service delivery of welfare income transfers paid by government to Indigenous families for the care of their children' are phenomena of Indigenous domesticity; some are features of Commonwealth government programs.[55] The research was funded by the Department of Family and Community Services (DFACS).

In designing the field studies of Kuranda and Yuendumu, the CAEPR/FACS researchers said that they would depart from ABS notions of Indigenous domestic units in three ways. First, they concluded that it was not possible to apply the ABS family typology to Kuranda and Yuendumu households:

> It was apparent that in the great majority of cases, household members were close kin relations. The sheer complexity of the extended family relationships present in the majority of households in both communities, defied, indeed defeated, any neat categorisation or artificial disaggregation according to ABS census definitions of family type.[56]

Second, in their description of households, the researchers classified as 'usual residents' those whom the Census would have noted as 'visitors'.[57] More recently, they have discovered that some Kuranda residents are classified as 'boarders' by others with whom they live.[58] Third, the CAEPR/FACS researchers broke with the ABS tendency to equate dwelling with household; instead they counted as households 'those groups who shared food, allowing the identification of separate households within one dwelling and across kin-linked dwellings'.[59] They defined 'family' and 'parenting' in 'flexible' and 'broad' terms.[60] The central concept of Indigenous domestic group in this study was therefore 'household'.

However, the field study of Kuranda did not always report its findings in terms consistent with these ethnographically informed definitions. First, the authors judged Kuranda's 28 households to be 'overcrowded'.[61] It is not clear how a 'household' defined in the above terms could ever be 'overcrowded'. A household defined in ABS terms (co-residents of a dwelling) is implied here, though the researchers do not tell us how many of the 28 'household' boundaries in fact coincided with the physical limits of dwellings. Second, the Kuranda researchers *did* in fact distinguish ABS family types within households, finding 41 putative sole-parent families among the 28 households (putative, because 15 of the sole parents were absent at the time of the study, though their children were there). Indeed, they commented that 'sole parents and their children are *key units* within extended family households'.[62] Third, although they counted visitors as household members, they also distinguished between 'core' and 'transient' members.[63]

The Yuendumu study maintained the distinction between 'household' and 'dwelling': there were 30 households, occupying 22 dwellings. However, Musharbash lost confidence in the notion 'household' when she realised that she had recorded some mobile individuals as members of more than one household. Her solution was to treat the dwelling as her unit of study and to substitute sleeping for eating, as the activity defining membership. Musharbash recorded the nightly fluctuations of numbers of people sleeping in particular dwellings. She also offered a case study of an individual who changed her sleeping place very frequently.[64] Musharbash's specification of 'sleeping' as the activity defining household membership had important consequences for her differentiation of 'visitors' from 'household members'. In Musharbash's ethnography, 'visitors' are those whose presence within the household did not include sleeping there. They were in other respects 'an integral part of [the household they were visiting], sharing the same rights and duties'. Though Musharbash defined 'visitors' as those who do *not* sleep in a household, she also considered them to have the characteristics that match the ABS notion of 'usual residents'.[65] Those whom the ABS terms 'visitors' she included as 'full household members', presumably because they fulfil her criterion of being among those who sleep there. Though Musharbash differentiates 'core' and other members, her grounds for doing so are not made clear. Perhaps it was according to the degree of persistence in their choice of sleeping place.[66]

Musharbash returned to the term 'household' in order to generalise about the significance of people's mobility:

> People move between households in an attempt to maintain economic viability. The addition of personnel to a household may either strain or improve the financial status quo. Failing to achieve such viability, households will break up and members disperse to other existing households, starting the cycle anew.[67]

She later added other motives for individuals' movement: overcrowding, conflict with other residents, disorderly behaviour by other residents, death of another resident, the desire to be with others. Because all individuals are subject to these motives, all have a network of places at which they can sleep. This includes children. In her recent paper reporting the second stage of her Yuendumu work, Musharbash has developed a typology of 'intra-community mobility for key reference persons'.[68]

Both the Kuranda and Yuendumu studies paid particular attention to children's relationships with adults. Women other than the natural mother were reported to do much of the looking after of children. The resulting network of care and economic support extended across households.[69] At Yuendumu 'respondents had a range of kin relationships to the children they looked after ...'.[70] When Kuranda children were in a household that did not include their natural mother or father, 'the costs of caring for the children are met by a range of people potentially including the parents, grandparents, adult siblings of the parents and other relatives — with these carers residing both inside and outside the household'.[71] When asked, Kuranda people thought it fitting that non-parent carers be compensated by getting all or part of the natural parent's Family Allowance and Parenting Payments. Some preferred to formalise this diversion of money (by arrangement with Centrelink); others liked to keep it on an informal basis. Yuendumu adults told Musharbash that they would like some way to distinguish between welfare money allocated for them to spend on themselves and that which was intended to be spent on the children. Half the Yuendumu respondents said that they had asked Centrelink to redirect the latter portion to another adult; the others preferred more informal arrangements.[72]

The CAEPR study was not conclusive in its view of whether the government could be doing more to assist adults to redistribute welfare money among the adults caring for children. On the one hand, Finlayson, Daly and Smith saluted 'the extended family structure' as:

an Indigenous 'welfare' network, providing individuals with a place to stay when they fall on hard times, giving support to young families, to children when their parents leave them to the care of older relations, and when the fortnightly welfare or CDEP money runs out ... [and as] a central social arrangement, constituting a form of social or cultural capital that makes an invaluable contribution to socio-economic wellbeing of families, their children, and the households in which they live.[73]

They observed mutually helpful arrangements among 'sole parents' and between 'sole parents' and their relatives, so much so as to question whether the (administrative) term 'sole' had any sociological validity.[74]

It is puzzling, after all this, that they speculated that 'the dynamic practices of Indigenous child-care may well be putting children (especially those of sole parents) and their carers at great risk'.[75] Without denying that some Kuranda children may be 'at risk' (of what?), I see no reason, on the basis of their study, for speculating that such risk would be altered by changes to 'the dynamic practices of Indigenous child-care'. Indeed, the researchers went on to recommend changes in *government*, not Aboriginal, practice. They proposed that the government recognise and financially underwrite those 'dynamic' practices, so that the 'actual carer' would get more money. They suggested that the 'great risk' would be reduced if 'welfare payments provided for the care of children' were 'more effectively targeted to the actual carer of the child'.[76] However, the evidence from the Kuranda and Yuendumu projects shows that there is no consensus among Aboriginal adults about whether informal arrangements or new arrangements with government agencies is the better course.

When the researchers spelled out the risk factors in the lives of Kuranda children, it was not clear that 'the dynamic practices of Indigenous child-care' were the problem. On the contrary, that dynamism is as likely to be a *solution* to, or an amelioration of:

the recycling status of sole parenthood within families; the excessive burden of care assumed by some older women for children; inexperienced young parents; children in receipt of marginal or erratic care; inadequate housing for young families; lack of training and employment opportunities for youth and sole parents; lack of services and facilities for youth; risks from substance abuse, family violence and crime; and the impact of absent fathers.[77]

In her summary of the Kuranda and Yuendumu studies, Smith pointed to another category of Aboriginal person whose well-being may suffer from the 'dynamic practices of Indigenous child-care': the carers themselves 'such as older women and men on stable pension incomes ...'. They are central figures in 'a network that operates under considerable duress', a network that 'can be quickly overburdened with demands'.[78] When that burden becomes too great, some children, responding to inadequate provisioning, 'may have to "hunt" for meals and a place to sleep at different households'.[79] In this sentence Smith has redescribed a property of the multi-household network — children's mobility across households — as if it were an instance of the failure of that network. Nothing could more clearly illustrate her ambivalent judgment about whether the extended network of care 'works'. Smith listed the factors which put the network under stress as: 'the extent of the burden of care, levels of mobility, and the limits of welfare income'.[80] We can rule out the first two factors. The first is a circular explanation. The second is elsewhere described as being an essential feature of the network, so to adduce it as a factor in the stressing of the network tells us more about the writer's ambivalence about the network than about the qualities of the network. The third factor is a matter on which only governments can act and is certainly not a property of the extended family network itself.

In their recent paper reporting the second phase of the Kuranda research, Henry and Daly are more cautious in discerning 'risk'. They do not 'view child mobility as pathological':

> It is not mobility, in and of itself, which makes children objects of social concern. In fact, mobility may be a reflection of the existence of an elaborate network of social support, as well as an expression of individual autonomy. However the mobility of some children who are 'doing the rounds' may be a reflection of their marginal status and vulnerability.[81]

The CAEPR study found that some Kuranda and Yuendumu people who were entitled to welfare payments were not getting them. Perhaps the most useful results of this study could be greater diligence in government service delivery and heightened awareness of entitlement on the part of Kuranda and Yuendumu people.[82] As I read the study, the single most important stressor of the extended family network is that the adults have too little money to meet the needs of those for whom they are responsible. Reporting an early phase of this research, Finlayson and Auld mentioned that 'a common suggestion to help people to move beyond the boom-to-bust cycle of Indigenous domestic economies' was for clients to be trained in 'simple budgeting skills'.[83] The authors were sceptical that the problem was one of skill deficit. Rather, they suggested, Indigenous adults had continually to choose between worthy claims — 'stew or shoe?' — often a choice between 'the material needs of children and youths, and that of the regular and daily demand to eat'.[84] The difficulty of such choices is not a property of this or that form of domestic organisation; it is a consequence of having too little money.

CONCLUSION

CAEPR research on Indigenous welfare has paid attention to the characteristics of Indigenous domestic groups. Poverty relief policies have no choice but to consider domestic dynamics, for it is in domestic groups that those without income (for the most part, children) are best able (excluding begging and theft from strangers) to access the money and goods of those with income. Such research aspires to do two things: to identify those domestic groups which are in poverty or in some condition of relative deprivation; and to identify those within the deprived domestic groups who can be deemed by governments to be responsible, to some degree, for the wellbeing of the more vulnerable members of those deprived domestic groups. To those responsible ones (adults of various kinds) the state will give conditional monetary support. It is in answering this second question — pinpointing the adults to be paid for looking after children — that CAEPR research has faced a challenge that is at once conceptual, empirical and ethical.

Two kinds of knowledge have been available: ethnographic case studies and Census data. CAEPR research in this field has been dogged by the problem that ethnographic studies cast doubt on the sociological validity of the units of statistical comparison ('households', 'families') through which Census data are organised. Much CAEPR research has been devoted to considering the problems of three concepts: household, family and visitor. CAEPR researchers have sometimes proposed definitions of these three terms which draw on both bodies of knowledge, though in reporting their own field work these synthetic concepts have not proved easy to apply. In my opinion, it is not possible for CAEPR to resolve the inconsistencies between ethnographic and Census categories. All that can be done is that researchers say clearly in which sense they are using such key terms as 'household' and 'family'. The CAEPR authors have not always done so.

Throughout the CAEPR literature on Indigenous domestic groups, to which Diane Smith has been the most prolific contributor, I have detected an emerging uncertainty about the policy significance of what are understood to be the fundamental features of Indigenous domestic life: the relatively rapid changes in the size and composition of 'households' (co-residents of a dwelling), the strength of kin-based associations between 'households' (occasioning flows of money and goods), the relatively large proportion of people (visitors, transients) who claim membership of more than one 'household', the ease with which responsibility for children passes among adults and between households.

In the most recent instalment of the Kuranda study, Henry and Daly are clearer in their conceptual preferences than any previous writers in this CAEPR research program. They argue that 'child-care is a family-centred rather than a household-centred activity':

> The fact that child-care extends beyond the boundaries of ... households leads us to question the salience of households as child-care units in the Indigenous context in Kuranda. This is not to discount the importance of households entirely, but to stress that the ultimate experiential location of domestic order and care for children among Indigenous people in Kuranda lies somewhere else. Households in Kuranda are integrated into wider socio-economic and kinship networks, or 'families'.[85]

As I have shown above, these 'family' (in the wider, ethnographic sense) processes can be (and have been) described by researchers both as ways that Indigenous poverty and its risks are palliated and as ways that poverty and its risks are perpetuated. I have detected a trend in the CAEPR literature (until very recently): an increasing willingness to pathologise Indigenous domestic processes. The unpersuasive promotion of the category 'sole-parent family' was a symptom of that pathologising trend, but its primary expression has been a rereading of the significance of the flows of money, people and goods within Indigenous networks — what some anthropologists call 'demand sharing'.[86] There is no resolution of the factual or logical inconsistency between the optimistic (levelling, supportive) and pessimistic (permissive of predation, actual child-carers missing out on money) readings of 'demand sharing'. However, they differ in their political implications. The more negative representation resonates with older (and much-debated) social programs of government intervention into Indigenous families. Finlayson and Auld ask 'whether bureaucratic intervention simply undermines the agency of Aboriginal clients to determine, according to their cultural mores (through mechanisms of shame, embarrassment and diplomacy), intra-community relations ... whether there are areas of Indigenous domestic life that should be off limits to bureaucratic intervention through program delivery'.[87] The pathologising emphasis also helps to distract attention from a significant contributor to poverty that only governments can address: the lack of purchasing power in welfare benefits.

The pathologising trend has been interrupted by those reporting the second stage of the Kuranda and Yuendumu studies. The emphasis in the recent papers of Henry, Daly and Musharbash has been on challenging the Commonwealth to improve, in a number of ways, its delivery of welfare payments.[88] Indeed, Musharbash has suggested that the government cease trying to align payment rules with 'the central social arrangements of Indigenous family life', whether 'households' or 'families'. The Commonwealth should treat the same way all welfare recipients over 16 years of age, suggests

Musharbash. Their payments should be graded by age, but whether they had responsibility for children or spouse would be irrelevant. 'By administering payments to individuals calculated on an age-graded needs basis only, the existence of social networks in Aboriginal communities would be both acknowledged and strengthened.' If the Commonwealth wants 'culturally-informed policy and service delivery', Musharbash has concluded, it must 'acknowledge the existence and importance of strong and wide-ranging social networks' that do not correspond to any model of the 'family'.[89]

Henry and Daly decline to endorse, for Kuranda, Musharbash's recommendation for Yuendumu. Kuranda folk, they say, are less mobile than Yuendumu people; and Kuranda's households seem to them more stable in composition.[90] In promoting such differences as relevant to policy, Henry and Daly are undermining one of the ideas with which this CAEPR research program began — that it would be possible, with enough research, to discover the 'central social arrangements of Indigenous family life'.

10
GENDER REFORMING

Within CAEPR's body of research, the topics of male–female interaction and male–female differences are prolifically represented. The information is scattered, and in this chapter I have tried to pull it together. There is a pattern. According to AEDP indicators such as income and employment, Indigenous women seem to have progressed relative to Indigenous men under the impact of the welfare and labour market programs of the last quarter of a century. As well as demonstrating this proposition, however, I want to ponder its significance. 'Family violence' is widely agreed to be one of the scourges of contemporary Indigenous life. I pose the question: has one of the unintended consequences of the 'self-determination' era been a raising of tensions between Indigenous men and women?

GENDER AND SOCIAL CHANGE

One of the defects of the CAEPR literature is the use of the terms 'sex' and 'gender' as if they referred to the same thing. Contemporary social theory differentiates these terms: 'sex' refers to biological difference; 'gender' refers to the social organisation and cultural signification of sexual difference. 'Masculinity' and 'femininity' are not biologically given; rather they are defined in relationship to one another by a myriad of social practices and structures: economic, political and cultural. CAEPR authors, as I will soon show, have told us a lot about sex differences in income, employment, education and training. But they have had little to say about 'gender' — the social organisation and cultural expression of the relationships between Indigenous men and women. To the extent that I speculate in this chapter on the *significance* of changes in sex differences in socio-economic status I am writing an essay about gender in contemporary Indigenous affairs.

I am encouraged to take on 'gender' in this way by a number of suggestive studies and comments about changes in gender relations in contemporary Australia. First, let me offer two cameos of the ways that the gender relations of non-Indigenous Australians are being affected by economic change. In 1994 and 1995, historian Mark Peel asked hundreds of working class men and women, living in outer suburbs where job security is a thing of the past, to discuss with him their experiences of disadvantage and injustice. A gendered pattern is clear in what he heard:

> Women, in particular, share a common story of persistence and battle ... [I]n the neighbourhood houses and the community centres and the streets, ... local women, both residents and workers, have had to manage the good and bad social experiments of the last fifty years. They have managed — generously, carefully and with an often incredible grace — the human consequences of policy innovations like 'deinstitutionalisation'. In playgroups and cooking classes and child-minding networks, they have built some of the sturdiest bridges of a multicultural Australia. Here, Aboriginal and non-Aboriginal groups also meet, sometimes with conflict and sometimes with common cause. And while women take the lead in interpreting and managing a harder and harder world, here, amidst all the devastation of entrenched unemployment, older men explore how to be a man without work, and younger men gather in small groups to care for children while their partners work in McDonalds or Coles.[1]
>
> Employment is a huge issue for these people, and in these working-class families, tradition and experience demand a male provider. If you can't provide, then you can neither become nor remain a man. And being a provider means you can't take 'any old job'. Real men provide, they don't just work, so lower wages and insecure jobs are just as much a threat to manhood as unemployment ... At the same time, a really fair world is one in which the work of women, especially the work of mothers, is recognised and supported. In their stories, women embed themselves in a narrative about 'women's lot' which links 1960s activist mothers to the volunteers and battlers of the 1970s and 1980s, and records the ironies and the successes of 'liberation' for working-class women. In this shared narrative, the main protagonists are the hard-pressed, heroic mother and those who would stand in her way. Even when they had worked or were working for wages, women's primary focus remains mothering, as both a personal and collective commitment. It is a struggle shared with others to get resources for the school, keep a health centre open, confront the rental manager ...[2]

In rural Australia as well, as Geoff Lawrence and Ian Gray have shown, gender identities and relations are under challenge. Studies show that a conventional depiction of farming as being 'men's work' seriously understates the importance of women's labour. However, patriarchal inheritance patterns and political cultures have long marginalised women and still resist their initiatives. 'Things are, however, changing rapidly.' [Women] 'have increased their participation in farm politics, and they are involved in newly formed rural women's networks. Social attitudes continue to restrict women adopting a more involved role in rural affairs, but what cannot be denied is their success in "forcing" such initiatives as the formation of rural women's units, various rural alliances, and government attention to women's issues'. Lawrence and Gray find it difficult to 'predict the fate of farm patriarchy which, while still apparently pervasive, is under attack from the further depletion of the structural relations which underpin the image of the male farmer as one who supports family and community'.[3]

Among those who write about Indigenous Australians there are different views about the way 'gender' has been changing under the impact of their recent (since the 1960s), rapid inclusion in a cash-based welfare system. For example, Noel Pearson and Julie Finlayson — both knowledgeable about Cape York people — have written rather differently about what has happened to such central Indigenous values as 'reciprocity' and 'nurturance'.

Pearson has characterised the last thirty years of government policy as an era of 'welfare poison', in which easier access to cash welfare payments has corrupted Indigenous society, undermining the socially regulatory principle of 'reciprocity'. Pearson has not gone so far as to specify that male–female relations, in particular, have been a casualty of 'welfare poison'. However, in his evocation of one major social pathology on Cape York, alcohol abuse, he implies that men's behaviour towards women and children manifests one of the main fault-lines of Indigenous society. The social relations of alcohol consumption, as Pearson describes them in *Our right to take responsibility*, include pathological solidarities among men:

> When you look at the obligations which are set up around the drinking circle, you see the drinkers under reciprocal obligations to contribute to buying the grog. When I have money it's my turn to shout. When your money comes, it's your turn to shout. *Outside of this drinking circle are the women and the children and old people and the non-drinkers.* The resources of these non-drinkers are used to feed the families — including those who have spent most or all of their money on grog, when they are hungry. But more than that, these non-drinkers are placed under tremendous social and cultural pressure to contribute resources to the drinking circle for buying grog. So the drinking circle becomes the suction hole for the family's resources. *Wives and girlfriends, parents and grandparents, are placed under tremendous pressure* — social and cultural and ultimately through physical violence: 'Why you wanna stop me from having *fun with my brothers*?' — to contribute to these pathological behaviours.[4]

Eleven years before Pearson's book, and not long before CAEPR started, Julie Finlayson published an ethnography that attempted to estimate the impact of women's enhanced access to welfare payments on gendered notions of nurturance in a north Queensland community.

Finlayson's account of male–female relations assumed that there was potential for competition between men and women for status, power and resources. However, in that contest, having money was not necessarily decisive; or, as she put it: 'the potential for social stratification or effective power arising from differential income is not always, nor necessarily realisable in Aboriginal communities'.[5] Certainly, history *seemed* to favour women's ascendancy over men. Colonial impacts have tended to collapse into a single domestic world the previously gender-divided daily life of the Aborigines of 'Rubyville'. There, 'domesticity is the dominant context of socioeconomic activity of both sexes. This fact of life has largely advantaged women since they are capitalising on their own sexuality through their role as mothers. In effect they "earn" income from the state for their domestic labour'.[6] Men have had to find ways to resist the resulting potential for women's hegemony. They have been greatly assisted by the currency of a social ethic of 'nurturance'. According to Finlayson, the Rubyville men make claims on women's nurturance. 'If women nurture, men relate to women as quasi-dependents. With this status, they are able to demand access to the resources women acquire through their own labour and status ... [and so] ... economic advantages women gain through the welfare system remain unrealised.'[7]

Violence is not essential to males' access to women's incomes. This does not mean that there is no violence; it's just that Finlayson emphasises ideology rather than force in describing men's suasion of women. Appealing to norms of nurturance, men are able to influence women's sense of social responsibility. The result is that a woman spends much of her money on her offspring (whether adults or children) and on anyone else who makes appeal to her as a proper object of her nurturance. Evidently, these others may include husbands, boyfriends, brothers and fathers, for 'relationships of claim between mother and son are little different to those between husband and wife, or between brother and sister'.[8] Warning the reader not to assume that these acts of nurturance are unreciprocated, Finlayson describes the relationships between women and men as 'symbiotic', adding that 'women expect certain assistance from men, particularly physical protection from harm or violence from others'.[9]

By symbiosis, does Finlayson mean symmetry — a balance of male and female powers? Or rather, is it the case that because men are so successful in their appeals to 'nurturance', they are effectively in dominance over the women of Rubyville? Finlayson answers these questions in the final paragraphs of her paper, concluding that in Rubyville 'gender domination resides in the ability to have few, rather than many, material resources'. She writes of 'men realizing a greater command over the resources of women than ... women over those of men'.[10]

Finlayson's and Pearson's remarks on welfare payments and gender relations are not identical, but they are convergent. Both pose the issue of a power struggle between men and women in the context of women's increased access to welfare incomes. Pearson mentions alcohol as a significant item of men's expenditure, whereas Finlayson is more interested in money's capacity to signify social relatedness than in what money buys. Finlayson's essay was not about a crisis in social relations, but about the persisting pertinence of an idiom of nurturance. Pearson, by contrast, is warning us that the social fabric of Cape York people is badly torn. Notwithstanding these differences of emphasis, both Finlayson and Pearson, a decade apart, are telling us that access to welfare money has affected the terms in which men and women live out their gender identities. If this is true in Cape York, it may also be true in many other regions of Indigenous Australia.

What light can CAEPR's research shed on the changes and continuities in male–female relationships in Indigenous Australia? First I will review some of the statistics on Indigenous men's and women's income, employment, job-seeking, training and 'social capital'. Then I will examine some of the cultural models, available in CAEPR writings, of the circulation of goods and money among Indigenous Australians. Through these two kinds of data, statistical and ethnographic, the CAEPR's corpus of research affords us a glimpse — through a glass darkly — of the contemporary restructuring of relationships between Indigenous men and Indigenous women.

MEN'S AND WOMEN'S INCOMES

From 1976 to 1991, men contributed a falling proportion of total Indigenous income. The main reason for this decline was that men's employment was of reduced importance as a source of all Indigenous income. Women's contribution to all Indigenous income rose from 32 to 45 per cent, an increase reflecting rises in both their rate of employment and their access to welfare incomes. One likely reason for women's greater power to get welfare incomes is that between 1976 and 1991 the welfare system changed in such a way as to increase women's eligibility.[11] Examining Census data for 1976 and 1991, Daly and Hawke showed by several measures that Indigenous women had rapidly narrowed the gap between their incomes and men's. That is, women had vastly increased their median income as a proportion of men's median income, and whereas in 1976, the ratio of all female income to all male income was 0.36, by 1991 it was 0.9.[12] Comparing 1976 Census data with DSS administrative data for 1991–92, it would appear that in 1976, for every one hundred Indigenous women there were 33.1 on some kind of benefit; by 1991 that rate had risen to 47.1.[13]

Compiling data from various publications by Taylor, we can construct a time series, 1986–96, for the growth in median incomes of men and women, in Queensland, New South Wales, Australian Capital Territory, Victoria, Tasmania and Western Australia.[14] In all five of these States and one Territory, Indigenous women's median income grew much faster than Indigenous men's. Men's median income growth was in the range 21–51 percent, while women's income growth was in the range 48–87 per cent.

In short, over the twenty years 1976–96, there is a persistent pattern in Indigenous income growth: Indigenous women are catching up to Indigenous men in their ability to earn money by employment and to get money from welfare.

MEN AND WOMEN IN THE LABOUR FORCE

In the final quarter of the twentieth century, structural changes in the Australian economy have tended to reduce the demand for unskilled labour and to maintain the employment rate and to increase relatively the incomes of those with some kind of formal training. These changes have differentially affected Indigenous men and women, a point noted by Gregory who related the fall in male Aboriginal employment to the changing demand for labour.[15] According to Tesfaghiorghis and Altman there was a fall in the ratio of male employed to female employed among Aborigines, from 2.9 in 1971 to 1.7 in 1986.[16] Taylor's analysis of 1986 and 1991 Census data showed that female employment grew proportionately more than male in every State and Territory.[17] In further analysis he showed that Indigenous women improved their position in the labour market (employment and participation up, and unemployment down) more than men in 1986–91 across all three sections of State (major urban, other urban and rural).[18] The male–female difference was least in 'rural' regions.

Both men and women were affected — but men more so — by declines in the demand for Indigenous labour in the industry divisions 'agriculture' and 'electricity/gas/water'. Men, but not women, were also negatively affected by declining participation in 'transport and storage'. Industry divisions that grew in their demand for labour tended to be those in which women were already strongly represented: wholesale/retail, public administration and community services.[19]

In those growing occupations that reward more advanced levels of formal education — manager and administrators, professionals and paraprofessionals, personal services and sales — women's employment rose faster than men's.[20] These data can be linked to the gender-based specialisation in training that Daly noticed when she investigated Indigenous investment in education and training.[21] Men were disproportionately attracted to 'trade' and 'transport', women to 'management', 'clerical', 'sales', 'general computing' and 'personal development'. This comparison holds true even when CDEP is differentiated from non-CDEP employment.[22] Women were much more likely to be in management, general computing, personal development and general health training in non-CDEP employment. Women also were more likely to be at university, and, when unemployed, more likely than men (unemployed) to go into training.[23] Daly's paper, read against other information presented in this chapter about the occupational and industrial differentiation of the sexes, suggests the emergence of a white collar/blue collar gender distinction among Indigenous Australians.

From Taylor's studies a gender difference is clear, in 1991–96, across the seven States/Territories.[24] While the trends in the employment and unemployment rates (counting CDEP as employment) of both men and women were positive, the magnitudes of improvement slightly favoured women. The trends in labour-force participation rates were largely negative for men, positive for women.

In short, in the period in which AEDP has been applied (1987 to present), women seem to have benefited more than men from the effort put into improving Indigenous labour force status.

THE SIGNIFICANCE OF CHILDCARE

Notwithstanding their gains in labour market status relative to men, Indigenous women remain less attached to the labour market than Indigenous men. Daly's regression analysis showed that a relatively low labour-force participation rate for Aboriginal women was associated with being married, widowed, separated or divorced and having children.[25] Poor English and non-urban residence also had a greater negative impact on women's participation rate than on men's. Hunter concluded from NATSIS data that 'studying or returning to studies was the main reason given by youth for not actively seeking work. Young and prime working-age females also cited a lack of available child care and other family responsibilities. For older people, the most prevalent reason was ill health'.[26] Using 1991 Census data, Daly argued that the employment income differences between Indigenous men and women were despite the 'human capital superiority of women. Women's lower income is associated with rural residence and with family characteristics'.[27] Hunter and Daly asked in 1998 whether women's partnering with men had an effect on their incentive to seek paid work. Using NATSIS data, they concluded that the financial disincentives to move from welfare to work 'were higher for females than males and higher for those who were married or in a de facto relationship. The first result reflects the lower earnings of females compared with males and the second, the fact that the welfare system explicitly recognises the additional costs of supporting a dependant spouse while employers do not'.[28] Having children was thus associated with a lower incentive for females to seek paid work.

Taylor and Hunter analysed data from DEETYA and NATSIS on participation in labour market programs. They showed that female participation in training was less than half of men's.[29] Their Table 5 showed a lower proportion of the female Indigenous population of working age attending training courses in 1994, with the male–female gap consistent across 'capital city', 'other urban' and 'rural'.[30] Lack of childcare was the reason most frequently given by females for non-participation (though lack of transport is equally significant for rural females); childcare was a minor consideration for males.[31] The demands of childcare on women may also be behind their finding that attendance at a training course was less strongly associated with females' employment than with males, except in rural areas.[32] Using NATSIS data, Hunter and Gray found differences between men and women in their stated reasons for not looking for work. 'Childcare and other family responsibilities' were much more prominent reasons for women than for men. The main reason given by men was that they were studying or soon to return to study.[33] In their regression analysis, the variables most strongly associated with being a 'discouraged worker' overlapped for men and for women. For women the most important factors discouraging participation in the labour force were living in a capital city and having responsibility for the care of children. For men they were age and having responsibility for care of children.[34] The authors highlight the significance of age, educational attainment and family responsibilities in people's job-searching.

Arthur and David-Petero give a Torres Strait vignette of young women, more than young men, having to take on wider 'family duties' than child-rearing:

> Family commitments are mostly to parents, grandparents, and children. The commitment to parents and grandparents invariably involves taking care of them when they are ill or in their old age. Hence, people suggested that they have often been stopped from doing things, or may be stopped in the future because of illness in the family or by the expectation that they must look after ageing parents

and grand parents ... Generally ..., and certainly amongst females, the expectation is that family obligations will take precedence over personal aspirations.³⁵

In short, childcare and other family work has repeatedly been shown to be a factor determining female Indigenous Australians' employment and job-searching. In this light, it is useful to know something of trends in Indigenous fertility. Gray commented in 1992 that he would like to see a survey 'directed specifically at mothers of reproductive age ...'. He lamented the paucity of 'national information about the patterns of use of family planning by Aboriginal women, the choices which they can exercise in family planning, and their access to appropriate services and advice'.³⁶ Despite the many ways in which CAEPR has found children to be a significant factor in the forms of Indigenous livelihood, CAEPR has paid attention to fertility largely as an aspect of the problem of predicting the size and age structure of the Indigenous population. The significance of fertility in the Indigenous life-course awaits its investigator.³⁷

In the early 1990s, demographers thought that Aboriginal fertility, having declined sharply in the 1970s, was stabilising in the 1980s at a level higher than for the Australian population as a whole. Gaminiratne (1992b) used Census data from 1981 and 1986 to examine this trend further. He found that Aboriginal women (1981–86) had higher fertility than Islanders, that both Indigenous fertility rates were higher than for the Australian population as a whole, that Aboriginal women had greater 'speed of reproduction' (more children at younger age of mother) than either of the other two groups, and that fertility (measured as the mean number of children ever born to each woman in the Census) for all three groups was still declining 1981 to 1986.³⁸ However, using 1991 Census data, Gray and Gaminiratne compared the enumerated young children with the enumerated women of childbearing age, reaching the conclusion that Indigenous fertility had increased in the second half of the 1980s.³⁹

Australia's birth registration methods began to improve in the 1980s and 1990s, and the National Aboriginal and Torres Strait Islander Survey of 1994 included fertility data. These two developments enabled Tesfaghiorghis, among others, to do further work on trends in Indigenous fertility. He concluded that Aboriginal fertility had not declined since the mid-1980s.⁴⁰ The current Aboriginal fertility rate could not be stated precisely, but it seemed to fall within a range of 3.1 to 3.5 children per woman, compared with 1.9 children per woman for the entire Australian population. Tesfaghioghis noted age differences: 'although teenage and young Aboriginal fertility has remained very high by any standards, there has been considerable fertility reduction among Aboriginal women over 25 years to a level that is comparable and even lower than that of total Australian women'.⁴¹

Gray's 1997 estimates of Aboriginal fertility showed it to have declined steadily over the forty years to 1996, and quite sharply within the fifteen years from 1966 to 1981.[42] When Taylor reproduced these estimates, he pointed out that the current Total Fertility Rate of 2.7 represents a fall of about 50 per cent in Indigenous fertility since 1970.[43]

I know of no study which tries to relate these trends to changes in Indigenous gender relations.

GENDER, 'WORK' AND 'SOCIAL PARTICIPATION'

In her two early papers that I have mentioned already in Chapter 2, Diane Smith discussed the complexity of Indigenous decisions about whether or not to participate in the formal labour market.[44] She sought to undermine a culture-blind assumption that not to be in the labour market was to have nothing useful to do. Her argument encouraged us to imagine that a person who was neither employed nor looking for work was not necessarily forsaking the task of trying to support him- or herself; that person might very well be supporting him- or herself 'socially' by giving priority to unpaid services that he or she performed for other Indigenous people. To describe someone as 'not participating in the labour market' begged the question of what that person *was* participating in. Smith and Roach compared the types of voluntary work undertaken by men and by women, aged 15 and over.[45] Women made up the majority of Indigenous voluntary workers in the following fields: 'caring for sick or aged people', 'school or youth group' and 'committee work'; men were slightly over-represented in 'community or sports' and more clearly over-represented in 'hunting, fishing and gathering'. (It is unfortunate that 'childcare' was not among the NATSIS's list of types of 'voluntary work'.)

Using NATSIS data Hunter identified five indices of 'social exclusion', and four of 'civic engagement'; he has cross-tabulated them with four labour-force statuses. Within each of the cells of this matrix he has differentiated males and females, and subdivided each gender category according to whether they are part of urban or non-urban households.[46] On the criterion 'arrested in the last five years', the NATSIS showed that men are far more 'excluded' than women — that is, a higher proportion of men than of women had been arrested in the last five years, whatever their employment status and whether urban or non-urban. On the criteria 'arrested for drunkenness' and 'hassled by the police in the last five years', the disparities between men and women were again great, with men again worse off, in every region and whatever their labour force status. How are we to make sense of the fact that Indigenous men are much more likely than Indigenous women to fall foul of police and to be arrested? At the very least, one can say that Indigenous women's lives are less disrupted by the coercive arms of the state, enabling them to get on with other rewarding activities such as education, paid employment and looking after children.

Hunter also identified variables which captured Indigenous Australians' levels of 'civic engagement'. Women of all categories were more likely to have voted in a recent election, and, more commonly than men, women had gone to Indigenous festivals and carnivals. In their tendency to do voluntary work the NATSIS found men and women to be about the same, though the data showed that men and women are drawn to different kinds of voluntary work.[47] In their aspirations 'to do further study or training', women far outscored men. It is consistent with these results that when the NATSIS asked Indigenous parents whether they were involved in decision-making at their children's school, 'only 30 per cent of males described themselves as involved … while 45.6 per cent of females indicated they were involved'.[48]

If we read Hunter's 2000 paper on 'social exclusion' and 'social capital' simply for its information about gender difference, we find that, on a number of measures — particularly to do with alcohol abuse and adverse encounters with the police — Indigenous women tend to be less socially 'excluded' (in Hunter's sense) and more socially 'engaged' than Indigenous men. Hunter's main point is that the unemployed, particularly the long-term unemployed Indigenous person, is more likely to suffer the measurable characteristics of 'social exclusion'. This makes even more remarkable the gender differences that I have noted above, for the NATSIS showed a lower rate of employment (and higher rates of unemployment and non-participation in labour force) among Indigenous women than among Indigenous men.[49] In short, we can read Hunter's paper as showing that in 1994, Indigenous women were far more successful than Indigenous men in overcoming the 'social' handicaps associated with being without a job. This possibly has something to do with women's centrality to those processes that Finlayson describes as 'nurturance'. The social participation of women is effected either by their employment (participation in the formal economy) or by their involvement in childcare (the informal, Indigenous 'economy') — or perhaps by a combination of the two.

CAEPR'S MODELS OF DOMESTIC REDISTRIBUTION

It is clear from the studies summarised above that Indigenous women generally have been more able than Indigenous men to adapt to the pressures and to embrace the opportunities that are characteristic of the era of 'self-determination' — at least in training, employment and income. This conclusion is possibly consistent with a theme in studies of modern Indigenous gender relations. In their recent survey of studies of violence among Indigenous Australians, Memmott and others head one section 'Powerlessness and helplessness amongst Indigenous men' in which they cite work by Judy Atkinson, Audrey Bolger, David Martin, Ernest Hunter, Marcia Langton and Fay Gale.[50] Memmott and others interpret male violence inflicted on the self and on others — particularly on women — as a response to their sense that they have lost status and power. Later in their literature review, they find 'alarming' the incidence of male assault on female partners.[51] They worry that young men lack 'healthy, functional role models for the transition into manhood'.[52]

CAEPR writings on contemporary Aboriginal culture do not speculate about the development of gender relations among Aboriginal people. However, within the CAEPR corpus there is some oblique commentary on this issue. In a series of statements on the themes of reciprocity, demand sharing and the socialisation of money, the CAEPR writers seek a general model of Indigenous domestic processes, in particular Indigenous understandings of day-to-day giving and receiving.

In 1992 Smith wrote of the basically egalitarian effects of:

> the process of sharing and demanding access to the cash and resources of others. Such cash redistribution does not occur indiscriminately as a result of some generalised ethic of reciprocity. Kinship and a range of historical ties are key idioms used to negotiate access to dollars and other goods and services. This redistributive mechanism is sufficient to ameliorate considerable income disparities and associated differences in expenditure capacity between households, especially those with low or intermittent incomes. Aboriginal economic well-being is, in this manner, supported by a fall-back system; an informal network of personal borrowings and repayments used to fulfil obligations and promote economic survival.[53]

These words do not address the issue of how the practices of demand sharing are implicated in gender relations. In the absence of such comment, the general impression conveyed by Smith is of equilibrium and symmetry among Indigenous actors.

However, in their 1994 paper on the impact of welfare payments on the economic status of Aboriginal women, Daly and Hawke declined to generalise about the redistributive effects of domestic giving and receiving. With Census and DSS data it was not possible, they pointed out, to gauge changes in the relative welfare of Indigenous women in the period in which the welfare system has reached out to include them. These data tell us too little about women's domestic circumstances, such as the income transfers within the household, and the ways in which responsibility for dependents is shared between adults.[54] Daly and Hawke thus allowed the possibility that men and women might fare differently as goods, money and people flowed through Indigenous domestic groups.

In a 1996 paper, as I have already mentioned, Daly and Smith sketched a sombre view of such flows. That is, they speculated that among the likely effects of 'high visitation rates' was 'stress on the expenditure capacity of core household members and their potential to save cash and other resources'.[55] With this acknowledgment that visitors might take out of households more money and resources than they put in, the equilibrium or egalitarian image of Aboriginal exchange became no more plausible than a model highlighting the opposite possibility: some households raided by predatory individuals, with other households, or individuals, benefiting thereby. What are the implications of this second possibility for our picture of gender relations? Jerry Schwab confronted this issue in 1995:

> It is no secret that particular individuals sometimes abuse the generosity of others. In this way Aboriginal people are no different than other people. While demand sharing is the traditional pattern and Aboriginal people have developed appropriate mechanisms to ensure it is not abused, those mechanisms sometimes fail. For example, alcohol is often associated with aggressive demands and many Aboriginal households have known the frustration of dealing with aggressive drunks who appear in the middle of the night demanding food and shelter. *Most often these individuals are young men.* In many cases the behaviour is a bluff, with normal inhibitions and subtleties about the boundaries of demands dissolved by alcohol. Yet *households without permanent male membership* are sometimes singled out by such individuals since women will often give in to ensure their own safety.[56]

Schwab then warned readers not to infer that there was any problem with the normative framework by which Aboriginal people reckoned what they owed one another. '*In no case*', he assured us, 'are such threats encouraged by *any corner of the community* and *without exception* these individuals are seen to bring shame on themselves and their families'.[57] His words implied Indigenous consensus about the way that norms of demand sharing are applied to actual cases, and that this consensus would *uphold the refusals of those who have been put upon*. However, when Julie Finlayson and Tony Auld cited Schwab's paper four years later, they glossed its argument in terms that seemed to make the opposite point: '… people generally, and some individuals in particular, have much to lose by refusing requests. The social pressure brought to bear on these individuals is usually sufficient to modify their aberrant behaviour'.[58] That is, the norms of 'demand sharing' may be invoked as easily to pressure those who have money and goods as to restrain and shame those who importune. If that is so, a consensus about the fairness of a redistributive outcome might be harder to achieve than Schwab supposes.

David Martin's account of the social uses of cash, published at the same time as Schwab's paper on reciprocity, was more explicit than Schwab about the social tensions that might imperil the performance and reproduction of norms of sharing and desert. Martin gave more emphasis than Schwab to what he called the 'internal hierarchies and divisions (including those between age groups and between genders)' of Aboriginal life.[59] Welfare cash enables people increasingly 'to assert their independence from others through the means which cash offers: men from responsibilities towards domestic units, wives from their spouses and children, and younger men from older ones ...'. He added that men's aspirations to autonomy from the demands of 'family' are now especially favoured by their access to cash income, which:

> enables them to become involved as relatively autonomous actors in establishing credit and prestige, through such means as the direct distribution of cash from their wages, the purchase and sharing of alcohol, and the distribution of gambling winnings. Many young men in particular use the bulk of their CDEP scheme incomes for gambling, purchasing alcohol, and travel. Of course, having spent all their money young men are dependent upon others for their basic sustenance, and these others are usually women — their mothers, grandmothers, and older sisters ... The capacity of men to draw upon the intangible resource of women's affections for and bonds with them in order to appropriate their labour and money, reduces the potential of women's independent cash incomes to generate increasing autonomy and independence.[60]

And 'men's access to cash incomes allows them to create a contemporary style of life defined in opposition to that of women and the requirements and demands of the domestic sphere'.[61] Like Schwab, however, Martin saw checks and balances in all this: any tendency to assert autonomy is held in check by counterassertions of reciprocal duty and relatedness.

Finlayson and Auld referred to the complexities of Indigenous household financial management. 'For many Aboriginal households the critical budgetary decision is often a prioritising choice between the material needs of children and youths, and that of the regular and daily demand to eat.'[62] They did not say who (in age and gender terms) makes this choice and by what process, but they reported comments from recipients of Parenting Payment (mostly female, and growing in number) that '"humbugging" by others, especially men, including the children's father, was a hassle on pension days. Colloquially, these payment days were referred to in Kuranda and

Cairns as "father's day" or "pram day", and it was not uncommon to see men steering prams in the company of women en route to the local bank or building society for a cut of income support money'.[63]

CAEPR's ethnographic researchers have not consistently made gender tensions the focus of their generalisations about Aboriginal 'demand sharing'. On my reading, those who have done so (Finlayson and Martin) have put more emphasis on the difficulties of living peacefully in a normative regime in which one is permitted, if not encouraged, to ask for help from those whom one can address as 'family'. Alternative evocations of Aboriginal demand sharing — emphasising its foundations in a normative consensus and its equilibrating outcomes (such as Smith and Schwab) — have been less likely to focus attention on the differences between males' and females' implication in 'demand sharing'. I suggest that it is better to highlight male–female difference and more realistic to emphasise the contemporary strains and difficulties between Aboriginal men and women.

CONCLUSION

By making gender tensions a CAEPR theme, I have been able to bring together the two kinds of knowledge that CAEPR has produced: ethnography and quantitative (mostly Census-based) studies. They show:

- women gaining relative to men according to certain socio-economic indicators
- women held back from training and paid employment by being primarily responsible for children
- many women in the 1990s seizing the opportunity provided by Sole Parent Payment to get their own welfare cheque
- men financing their homosociality from CDEP payments and from their ability to get money from female relatives.

Noel Pearson has recently painted a depressing picture of this relatively new, welfare-based system of gender relations. The era of what he calls 'welfare poison' has produced new pressures and opportunities for Aboriginal Australians. It is possible that men are generally not dealing with these challenges as effectively as women. And it is possible that the cost/reward of this new disparity is some combination of a rise in anti-social behaviour by Indigenous men and an increasing differentiation of aspirations and expectations on the part of Indigenous women.

11
HOUSEHOLDS, INDIVIDUALS AND THE INDIGENOUS POPULATION

Under Australian practices of population enumeration, the categories 'Aboriginal', 'Torres Strait Islander' were artefacts, until 1966, of choices that people make when answering the 'race' question in the Census and of choices made by officials when formulating questions, when administering questionnaires to institutionalised populations and when encoding the answers given by non-institutionalised respondents. From 1971 the Bureau of Census and Statistics established a new approach that minimised officials' influence on the enumeration of 'race' and maximised the impact of respondents' discretion. 'In consultation with persons and organizations concerned with Aboriginal affairs, the Bureau decided to abandon the "biological" or "genealogical" concept of race in favour of an entirely social or self-identification concept.'[1] That is, people were asked to choose whether they were to be recorded as Aboriginal, Torres Strait Islander, European or 'other'.

In 1980, the foremost historian of Indigenous enumeration, Len Smith, concluded that it had long been possible for individuals to 'migrate' from one ethnic category to another (including between 'half-caste' and 'full-blood') either by their own changing identification or by being subject to varying official classifications. The balance of such 'migration', he argued, was that more people were becoming 'Aboriginal' than were ceasing to be 'Aboriginal'. He was sure that this had been the trend, in New South Wales and Victoria, since before World War II. He inferred that part of the Aboriginal population increase between 1961 and 1971 was due to changes in identification mainly by 'parents with growing families in most parts of the south-eastern States, and urban areas of the other States'.

There were probably many thousands more, he estimated, whose mixed descent gave them the option of a similar change in future Censuses.[2]

CAEPR researchers studying the growth and age structure of the Indigenous population since 1971 have been sensitive to the significance of identity choice in the constitution of an Indigenous population. 'It should ... be kept in mind', wrote Gray and Tesfaghiorghis, 'that the concept of a separable "Aboriginal" component of the population is based on a number of problematic assumptions, and Aboriginality can to some degree be considered as a constructed identity which may not correspond closely with the identity within which a person operates as a social being from day to day'.[3]

The primary site in which the Census identity question is determined is the household. The Census is for the most part an interaction between governments and households. Five types of 'Aboriginal families/households' (with or without children) are revealed by Census data. The first three are:

- Aboriginal man and woman
- Single Aboriginal man
- Single Aboriginal woman.

The identity 'Aboriginal' for these three types of household is unlikely to be unstable. However, there is great potential for variation in the identification of members of households of the following types:

- Man Aboriginal, woman non-Aboriginal
- Woman Aboriginal, man non-Aboriginal.[4]

There would seem to be more and more of the latter two kinds of household in Australia. They are significant in enumeration in a number of ways. First, the children of such a household could be classified as Aboriginal or non-Aboriginal according to parents' wishes, and this judgment could change from Census to Census. Second, we should not presume that a baby born to an Aboriginal/non-Aboriginal couple and assigned an 'Aboriginal' identity for Census purposes by those parents will remain always 'Aboriginal' in identity. When he or she grows up that individual might choose a different identity when filling out the Census form or when advising a fellow house-holder how to fill it out. Third, demographers have begun to notice that the births of some Indigenous Australians have nothing to do with the fertility of Indigenous women. They were births to non-Indigenous women married to Indigenous men. It was a matter of 'household' identity that those offspring were enumerated as 'Aboriginal' or 'Torres

Strait Islander'. Increasing levels of such intermarriages combined with the evident readiness of these non-Indigenous mothers to identify their offspring as Indigenous has resulted in higher than projected Indigenous birth rates. By analysing birth registration data, Alan Gray was able to confirm that 'there are indeed rapidly increasing numbers of Indigenous births to non-Indigenous women ...'.[5]

The proliferation of Indigenous/non-Indigenous households means that by the late 1990s demographers were no longer confident that they could infer changes in future Indigenous population structure simply from contemporary changes in Indigenous fertility. The phenomenon of the 'mixed household' was introducing another element of uncertainty into the projection of Indigenous population growth. In the 1996 Census eight per cent of mixed household children who could have been identified as 'Indigenous' were not. Was it not possible that some of those children would, as they matured, identify as Aboriginal or Torres Strait Islander when filling out the Census? Some, of course, would 'migrate' in the opposite direction.

Naturally, it is not only the offspring of mixed marriages who might change their identification in the course of their life. As the research of Len Smith cited above shows, many people have found that they would now prefer to be identified as 'Aboriginal' or 'Torres Strait Islander', whereas once they did not. There is less shame and more pride in these categories than once there were. As a result of all the factors discussed above, those interested in a precise enumeration of the 'Indigenous population' find that 'what appears to be a firm definition is actually extremely fuzzy'.[6]

Gray acknowledged that demographers knew too little about how 'Aboriginal and Torres Strait Islander people answer questions about Indigenous origin'.[7] As he had acknowledged in an earlier paper with Gaminiratne, 'the uncertainties of self-identification actually occur where no-one expected to find them, that is among young children, not among adults who in theory have a choice about the matter'.[8] One implication of demographers' recognition that many Indigenous households are 'mixed' and that offspring may not follow what their parents said about their identity is that projections of the size and composition of the Indigenous population — and thus of the future needs of the Indigenous population — have become more 'experimental'.[9] By recording a one-third increase in the Indigenous population since 1991, the 1996 Census, in the words of John Taylor, was helping to return demographic analysis to the 'familiar condition of uncertainty about intercensal projections'.[10]

The startling 1991–96 increase in the Indigenous population (with its implied annual growth rate of 6.6 per cent) cried out for analysis. There has been some debate about whether this count reflects technical problems in enumeration or the intrinsic complexity of the question of 'identity' for many of those Australians filling in the Census.

Gray was among those who thought that technical problems in the administration of the Census might be part of the problem. He found in a 1997 analysis that about half of the 1991–96 increase in the Indigenous Australian population could not be accounted for by considering: births to Indigenous women, deaths of Indigenous people, and births to Indigenous fathers with non-Indigenous partners. He referred to this unexplained component, without prejudice, as 'the "new" Aborigines' (a term in which he appears to have included 'new' Torres Strait Islanders). Their age distribution matched that of the 'old' Aborigines (and Torres Strait Islanders). He warned against explaining the 'new' as people who had changed their identification, preferring to hypothesise unspecified defects in the Census. However, even were the Census to be perfected as an instrument for reflecting the true numbers of people willing to identify as Aboriginal or Torres Strait Islander, there would remain an element of uncertainty in population growth projections, Gray pointed out. Here he referred to the trend (discussed above) for Indigenous Australians to have children with non-Indigenous partners.[11]

While agreeing with Gray that the 1996 Census had probably not resolved all problems of enumeration, Taylor's example of a methodological problem did nothing to account for what Gray called 'new' Aborigines. That is, Taylor pointed not at the cities, where Gray's 'new' Indigenous people were likely to be found, but at the remote regions' methodological challenges. Those challenges were evidently being met, for in remote regions Indigenous population growth was closer to projections based on the relatively well-known biological facts of Indigenous fertility and mortality. Taylor was evidently more willing than Gray to consider 'identification change', rather than Census failure, as part of an explanation of the extraordinary increase in Indigenous Australians in 1991–96.[12] Taylor's confidence in the 1996 Census was founded partly on his first analysis of the social composition of the 1996 population. This showed that the housing needs and job requirements of those counted as Indigenous Australians in 1996 were no different *in kind* — if far greater in number — from those revealed in the 1991 count.[13]

CAEPR researchers have tended to trust the 1996 Census, notwithstanding its startling enumeration. By considering the Indigenous responses not only to the Census questions but also to the 'Post-Enumeration Surveys' conducted in 1991 and 1996, Hunter concluded that there was more stability than was at first apparent in the numbers identifying as Indigenous Australians.

Nonetheless, from these data, he could distinguish between 'the "marginal" and the more consistent Indigenous identifiers'; he found the two groups to be similar in age profile.[14] As well, his comparison of three successive Censuses, in respect of the revealed educational qualifications and place of residence, did not demonstrate that the 'new' people differed in socio-economic profile from the 'old'. He warned against doubting that 'these newly identified population are Indigenous'. The 1996 Census was 'sufficiently credible ... to be taken at face value'.[15]

Accordingly, Taylor and Bell felt confident that they could use the 1996 Census as the basis for revising the 1991 Census. That is, they decided to take 'the 1996 Census-derived population' as 'the best estimate yet of an ultimately unknown number of individuals of any Aboriginal or Torres Strait Islander ancestry'.[16] Making allowance for the death rates of all age groups (in order to estimate people who could have been in the 1991 Census but died before the 1996 Census), Taylor and Bell could 'fill in' people who, for one reason or another, were not counted as Aboriginal or Torres Strait Islander in 1991 but were so counted in 1996. They performed this recalculation, however, only in respect to those Indigenous Australians aged 15 years and over, as their immediate concern was to measure changes in labour market characteristics. They estimated that out of 188 586 Indigenous people in 1991, 28 874 (or 15.3 per cent) had not then identified as Indigenous.

These demographic studies tell us that the Indigenous constituency is an artefact of a method of enumeration in which people's *choices* (usually as 'households') are of central importance. One way to register the significance of this element of choice is to concur with Taylor that 'there is no sense in which the Indigenous population can be described as clearly defined for statistical purposes'.[17] Yet his own research practice (and that of others who calculate trends in social indicators) has been to make a pragmatic commitment to the notion of a defined Indigenous population. Otherwise it would not be possible to evaluate the impact, over time, of government programs to improve measurable features of Indigenous welfare. Taylor has recently summarised the problems and possible solutions to variability in Census counts:

> First, it raises questions about the intercensal comparability of social indicators, although one option ... is to adjust base year indicators to the level of the newly-revealed population using reverse survival techniques; another is to treat census cross-sectional data as panel data by grouping individuals into cohorts and treating the averages within these cohorts as individual observations.
>
> Second, where the count has varied largely because of identity change, it is not clear whether aggregate change ... involves an alteration in the circumstances of the original population or whether it

merely reflects the particular features of individuals appearing in the population for the first time. The problem for the analysis of transformation is that change in the condition of the original population is undetectable. All that can be noted is different aggregate status in respect of 'different' populations.

Third, variability creates an 'ever-shifting population base against which rates of events (such as hospitalisation or school enrolments) have to be calibrated'. And finally, variability due to changed identification 'undermines the robustness of population estimates and projections'.[18]

The demography of Indigenous Australians is a rigorous, but hardly an exact science. That is because the phenomenon that we call 'the Indigenous population' is an artefact of its procedures of data generation, the most important of which is an interaction between the government and the household. When households answer the 'identity' question, they are not constrained by any 'natural' features of their membership. Rather, the 'Indigenous population' is a cultural phenomenon, the aggregate of thousands of decisions about 'identity', taken privately in millions of Australian households.

PART 4

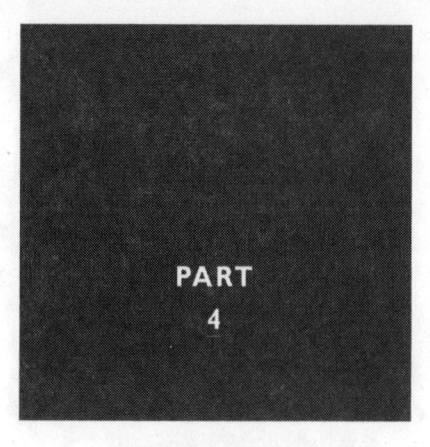

INDIGENOUS AGENCIES OF COLLECTIVE CHOICE

INTRODUCTION

In my introduction to this book, I promised that I would follow the way that CAEPR research into Indigenous self-determination policy has operationalised 'the Indigenous choosing subject' — the 'self' in 'self-determination' — at three levels of social organisation: the individual, the domestic group and the organisation/community.

In Part I, I have shown that CAEPR's studies look at labour markets and human capital formation as if they were made up of thousands of decisions by individuals. In making sense of the outcomes of those choices (the mixed results of the AEDP programs), it was possible for CAEPR researchers to go beyond an analysis focused on individuals. An important part of the CAEPR analysis emphasises the structural constraints within which labour markets do and do not work for Indigenous Australians: structures of spatiality and demography, deep residues of history in the formation of people's aspiration, and so on. As well, CAEPR studies have paid attention to collective Indigenous choices made through institutions (such as CDEP) that enable Indigenous people to distance themselves, as groups, from the mainstream labour markets.

In Part II, I surveyed economic development issues in which the 'choosing Indigenous subject' is characteristically a collective rather than an individual agent: the holders of communal title and the organisations (Land Councils, royalty associations and Native Title Representative Bodies) set up to give an effective voice to those holding, or aspiring to hold, communal title.

In Part III I said nothing of this communal/organisational level of Indigenous agency. Rather, my focus was on the terms in which CAEPR researchers have imagined the domestic unit as a locus of

Indigenous decision-making, decisions about the management of children being of particular concern. I concluded Part III by suggesting that what we refer to as 'the Indigenous population' is best understood as an artefact generated by one particularly important decision made at the individual and household levels: identity choice in the Census. That is, by administering the Census the government addresses individuals and 'household' heads as subjects of choice about 'identity'. In looking at the Indigenous population in this way, I have been building up to an important theoretical point: the category 'Indigenous population' is not to be confused with the category 'Indigenous Sector'.

The purpose of Part IV is to focus attention on 'the Indigenous Sector'. I have already begun to touch on 'the Indigenous Sector' at many points in Parts I and II. That is, in my account of CAEPR's research on labour markets and on land use, I have found it impossible not to include CAEPR's research on CDEPs, royalty associations, Land Councils and Native Title Representative Bodies. However, I now want to go beyond these empirical illustrations of the Indigenous Sector in order to theorise that sector. To do so, it is necessary to leave the 'individual' and the domestic group behind. That is why I wanted to deal with 'the Indigenous population' where, in my conceptual scheme, it belongs — an artefact of the state's addressing of households and individuals about their identity. It would doom my theoretical presentation of the Indigenous Sector if I were not able to distinguish it analytically and empirically from the Indigenous population in that way.

A person who says they are 'Aboriginal' or 'Torres Strait Islander' when filling out the Census will not necessarily be a client or a participant of an organisation of the Indigenous Sector. For example, most of those who are thought to be eligible to vote in the (voluntary) ATSIC elections choose not to.[1] Another example: when the NATSIS asked Indigenous adults what they would do if they had the option of sending their children to an Indigenous community-controlled school a very large proportion said that they would choose a 'mainstream' school. Clearly, the clients and participants of the Indigenous Sector, as a suite of organisations, are not to be confused with the Indigenous population. Not every person in the Indigenous population will have some role in the Indigenous Sector as a client, an employee or an office bearer within that sector. And it is not only that some 'Indigenous people' (in the Census sense) are not clients, employees or participants of Indigenous organisations. It is also that among these organisations' most important clients and employees (though rarely office-holders) we find many non-Indigenous people and organisations. Much of what Indigenous Land Councils, Native Title Representative Bodies and Prescribed Bodies Corporate do they do with non-Indigenous resource development companies. Many CDEP organisations employ non-Indigenous staff in management positions. The Indigenous Sector, as a suite of organisations, has to be portrayed in terms that are rather different from the ethnic descriptors that we apply to the Indigenous populations (and to its sub-populations, as we shall soon see).

Students of 'Indigenous affairs' would do well to be clear about whether, in pursuing any particular question about 'Indigenous Australians' en masse, they are looking through the lens of 'the Indigenous population' or of the Indigenous Sector. Both lenses are in use in CAEPR's body of research and in this book. It is helpful to keep the difference between them in mind when considering the aims of public policy and what 'self-determination' means. The 'Indigenous population' and 'the Indigenous Sector' are each important categories in the story of 'self-determination', but in different ways.

For example, I have suggested in my introduction that one of the reasons for supporting the Indigenous Sector is that it expands the field of choices that Indigenous Australians face, even if their choice is to avoid using the services of that Sector — to go 'mainstream' for the services that matter to them. To say this implies a subtle but important reformulation of the objectives of self-determination. Self-determination is advanced not only by the fact that the Indigenous Sector actualises an institutional challenge to the settler–colonial jurisdiction. Self-determination is also advanced by the mere fact that an individual or a family group can make a choice about whether to avail themselves of the resources of the Indigenous Sector. In this way, the Indigenous Sector — like the enumeration strategy that relies entirely on self-identification — is the condition of the enhanced liberty of individuals and family groups. In these evocations of 'self-determination' the 'self' in question may be a person, a household, a family unit or perhaps a 'community' (as in the 'community' decision to have CDEP rather than individualised welfare payments).

To give an account of Indigenous 'self-determination' in such terms, with 'self' defined so as to include individuals, is to make an ethical argument that I find appealing. I think that the liberty of individuals is so important that it should be the ethical basis of social policy, including the social policy of Indigenous self-determination. However, I do not match this ethical primacy of the individual by any concession that the individual should be central to social and historical analysis. In upholding the human rights ideal of individual autonomy, one need not be a 'methodological individualist'. That is, to value individual autonomy in ethical terms does not entail that we must explain a rate of unemployment as no more than the sum of thousands of decisions made by individuals. I wish to make a strong distinction between the ethical individualism that I embrace and the methodological or analytical individualism that I continue to refuse.[2]

This distinction frees me to make a move that might strike the reader as strange (it confused me for quite a while). My ethical individualism is no barrier to a social ontology in which entities other than individuals are important. I believe that it makes good analytic sense to think of humans as making choices not only as individuals but also as collectives. Throughout the global discussion of Indigenous self-determination, it is assumed that the Indigenous 'self' can and should refer not only to individuals but to collectives, both small (for example, families) and large (organisations). Although we might refer loosely to such large Indigenous collectives such as 'the Indigenous Australians' or 'the people of Arnhem Land' or 'the Torres Strait Islanders', these are not, strictly speaking, adequate terms in a thoughtful account of collective Indigenous agency. If we understand Indigenous people to have rights as 'peoples', we are not compelled by that understanding to conceive 'the Indigenous people of Australia' as a collective subject, as if its collective mind, mentality, wishes or interests could be understood and invited to a dialogue with the 'collective mind' of non-Indigenous Australians. 'The Aboriginal people' and 'the Torres Strait Islanders' are abstractions, not collective agents. In social analysis and in political practice we must think of 'the Indigenous people' in all of its actualisations as choosing subjects and, in particular, in its actualisation as the Indigenous Sector — a suite of some 3000 organisations.

I see no point in trying to list these organisations or to define a precise boundary that would deal with ambiguous and doubtful instances of 'Indigenous organisation'. Rather I have exemplified the Indigenous Sector by reading CAEPR's research as an unsystematic exploration of its many forms and issues. If I insist on this organisational sense of 'Indigenous Australians', it is in order to come to terms with the way that Indigenous people actually make *collective* choices

Elsewhere, I have argued that the only way that Indigenous 'group rights' can be realised is through political organisations that can credibly maintain that they actualise and represent the 'group'. When Equal Opportunity and Human Rights Commissioner Zita Antonios inquired into the group rights of Pitjantjatjara people who sought to limit sales of liquor on their homelands, her practice was to accept the representations of the litigant group by the Pitjantjatjara Council. Without that representation to refer to, 'the Pitjantjatjara' could not be recognised, in legal and political processes, as a 'subject' of rights. Without that political work, in other words, 'the Pitjantjatjara' would have been an ensemble of individuals, with a variety of opinions, no doubt, about the need to limit sales of alcohol. The Council's representations made the 'group' real.[3]

I suggest that the group rights of Indigenous Australians are evolving in this piecemeal fashion, as a series of loosely integrated organisational projects. We might support the assertion that 'as a people' Indigenous Australians enjoy certain rights, but we should not let such rhetoric become our analytical vocabulary. In practical terms, the collective subject of these rights is neither 'the Indigenous people' nor 'the Indigenous population', but the organised instances of their mobilisation. 'The people' must be realised in an organisational form. To the extent that appeals to Indigenous rights are effective in shaping policy it is through the working out of specific arrangements, in specific places, mediated by specific organisational expressions of a 'group' of Indigenous Australians. That is one reason why contemporary advocates of a treaty (such as Mick Dodson and Marcia Langton) see it as a national framework within which many particular 'local treaties' could be negotiated. It is at the level of the locality and the organisation that the human rights of Indigenous Australians are to be realised.

I seek a social and historical analysis that breaks with methodological individualism not only in the sense that it can admit that our choices are constrained by structures but also in the sense that agency is sometimes collective and sometimes individual. Barry Hindess has pointed out that actors may be either individuals or collectives, as long as we conceive actors as making choices through 'forms of deliberation' whose nature and whose conditions of existence can, in principle, be studied. He distinguishes between real collective actors that do have 'means of taking decisions and of acting upon them' and fantasised collective actors that do not. 'Capitalist enterprises, state agencies, trade unions and community associations' are 'actors', but 'classes', 'societies' and 'peoples' are not, because they do not, as such, have the means of taking decisions and acting upon them. At best, there are people and organisations that claim to make decisions on behalf of these abstractions. It is through such an analytics of social action that an account of the Indigenous Sector may yield an understanding of 'the Indigenous people'.[4]

Robert Post has recently pointed out some implications of presuming that 'group rights' are realised through a 'group rightholder' or organisation:

> The institutional structure of a group capable of exercising rights will likely enable it to compete with the state in authoritatively articulating the nature of the group interests and group identity implicit in the nature of the special rights.

However, the state is likely to enjoy 'direct access into the internal institutional structure of a group':

Those who capture the right to speak for a group also capture the right to wield special rights granted by the state. Access to the state resources created by these rights thus becomes a prize to be won by competitive factions within the group, which the state can use to enhance national solidarity by co-opting group factions. This dynamic, in turn, can accelerate any potential divergence between institutional structure and group structure.[5]

It is in these terms that the study of Indigenous affairs can fruitfully be specified as the study of the organisations of the Indigenous Sector — their leading actors, the ways that they depict 'culture' as a ground of necessity, and the ways that members of the Indigenous population do and do not rally to the activists' political work of disseminating representations of their collective being.

So far I have argued that it is both logically possible and ethically necessary to imagine that Indigenous Australians are 'choosing subjects' in both the individual and the collective senses. However, those who are sceptical of 'self-determination' are likely to give ethical priority to the postulated agency of individuals. After all, it was the ambition of 'assimilation' to emancipate the Indigenous individual or household from the wider communal loyalties that were understood to hold them back. Those more positively disposed towards 'self-determination' should not discount the importance of individual choice. Indeed, I have asserted its ethical centrality to good social policy.

However, this ethical insistence on liberty and autonomy of the individual has been obscured or overlaid by two mistaken habits in the thinking of many those sympathetic to self-determination. One is the conflation of the ethical and the ontological senses of individual, so that in breaking with methodological individualism, one had also to abandon — as a Right-wing, neo-liberal fetish — the sanctity of individual liberty. The other troubling feature of much self-determinationist thinking has been the historic political necessity to distance 'self-determination' from 'assimilation'. To evoke 'self-determination' by emphasising the opportunities it gives for collective Indigenous agency and entitlement should not obscure the continuing pertinence of individual agency and entitlement to Indigenous Australians. The deregulation of Indigenous people as individuals was one of the hard-won victories of 'assimilation' as an ideology of reform. But 'assimilation' was not enough (and in some manifestations was actually retrograde). At a time when there is much unguarded nostalgia for 'assimilation' and despair about 'self-determination', I prefer to keep my faith that individuals and households are enabled more than disabled in their choices if they are part of a wider Indigenous community that has corporate powers of action and decision.

In the remainder of this introduction to Part IV I will briefly rehearse the evolution of policy thinking about Indigenous self-determination's organisational platform.

THE EMERGING PLATFORM OF SELF-DETERMINATION

In 1976, the Commonwealth passed two laws that define the Australian 'self-determination' approach: the *Aboriginal Land Rights (NT) Act* and the *Aboriginal Councils and Associations Act* (ACAA). The first Act gave Northern Territory Aborigines title to their extensive 'reserve' lands, set up a mechanism by which more land could be claimed and created 'Land Councils' to advise and represent 'traditional owners'. The opportunities and burdens of land ownership are the subject of an earlier chapter in this book. More important, for our present concerns, was the ACAA. The ACAA was based on the argument that Aborigines (and by implication Torres Strait Islanders) would be empowered were they to act as incorporated collectives. The Commonwealth would provide them with a statute of incorporation that respected their customary ways of doing political business with one another. The Minister, Ian Viner, commended the Act for recognising 'cultural differences between Aboriginal and non-Aboriginal societies' and for enabling 'Aboriginal communities to develop legally recognisable bodies which reflect their own culture and do not require them to subjugate this culture to overriding western legal concepts'.[6] A review of the Act in 1996 questioned whether it was so easy for such bodies — accountable to government, reliant on non-Indigenous professional staff — to 'reflect their own culture'.[7]

However, there is no doubt that the ACAA has been the statutory platform for the emergence of an Indigenous leadership that is seasoned in mediating between government agencies and an Indigenous constituency. When the Royal Commission into Aboriginal Deaths in Custody reported in 1991, Commissioner Johnston firmly endorsed the principle that services for Indigenous Australians be delivered by Indigenous organisations on a contractual basis, where such an organisation was available. He went on to discuss the difficulties — both the practical ones and those arising from competing notions of responsibility — of making such bodies accountable to governments for their funding. He recommended that 'performance indicators' for such organisations be determined by negotiation between governments and funded bodies. It would be necessary to devote more resources to training Indigenous functionaries of these organisations, he acknowledged. He envisaged, and indeed recommended, that funding be triennial (every three years), not annual or quarterly.[8]

If Johnston saw local, service-delivering Indigenous organisations as the concrete realisation of 'self-determination', by the time he came to write his report he had also to take into account their relationship with a new (1990) national body, the Aboriginal and Torres Strait Islander Commission (ATSIC), dedicated to the same policy principle. ATSIC was the product of a series of experiments, by both Labor and Liberal governments, in the recognition of an Indigenous constituency and the encouragement of a national leadership. In 1973, the Whitlam government established the National Aboriginal Consultative Committee (NACC) with 41 members elected from 41 electorates by Aboriginal and Torres Strait Islander voters. The NACC had no executive powers. Nor did its successor, the elected National Aboriginal Conference (NAC, 1977–85). However, the Fraser government did give powers to spend money (on land, housing and enterprises) to the Aboriginal Development Commission (ADC), set up in 1980. The Board of the ADC was composed of Commonwealth government appointees. In the second half of the 1980s, the Hawke government reviewed these attempts to empower a national Indigenous elite. From this review came ATSIC in 1989. ATSIC's Commissioners are elected; they are responsible for the delivery of some of the Commonwealth programs directed to Indigenous Australians.

ATSIC's structure was an attempt to bring together the regional and local Indigenous political mobilisations enabled by the ACAA with the national electorate inaugurated by the NAC and continued in the NACC. Accordingly, the Indigenous electorate elects Regional Councils. Regional groupings of these councils make up a 'zone', and each zone is represented by an elected national Commissioner. The Board of Commissioners governs ATSIC, whose staff are Commonwealth public servants. Many incorporated Indigenous organisations are the funded clients of ATSIC. Functionaries and leaders of these organisations are among those who seek election to ATSIC's regional and national bodies.

There are 35 Regional Councils (reduced in 1993 from the initial 60), each with up to twelve members elected every three years. Every year, each Regional Council formulates or revises a regional plan that proposes the level of expenditure within those programs that fall under Regional Council jurisdiction. About half of ATSIC's program funds are administered by the Regional Councils. The 'devolution' does not stop there. Of $1092 million spent by ATSIC in 1999–2000, $770 million was granted (either by regional or by national decision) to 1058 Indigenous organisations, each of which has to satisfy stringent acquittal requirements. That is, more than three-quarters of ATSIC's money is used to fund non-government Indigenous agencies delivering public services such as employment, heritage protection, housing and community infrastructure and native title advocacy. ATSIC is both a major agency of the Indigenous Sector and a significant source of the funds on which the Indigenous Sector runs.

To put this in perspective, however, it must be recalled that ATSIC is responsible for only half of what the Commonwealth spends on programs dedicated to Indigenous Australians. Other Commonwealth agencies contributing to Indigenous programs include the Department of Education, Training and Youth Affairs (DETYA), the Department of Employment, Workplace Relations and Small Business (DEWRSB), the Department of Family and Community Services (DFACS) and Environment Australia. Each of these agencies grants some of its program funds to Indigenous organisations. At the two other levels of government, there are also many programs with Indigenous clients, both individuals and organisations. However, it is not possible to quantify on a national basis State/Territory and local government expenditure on Indigenous programs, because the States and Territories do not collect (or do not publish) the data required for such a calculation. In short, ATSIC is a significant, but hardly a dominant, agency in a multi-agency approach to the administration of services to Indigenous Australians.

ATSIC is an experiment in regional devolution, and much of CAEPR's comment on ATSIC has regionalism as its theme. Because ATSIC is unique in its representative and regional structure and because it has sometimes functioned as the main vehicle of the Indigenous leadership's advocacy of Indigenous rights, it has attracted much scrutiny. CAEPR research, funded by ATSIC but independent of its supervision, has illuminated two issues of regional devolution that I will examine in the next two chapters. In Chapter 12, I ask a question prompted by political pressures to consider inter-regional 'equity': are the needs of ATSIC's regions objectively comparable? In Chapter 13, I examine impulses towards regionalism that derive more from the popular desire for regional autonomy (with a case study of the Torres Strait) and from the stimulus of the recent recognition of native title.

12
ATSIC'S REGIONS: THE 'EQUITY' ISSUE

ATSIC's accountability for its expenditure has been a topic of parliamentary and public debate for many reasons. One of them, as Sanders explained, has been that:

> [e]xecutive control over almost all Commonwealth Aboriginal affairs portfolio expenditure would be handed over to a largely-elected body of Aboriginal Commissioners. There was also provision for the devolution of grant-funding decision-making within ATSIC to the level of elected Regional Councils, at least in an advisory capacity.[9]

To make this publicly acceptable, the Hawke government demanded 'more stringent accountability for the expenditure of public funds':

> There would be greater ministerial oversight of the organisation's estimates and some other possibilities for ministerial intervention, albeit largely as powers of last resort. There would also be clearer specifications of procedures to be followed by ATSIC in assessment and administration of grants and loans, and clear statutory delineations of the purposes for which grants and loans could be made. This was the renegotiated policy bargain.[10]

ATSIC's Commissioners showed an early zeal in policing grant acquittal, noted Sanders. Their 'ongoing review ... of all grant administration processes within ATSIC' anticipated 'close scrutiny from bodies such as the parliament and the Auditor-General', and resulted in 'more stringent' oversight of large grants.[11] Pressure from ATSIC's internal Office of Evaluation and Audit (strengthened by 1993 amendments to ATSIC's Act) also produced a clearer distinction between the commercial and the social rationales of

ATSIC's support for enterprises. As part of what Sanders has called ATSIC's 'policy bargain', devolution to Regional Councils was permitted; the decisions of Regional Councils were laid open to OEA scrutiny in 1993.

Did these measures mean that ATSIC was 'succeeding in reconciling public accountability and Aboriginal self-determination/self-management'? Sanders asked.[12] To answer that question was difficult, he argued, given the essentially contested nature of its key terms. To Parliament, ATSIC was a 'success' to the extent that the OEA enforced a climate of strict financial accountability. On the other hand, Indigenous evaluations probably remained mixed at the end of the first term of elected Regional Councillors. The voter turnout in ATSIC's December 1993 regional elections would be one measure of its reputation among Indigenous people, suggested Sanders. '[I]t is too early to make a judgement on longer-term prospects of success' in 'ATSIC's delicate balancing act.'[13]

Michele Ivanitz has judged that ATSIC may have lost more than it won since that early 1990s 'policy bargain'. Regional Councils and funded organisations have survived the inspection of the Office of Evaluation and Audit. A special audit in 1996 found that only five per cent of funded Indigenous organisations failed to comply (mostly minor technical breaches) with acquittal requirements. Yet the Howard government cut ATSIC's funds in 1996; the Board responded by eliminating the Community Training Program, the Development of Industry Strategies, the Community and Youth Support Program and the Movement to Award Wages program. In 1998 the Minister exercised his authority under the Act to redirect money from the Community Housing and Infrastructure program to the Torres Strait Regional Authority, to the Commercial Development Program and to the Office of Indigenous Policy (which at first sat in another portfolio, Prime Minister and Cabinet, and then moved to the Department of Immigration, offering advice to Cabinet that competes with ATSIC's submissions). Ivanitz wondered whether it was the Howard government's intention to 'dismantle' ATSIC.[14] Evidently not, but there is no doubt that ATSIC has had to fight for its position as the principal vehicle for Indigenous self-determination. In the opinion of the Minister who set it up, ATSIC 'has been white-anted from the first day. It has been undermined'.[15]

Though it has not commented directly on the issue of ATSIC's political standing, one theme of CAEPR's research into ATSIC — the comparability of regions — gave the impression that ATSIC could 'prove' its administrative rationality by establishing an objective basis for appraisal of its clients' demands. The CAEPR researchers sought an objective basis for comparing regions in their neediness.

What are ATSIC's regions? In an early CAEPR Discussion Paper, Tesfaghiorghis explained what he understood to be their basis:

> The process of establishing ATSIC regions and zones was primarily undertaken in 1988–89 by the then Minister for Aboriginal Affairs, Mr Gerry Hand, and his staff assisted by a Task force set up in the Department of Aboriginal Affairs (DAA). The determination of the various jurisdictions and boundaries was essentially based on a process of extensive consultations with Aboriginal communities and organisations around the country, both as to the numbers of regions and zones, and as to their actual boundaries. There is little information on public record indicating how these regions were demarcated, but they were based on the following factors: Aboriginal cultural, linguistic and social factors, contemporary geographic realities (like location of service centres), and possibly other factors which Aboriginal organisations articulated.[16]

Smith has described the regional structure as 'a limited translation of diversity, subject as it was to prevailing government concerns about the need for financial and administrative efficiency, and the sheer difficulties involved in translating complex Indigenous cultural differences into a nationally representative organisational framework'.[17]

In CAEPR's quest, it was first necessary to consider whether regional populations could be defined. Do we know who lives where? When Taylor and Bell described Indigenous mobility, they concluded that some Regional Councils would find it easier than others to describe in statistical terms the needs of their constituents:

> [I]n most remote regions relative stability in population levels is characteristic. In other regions, however, migration contributes substantially to population change either through net losses, as in western Queensland, or net gains, as in south east Queensland. At the same time, the analysis of migration flows clearly reveals patterns of movement between networks of places that often straddle current regional council boundaries. This begs the question of what constitutes an appropriate population to plan for in any region as regional councils may not be just servicing their own clients as defined by the locally enumerated population.[18]

If each region of Aboriginal Australia were to have good data about its needs and progress, the local Indigenous organisations themselves would have to play a part in gathering information. Referring to Regional Councils as 'entirely new jurisdictions in Australian public administration', Gaminiratne and Altman warned Regional Councils about some defects of the regionally disaggregated data.[19] It would be difficult, in the short term, for regions to measure their progress according to social indicator data. However, 'with time, more detailed population data from censuses, vital registration and other administrative data sets will be available by regional council areas, which will provide substantial supplementary data inputs for the regional planners in deciding priorities and the evaluation of programs ... It might be that ... regional councils will need to become involved in primary collection of comparable data for their own regions ... [or in] special surveys that address issues of specific relevance in the division of resources between ATSIC regional councils'.[20] They added that Regional Councils might also find such data useful in deciding allocations *within* regions.

The potential utility of data gathered by Indigenous organisations was also highlighted in another CAEPR study. Working with Martin's Aurukun ethnographic data and 1991 Census data, Taylor and Martin investigated whether ABS remote area enumeration was a reliable way to measure the size and characteristics of remote regions. They warned that the Census was likely to under-enumerate the 'young, more mobile and more socially marginal', with consequent underestimation of the need for programs in education, housing and unemployment.[21] To reduce this risk, they argued, the ABS should try to make use of administrative data compiled by Land Councils, Community Councils and Outstation Resource Centres. The ABS should 'encourage ongoing links between State offices and relevant community organisations'.[22]

To what political uses could data on Indigenous regions be put? Here it is necessary to distinguish between two users: the Regional Councils, looking at their own needs, and national agencies, seeking to compare one region with another. As well as measuring regional program outcomes and estimating regional program needs, regionally disaggregated data could be worked up into indices of need, making objective comparisons of regions possible.

CAEPR researchers explored the potential of this 'comparative' perspective and in doing so they raised, but did not confront, an important policy issue. For example, Tesfaghiorghis outlined a possible 'socioeconomic status index' (combining percentage qualified, employment/population ratio and the median individual income). He intended this index to show relativities *within Indigenous Australia*, not to compare Indigenous with non-Indigenous Australians.[23] That is, the use of such an index as a guide to distributing ATSIC's resources could relieve inequalities among Indigenous people. However, Tesfaghiorghis did not explain why that should be an objective of government policy. Perhaps the point of Tesfaghiorghis's intra-Indigenous comparisons was that they would help to give legitimacy to the deliberations of ATSIC. Some CAEPR researchers presented these indices as a chance to *rationalise* political processes within ATSIC. That is, ATSIC — either its central, its State, or its regional offices — could use indices of Indigenous need as an objective basis for arbitrating competing resource demands between regions and within regions.

Smith devoted three papers to the possibility of basing resource allocation within ATSIC on the specific characteristics of regional populations. As she pointed out, it was part of ATSIC's intended innovation to encourage what she called 'the regionalisation of program initiatives and needs ...'. Pressure from regions 'will increasingly influence the functionally-based program structure', she predicted.[24] 'As regional councils and the communities within them progressively determine priorities in their service and funding needs, they will begin to negotiate service packages' and program monitoring will increasingly be regional.[25]

In Smith's work we find two different reasons for CAEPR's research to help ATSIC know the specific features of its regions. First, a regionalised ATSIC would be more responsive to, and more representative of, those whom it aspired to serve, for it had become clear to government since the 1970s that Indigenous people were regionally diverse in needs, aspiration and identity.[26] Secondly, a 'program structure based on regional packages would greatly facilitate the attainment of horizontal equity in the delivery of ATSIC's programs'.[27] I take her words to mean greater equality between regions, in respect of certain socio-economic characteristics. However, it is necessary to ask again: why should it be considered important to reduce inequalities *among* Indigenous Australians? Smith, like Tesfaghiorghis, did not address this question. Nor did she discuss the possible tension between, on the one hand, the central offices of ATSIC pursuing inter-regional 'horizontal equity', and, on the other hand, the 'growing regional vision of increased financial self-determination'.[28] A central office bent on equalisation would find good reasons to limit devolution of decision-making to regions.

We may wonder at the persistence of this unargued assumption that ATSIC should pursue a measurable levelling of socio-economic status among Indigenous Australians (defined as a series of regional populations). Possibly CAEPR researchers were prompted by ATSIC's Office of Evaluation and Audit (OEA). OEA's rationale was to assure the Australian public that ATSIC was spending public money honestly and effectively. Evidently the OEA saw the objective arbitration of inter-regional rivalries for ATSIC resources as a way for ATSIC to establish a reputation as a sound public agency. Smith referred to the OEA's interest in identifying 'relative disadvantage between regions' using 'an effective national policy instrument', which she called a 'fiscal equalisation model'.[29] Perhaps this instrument could eventually inform the approach of other agencies to inter-regional equity among Indigenous Australians, she speculated. An instrument to measure and promote 'inter-regional equity' would be 'a policy-neutral tool by which ATSIC's Board of

Commissioners could make consistent, equitable funding decisions and which could facilitate an integrated approach to ATSIC's financial planning'.[30] Its application 'for some regions ... may mean an increase in funding, for others a decrease'.[31] She asserted that 'a more geographically-based program structure and a system of resource distribution based on regional equity should facilitate accountable decentralisation'.[32]

That Smith should take achieving 'accountable decentralisation' as an important intermediate political objective of ATSIC perhaps reflected CAEPR's (and perhaps Smith's in particular) sensitivity to the fragility of ATSIC's mandate from the Commonwealth government.

CAEPR researchers continued to investigate the construction of an index of socio-economic status that would enable inter-regional comparisons. Altman and Liu acknowledged that the purpose of such an index was open to debate. 'Whether need should be defined in relative or absolute terms remains a contested issue.'[33] They used 1986 and 1991 Census data to formulate an 'Index of Socio-economic Advantage' (ISA), made up of education, employment and income, to apply to 36 Regional Councils and so to 'situate each ATSIC region in relation to others ...'. As they explained, 'ATSIC is quite legitimately seeking a systematic means to allocate scarce program dollars on some broadly accepted measure of need ...'. However, they made the important point that, because ATSIC was only one of many agencies with responsibilities to service Indigenous communities, 'any rational resource allocation will also need information on global allocation of resources from all levels of government, at the regional level ...'.[34] If ATSIC could not centralise all such data, then it would lack a rational basis for centralised allocation of resources in accordance with the (contested) ideal of inter-regional equality.

Notwithstanding these very significant limitations on the entire project of 'horizontal equity' among ATSIC regions, CAEPR researchers continued to research a socio-economic index. Gray and Auld found a way to rank ATSIC's 36 regions in terms of a composite index (made up of data on family income, housing, educational attainment and non-employment). It was possible to measure changes in ranking over time. Acknowledging data problems that reduce the soundness of comparison's over time, they found little change in 1991–96 in regional rankings. Their index was 'possibly' of use to the Commonwealth Grants Commission, they suggested, in its search for a method 'to determine the needs of groups of Indigenous Australians *relative to one another* ...'.[35] Though they discuss the empirical and conceptual limitations of their index, Gray and Auld do not discuss why the CGC (or anybody else) should think that intra-Indigenous comparisons of need were important in the formulation of public policy.

CAEPR's investigation of socio-economic indices of regional well-being has been predicated upon an unargued policy of striving for 'equity' within Indigenous Australia. It was as if Government agencies have been mandated to reduce inequalities *among* Indigenous people. However, that is at best a controversial goal. Its evident popularity among some researchers and officials is best explained as their 'rationalist' tactical response to the political attacks on ATSIC's unprecedented powers of devolution. What a trump card a regional algorithm might have been!

Putting issues of policy and tactics aside, any empirically adequate index of inter-regional need would have required much more sharing of data and plans among all the agencies servicing Indigenous Australians. One agency, perhaps ATSIC, would have to be entrusted with all such data, so that it could be analysed in its entirety. Such a pattern of co-operation has not, to date, appeared likely.

13
ATSIC'S REGIONS: THE IDENTITY ISSUE

In the previous chapter I reviewed one of the ways that CAEPR considered the potential of ATSIC's regional structure. In this chapter I trace an alternative 'regional' theme in CAEPR that owes more to the impulse to popular sovereignty and grass-roots legitimation than to the problems of achieving administrative rationality. For most of the chapter, my case study is the Torres Strait. At the end of the chapter I consider new impulses towards regionalism, that need not have anything to do with ATSIC's agendas of administrative rationality and popular sovereignty.

THE TORRES STRAIT: EXEMPLARY REGIONALISM?

The political assertiveness of one region, the Torres Strait, provoked CAEPR research into the difficulties of designing a regional instrument of Indigenous self-determination

The problems begin with the notion of 'Islanders'. When Arthur asked in 1992 whether there are 'any issues which are particular to Islanders', he in fact broached two understandings of 'particularity' — regional and ethnic.[1] That is, the phrase 'Torres Strait Islanders' can be used to refer to (a) people with that ethnic identity, regardless of where they live, and (b) people who live in the Torres Strait, regardless of their ethnic identity. Though people (a) and people (b) undoubtedly overlap in membership, they are not the same phenomenon politically, for most 'Islanders' do not live in the Torres Strait.

As a subject for demographic analysis, it is the first (that is, ethnic) sense of 'Torres Strait Islander' which has been of greater interest. Demographers, most of the time, use the data of the Census, and the Census defines Torres Strait Islanders not according to place but according to their answer to a question about ethnic self-identification. However, CAEPR demographers have not always been satisfied with the quality of the data on Torres Strait Islanders. When Gaminiratne examined the rise in the Torres Strait Islander population in 1986–91, he found it growing 2.8 times faster than the Aboriginal population, at an 'extraordinarily high' annual rate of 5.6 per cent.[2] Perhaps the 1986 Census had missed many Islanders who were now turning up in the 1991 Census. Perhaps there was an increased tendency for people to identify as Islanders in answering the Census. Perhaps people in the Bass Strait and people with Pacific Island ancestry thought that they too should identify as 'Islanders' when filling out the Census. 'The rapid annual growth rate of the Islander population in almost all States cannot be explained by natural increase or migration. Clearly, growth rates of this magnitude represent defects in the census counts, changed identification, or both.'[3]

The ethnically defined Torres Strait Islander people are dispersed. In 1986, almost four out of every five Torres Strait Islanders lived on the mainland. (This figure can not be stated precisely, considering Gaminiratne's worry that the 1986 Census may have undercounted Islanders. Indeed, Jeremy Beckett dismisses the mainland Islander count as 'wildly inaccurate'.[4]) According to Taylor and Arthur's account of these people's migration to the mainland since World War II, they were attracted by the greater employment and income opportunities in north Queensland towns and in places even further from home. Unskilled employment in the railways seems to have been particularly important, and family members have helped one another to get jobs and to settle, a long way from the Torres Strait, among people they know. The proportion of Islanders living no further away than mainland Queensland had fallen from two out of three (estimated in 1975, measured in 1986) to one in two in 1991. In short, Islanders were evidently dispersing further across Australia in the 1980s. Those remaining within Queensland were mainly to be found in Brisbane and coastal towns.[5]

Was this dispersion from the Strait into eastern seaboard cities irreversible? Taylor and Arthur discussed the possibility that mainland employment and living conditions could lose their comparative attractiveness; they acknowledged, as well, that it has become much easier and cheaper to travel back and forth between mainland and Strait islands. It was likely that Islander migration was shifting from a one-way dispersion pattern, to a more opportunistic, circular pattern.[6] Comparing Islanders' places of residence in 1981 and 1986 (and allowing for the characteristic tendency of the Census to understate short-term mobility) they noted the relative immobility of Islanders.

'Thus, they are either located in places where labour markets exist (metropolitan and regional centres), or they are located in the Torres Strait where ... conditions may be increasingly conducive to longer-term residence among many Islanders.'[7]

Arthur argued in 1996 that this history of migration and settlement, resulting in a diaspora, has made it both possible and desirable to 'consider the Islander population in two components, that in the Strait and that on the mainland, and to analyse statistics accordingly'.[8] He and Taylor had made such a comparison in respect to 'economic status', using 1991 Census data.[9] They found that, if CDEP jobs were counted as employment, Islanders in the Strait had a higher rate of employment, though smaller average incomes, than those on the mainland. Discounting CDEP jobs, Islanders in the Strait were worse off than mainland Islanders; indeed, the latter were 'approaching a position of statistical equality with other Australians'.[10] The educational attainments of Strait people were also lower than those of mainland Islanders. Arthur and Taylor concluded that, from the point of view of designing economic development programs, it made more sense to disaggregate the Torres Strait Islanders, in order to highlight the specific challenges facing those living in the Straits, than to treat Islanders as a single (ethnic) category of socio-economic need.[11]

But were these socio-economic differences more important than commonalities of ethnic identity? Arthur used NATSIS data to compare a subset of mainland Islanders (those residing in Queensland) with Strait Islanders. In contrast with their economic differences, he found evidence of strong similarities of cultural orientation between the two categories of Islander, including a 'high proportion of mainlanders who still view the Torres Strait as their homeland and who feel they can live there if they wish'.[12] Apart from having more non-CDEP jobs, mainland Islanders were arguably less well integrated into the society to which they had migrated: fewer of them had recently voted, and more of them had had difficulties with the police and had need of a lawyer. These data were consistent with Taylor and Arthur's earlier speculations that there were good reasons for the Torres Strait diaspora to feel, and occasionally to answer, the pull of home, and thus to practise 'circular' mobility between the Strait and the mainland places where they had settled and found employment.

However, because the reliability of Census data on Torres Strait Islanders continues to be of concern, it has proved difficult to research these patterns of Islander circulation and to examine the relative weight of employment opportunity in Islanders' decisions about where to live. Gaminiratne was sceptical about interpreting their 'extremely high growth rates in other eastern States' as evidence of Islander migration out of Queensland.[13] Who, besides Torres Strait Islanders, were identifying themselves as Islanders?

After 1996, there was a new reason to doubt the Census 'Islander' count. In the 1996 Census, the government for the first time allowed people the option of identifying as *both* Aboriginal and Torres Strait Islander. Some ten thousand people did so. The introduction of this 'hybrid' category made it harder to apply the two-part distinction upon which the enumeration of an ethnically distinct Torres Strait Islander population had rested. If those of mixed Aboriginal and Islander descent were counted as 'Aborigines', the Islander population grew by 7 per cent 1991–96; if they were counted as 'Islanders', the Islander population grew by 44 per cent in that period. 'Difficulty with defining the Torres Strait Islander population has been a regular feature of Census enumeration', complained Taylor, 'and this new category of identity seems to have added further complexity to the issue'.[14] Accordingly, he chose to conduct the rest of his analysis, in his 1997 paper, on the total 'Indigenous' population. So too did Alan Gray's projection of population growth from 1991 to 2001 refuse to distinguish the Torres Strait Islander from the total Indigenous population.[15] Similarly, when Taylor and Bell took advantage of another 1996 Census innovation to offer an analysis of short-term mobility, they could compare Indigenous with non-Indigenous, but they saw no opportunity to compare the now ill-defined categories 'Aboriginal' and 'Torres Strait Islander'.[16] So it has become impossible, for the time being, to document the continuing mobility characteristics of the Torres Strait Islander diaspora.

If 'Torres Strait Islander' has been a problematic category in demography, it has been no less troubling a category in the design of regional political institutions. Soon after its inception in 1990, ATSIC was quick to respond to criticism from Torres Strait Islanders that their interests were not being represented adequately. As early as 1936, the Islanders had demanded to be distinguished from Aborigines, and the Queensland government set what Islander leaders regarded as a good example from 1938, by having a separate law for governing Torres Strait Islanders. For the State government, this was a territorial, rather than an ethnic distinction. Accordingly, the Torres Strait Islanders who did not live in the Strait were not, except on their visits home, subject to the law governing Torres Strait Islanders. In 1989, when elected Torres Strait Islander Community Councils were brought into being by the Queensland government, only those with two years' residence on the relevant island could vote or stand for office. When the design of ATSIC was discussed in the Strait in 1987 and 1988, Islanders requested that the chairpersons of these elected community councils become members of the proposed Torres Strait Regional Council of ATSIC. After a 1992 review, ATSIC dissolved this Regional Council and replaced it with the Torres Strait Regional Authority (TSRA) on 1 July 1994. From 1994 to 1997 the TSRA negotiated its budget directly with the chair of ATSIC and the Minister for Aboriginal and Torres Strait Islander Affairs. After 1997, the TSRA budget was separated from ATSIC's and was negotiated directly with the Department of Finance.

The TSRA area consisted of the islands of the Torres Strait, excluding Barn and Crab Islands and also excluding the nearby mainland communities, Bamaga and Seisia. ATSIC's regional structure — the Council, succeeded by the Authority — followed Queensland government practice in one respect and departed from it in another. ATSIC followed Queensland in clearly distinguishing the governing structures of the Strait from governing structures for the rest of Queensland's Indigenous communities. That is, its sense of 'Torres Strait' was regional, not ethnic. ATSIC 'largely incorporated and built on' the area of Queensland government's Island Coordinating Council (ICC) which was set up in 1984 and continues, concurrent with the TSRA.[17] Under the ATSIC Act of 1989, members of the ICC, by virtue of holding that office, would become ATSIC's Torres Strait Regional Councillors.[18] From 1994 to 1997, this relationship was facilitated by the fact that the same person chaired the TSRA and the ICC. However, ATSIC departed from Queensland practice by including more than the ICC. ATSIC included the 'inner island' areas (Thursday, Heron and Prince of Wales Islands) served by Torres Shire in the area represented by the TSRA.

CAEPR research on the implementation of the AEDP in the Torres Strait took note of the TSRA's expressed economic development goals: targeting tourism, agriculture and fisheries, and aspiring to move Islanders from part-time to full-time employment. Using 1986 and 1991 Census data, Arthur described the economic status of those within the TSRA's jurisdiction. He advised the TSRA to be realistic about the limited possibility of full-time work in the TSRA area.[19] His warning paralleled Davis's observation that the TSRA's economic development goals were 'to a large extent countermanded by the Saibai Islanders, who maintain an economic strategy which balances traditional subsistence practices with government transfers to retain a desired standard of living'.[20] Arthur and Taylor, after comparing the socio-economic status of Torres Strait Islanders living inside the TSRA with the socio-economic status of Islanders living outside the TSRA, concluded that the latter were much better off in terms of employment and income. If the TSRA wanted to bring Strait residents to socio-economic equality with other Islanders, they advised, the economic development efforts of the TSRA 'will need to be doubled'.[21]

However, it is not clear, from their paper, whether the TSRA *had* defined its economic development goals in this comparative fashion.

ATSIC's Indigenous legitimacy in the Torres Strait rested partly on the economic and cultural realism of the TSRA's expressed economic development goals, and partly on Islanders' opinion of the representative adequacy of the TSRA. Sanders showed in 1994 why 'representation' was a complex issue in the Torres Strait. ATSIC thought it necessary to establish not only a regional body (the TSRA) but also an instrument of ethnic representation. ATSIC's Torres Strait Islander Advisory Board (TSIAB) represents Torres Strait Islanders who live outside the Torres Strait *as well as* those living in the Strait. The TSIAB was serviced by a distinct bureaucratic section of ATSIC, the Office of Torres Strait Islander Affairs (OTSIA). Both the TSRA and the TSIAB were chaired by the Torres Strait Zone Commissioner. However, the two bodies imply rather different tasks of representation and accountability. As Sanders explained, 'The TSRA is ... effectively an Island regional body, while the TSIAB is quite explicitly a national Islander body. There is thus a dual constituency structure for Torres Strait and Torres Strait Islanders'.[22] Sanders asked whether the conceptions of these two constituencies were diverging. He noted in 1994 that some regional leaders aspired to make the regional structure more 'regional' and less 'ethnic' in definition, by including Straits residents who are not, ethnically, Islanders. He speculated about the need for a 'confederal' structure for such a TSRA, allowing the persistence of the distinction between the Torres Shire constituency and the ICC constituency in the process of selecting the TSRA's members. He conjectured also, that if the TSRA became a multi-ethnic regional structure, and so moved outside ATSIC (which by law has an exclusively Indigenous constituency), the TSIAB would become more important to ATSIC as the representative instrument of a specifically ethnic Torres Strait Islander constituency. As Sanders points out, the idea of a multi-ethnic Torres Strait regional government owes nothing, in principle, to the notions of Indigenous rights with which ATSIC has often sought to define and justify its mission.

In Sanders' view, 'the marriage between Islander aspirations for regional autonomy and the ATSIC structure has only ever been one of convenience ...'.[23] Arthur cited Beckett's view that the Islanders have been effective, since the early 1970s is 'playing off the State and Commonwealth governments'.[24]

In 1996, the TSRA's future as an agency of regional self-government was referred by the Howard government to the House of Representative Standing Committee on Aboriginal and Torres Strait Islander Affairs (HORSCATSIA). The Committee asked: was more autonomy for 'the people of the Torres Strait' desirable, what form might it take, and how might it affect Islanders not residing in the Straits? In their submission to HORSCATSIA, Altman, Arthur and Sanders suggested that a 'Torres Strait regional government constitutional convention' should be convened to discuss possible forms of Torres Strait regional government.[25] They foreshadowed 'the possibility of some close derivatives of the existing Island Councils and the Torres Shire Council (TSC) coming together as a confederal regional government based on complementary Torres Strait Regional Government legislation passed by the Commonwealth and Queensland parliaments'.[26] HORSCATSIA's August 1997 report recommended 'that the existing Indigenous and non-Indigenous regional bodies in Torres Strait be replaced by an elected Torres Strait Regional Assembly which would have the power to formulate policies for all the residents in the region'.[27]

However, this 'regional' agenda was in competition with the 'ethnic' mobilisation of most of those making submissions to the Standing Committee. The latter construed 'the people of the Torres Strait' in ethnic, not regional terms. They sought a separate national commission for Torres Strait Islanders. This was indeed a direct challenge to ATSIC. HORSCATSIA did not support the call for a separate commission because 'the Torres Strait Islander population is too small and dispersed to make this efficient or effective'.[28]

Sanders and Arthur, acknowledging the importance of the two different 'Islander' agendas, suggested that both lines of reform could be 'progressed together'.[29] They suggested that by construing the problem of Torres Strait Islander autonomy in regional terms, ATSIC had not taken sufficient notice of the 'ethnic' or 'national' challenge by Islanders. 'Thus, the establishment of the TSRA in 1994 left intact the problems that Torres Strait Islanders, and particularly those living outside the Strait, perceived with ATSIC.'[30] They discussed the possible structure, funding and organisational scale of a representative national TSI Commission. As well, they wondered into which constituency would fit those Indigenous Australians who identified as both 'Torres Strait Islander' and 'Aboriginal'. Noting a number of difficulties with ethnically separate representation and government of Torres Strait Islanders, they discussed possible reforms to the representation of Islander interests within ATSIC. These were issues for Islanders to discuss, they insisted.

Mainland-dwelling Islanders demonstrated their continuing sense of belonging to their Strait homeland. Some have made native title applications to Strait areas, and in 1997, those attending a National Torres Strait Islander Workshop demanded that they be given full voting rights in any regional body governing the Straits. However, when Arthur surveyed the many interests that would have to be involved in furthering the cause of regional autonomy, he had little to say about the mainlanders, other than that their 'precise part ... in formulating any regional agreements is unclear'.[31] He concluded that 'a commitment [to regionalism] exists in the Strait', and that the Torres Strait was the region most likely, out of all Australian regions, to produce a regional agreement. This conclusion did not answer the question of the nature of the commitments of those not 'in the Strait'.[32]

The ethnic sense of 'Torres Strait Islander' continued to trouble the regional sense. Arthur turned his attention to the mainlanders' grievances in a survey of their access to government programs and services (a study commissioned by OTSIA). His respondents expressed the view that 'within the system of Indigenous programs and services, and *especially within ATSIC*, they are marginalised *with respect to Aboriginal people*'.[33] He elaborated:

> [E]lected regional councils decide which funding applications should be supported and Islanders believe that Aboriginal applications are favoured over their own. Islanders also claim that regional councils have, on occasions, referred their applications to the TSRA on Thursday Island, in the belief that the TSRA is the appropriate body to deal with all programs and services for Torres Strait Islanders.[34]

Of course, in that belief they were mistaken. Whatever use it might make of the rhetoric of 'ethnic' identity, the TSRA's constituency is defined spatially, as much as ethnically. So how to address that ethnically defined constituency, the Islander diaspora?

Arthur suggested some ways that governments could increase their efforts to identify their programs as being of service to Islanders, such as including the term 'Torres Strait Islander' in the naming of agencies and programs dedicated to Indigenous Australians. ATSIC could earmark certain funds for Islanders, so that they competed with one another, not with Aborigines, for grants. He also suggested that Islanders might increase their access, or feel themselves to enjoy better access, were they to increase what he called their 'links' with Aborigines. However, Arthur remained impressed by the weight of Islanders' sense of being an ethnically distinct group. 'It is likely ... that Islanders will continue to lobby for some greater degree of separation.'[35]

By 1999, Sanders had come to the conclusion that in the 1990s the 'ethnic' mobilisation of Torres Straits Islanders and the 'regional' mobilisation of the 'people of the Torres Strait' had tended to undermine one another.[36] He gave details of a number of instances in which the two perspectives clashed. First, when HORSCATSIA recommended in 1997 that the Torres Strait Shire be abolished because it was superfluous to the proposed Torres Strait Regional Assembly, Islander critics associated with the TSC argued the need for equity in the representation of different sub-regions of the Torres

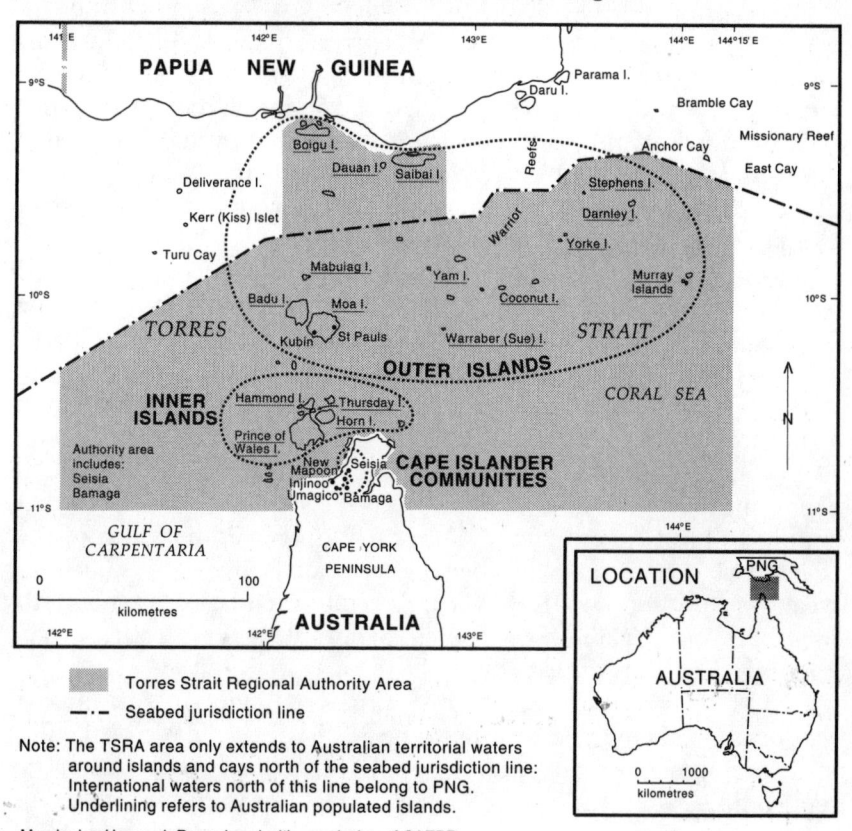

Figure 1. The Torres Strait Region

[Map showing the Torres Strait Region with Papua New Guinea to the north and Australia (Cape York Peninsula) to the south. Labels include: Parama I., Daru I., Bramble Cay, Boigu I., Dauan I., Saibai I., Anchor Cay, Missionary Reef, East Cay, Deliverance I., Stephens I., Kerr (Kiss) Islet, Darnley I., Turu Cay, Mabuiag I., Yam I., Yorke I., Badu I., Moa I., Coconut I., Murray Islands, Kubin, St Pauls, Warraber (Sue) I., Hammond I., Thursday I., Horn I., Prince of Wales I., New Mapoon, Seisia, Injinoo, Umagico, Bamaga, TORRES STRAIT, OUTER ISLANDS, INNER ISLANDS, CAPE ISLANDER COMMUNITIES, CORAL SEA, GULF OF CARPENTARIA, CAPE YORK PENINSULA, AUSTRALIA. Authority area includes: Seisia, Bamaga. Legend: Torres Strait Regional Authority Area; Seabed jurisdiction line. Note: The TSRA area only extends to Australian territorial waters around islands and cays north of the seabed jurisdiction line: International waters north of this line belong to PNG. Underlining refers to Australian populated islands. Map by Ian Heyward. Reproduced with permission of CAEPR.]

Strait. The significant point in the TSC's critique was that it drew on 'regional', rather than on 'ethnic', definitions of the 'Islander' constituency.[37] The regional political domain which emerged in the 1990s, under the representative framework of the TSRA, was multi-ethnic, blurring old distinctions between inner and outer island identities and between Islanders and non-Islanders. 'Uncertainty' is the word chosen by Arthur and Sanders to sum up Islander views of 'the idea of opening up the regional representative body to non-Indigenous residents'.[38] HORSCATSIA appears to have underestimated the importance of such regional thinking.

And yet, at the same time, HORSCATSIA also found it difficult, in its proposals about representing Islander interests at the Commissioner level of ATSIC, to honour the 'ethnic' solidarity of Torres Strait Islanders. Mainland Islanders saw in the committee's 1997 report a threat that they would be even further separated, in their political institutions, from the residents of the Straits. Sanders refers to HORSCATSIA's 'failure to come to grips with the strength and depth of Islanders' feelings of distinctiveness and separateness from Aboriginal Australians and their dissatisfaction with being placed in combined Aboriginal and Torres Strait Islander representative structures Australia-wide'.[39] As Sanders and Arthur have recently put it, 'once Torres Strait had allowed itself to be drawn into ATSIC, much of the energy of the autonomy movement was then directed at getting out of ATSIC again', and this 'has somewhat displaced the previous aim of gaining greater autonomy from the Commonwealth and Queensland governments'.[40]

Both the regional and the ethnic mobilisations of 'Islanders' were strongly expressed in different critical responses to the HORSCATSIA report and to the Commonwealth's subsequent (1998) proposals. The regional idea was re-asserted in 1999 by an 'Autonomy Task Force' whose proposal for a regional governing structure, eventually with 'territory status', 'returns once again to the idea of placing all Torres Strait Islanders in one combined representative structure separate from ATSIC. This is an idea that simply will not go away ...'.[41] Meanwhile, the 'ethnic' idea of the 'Islander' constituency is being kept alive by the Commonwealth's refusal of HORSCATSIA's recommendation that TSIAB members be elected by Torres Strait Islanders, rather than appointed by the Minister.

ATSIC's recent 'Report on Greater Regional Autonomy' (endorsed by the ATSIC Board in June 2000) discussed regional political development as an option for all Indigenous Australians. The report did not take the Torres Strait Regional Authority as a model for other regions. However, it could not resist drawing some lessons from the Strait. Regional Authorities, the Report asserted, 'were more appropriate in remote and northern regions, and ... following the regional example of the Torres Strait Regional Authority, it was easier to form a regional authority over a discrete geographic region where Indigenous peoples formed a majority'.[42]. As well, the Report noted, but did not explicitly endorse, a suggestion that 'an analysis of the Torres Strait Regional Authority' should be made available 'as a guide to successful options for progressing an authority'.[43] Strangely, the Report did not mention the (ATSIC-funded) CAEPR analyses that I have summarised in this chapter. When the ATSIC Report turned readers' attention to the problem of defining a Regional Authority's constituency, the main point of discussion was how the rights of a region's residents should be related to the rights of a region's traditional land/sea owners.[44] With one exception, the possibility that some 'residents' (most likely a minority) would not be Indigenous Australians passed without notice in the Discussion Paper. The exception was ATSIC's comment on the Northern Territory Department of Local Government's design for a regional authority in Arnhem Land.

With studied neutrality, ATSIC noted 'that the authority would not be comprised entirely of Indigenous peoples' and that non-Indigenous residents would enjoy a certain power within the proposed structure.[45] It made no comment on the advantages and disadvantages of a regionalism whose definition of constituency might depart from ATSIC's politics of identity. Yet Mick Dodson, when Social Justice Commissioner, declared that any regional agreement would involve 'equitable and direct negotiations between Indigenous peoples, governments and *other stakeholders*'.[46] Presumably Dodson would not rule out the *possibility* that the 'other stakeholders' would enjoy the same entitlements as the Indigenous peoples. Sanders and Arthur report that in local understandings of the attachments of non-Indigenous residents to the Strait the definition of 'Indigenous' may be under pressure. '... Torres Strait Islanders tend to acknowledge and respect the presence of long-term non-Islander residents, often saying that they too are now "indigenous".'[47]

The Council for Aboriginal Reconciliation has encouraged all Australians to consider new arrangements for co-existence between Indigenous and non-Indigenous peoples. In this light, CAEPR's commentary on the Torres Strait discussion should be more widely known.

NEW STIMULI OF REGIONALISM

Patrick Sullivan has argued that the arrival of 'native title' has given Indigenous regionalism a new opportunity. He contrasted this with the false or limited opportunity for regionalism presented by ATSIC's model of regional representation. Instead of conceiving the regional polity as an electorate made up of individual voters, he argued, the architects of ATSIC's regionalism should have acknowledged the political standing of the local ensemble of Indigenous organisations. ATSIC in effect diminished the potential of these organisations by making them supplicants of the funds disbursed on the recommendations of the elected Regional Councillors. ATSIC was unlikely to encourage these organisations to come together as the beginnings of an Indigenous regional government, as seemed possible in the Kimberley. It was rather more likely that ATSIC would follow DAA and treat these organisations, singly, as claimants for public money to fund specific tasks of service delivery. Even if ATSIC were to negotiate a regional agreement with these organisations in combination, that agreement would be limited to matters within ATSIC's program responsibility, such as the delivery of certain services and economic development. ATSIC's regional structure provided a narrow and unpromising basis for Indigenous regionalism, he concluded.

However, 'native title' offered new and better possibilities. Land use agreements presented a new agenda of regional governance. In regions where a lot of the land is owned by Aboriginal people — and 'native title' legislation (including the Indigenous Land Fund's acquisitions) will ensure that there are more and more of these — it makes sense to include land management among the array of governmental practices in which Indigenous people are significant players. The need for 'agreements over joint land use at the local and sub-regional levels' is a potent stimulus to 'involving Aboriginal land holders in strategic plans, consultation, negotiations, and finally binding agreements' about land management.[48] Of course, in 'land management' issues all three levels of government will have interests and responsibilities. Sullivan went on to canvass possible models of regional Aboriginal governance, in the Kimberley, with responsibilities for service delivery, economic development and land management.

Against this hopeful projection, Martin has sounded a caution about the scope of regional agreements founded on the new opportunity provided by the *Native Title Act*:

> [I]t is neither desirable nor practicable to negotiate a comprehensive 'regional agreement' ... covering such diverse matters as control of lands and resources, Aboriginal governing structures, service delivery, and so forth, as with certain Canadian models ... [N]ot only would this risk outright government rejection, or at the very least bring so many parties into negotiations that they would become unmanageable, but also it would be virtually impossible to manage from the point of view of the diverse Aboriginal constituencies and interest groups.[49]

Nevertheless, he could see possibilities in the region he knows best. After reviewing the 'administrative and political systems' of Cape York, Martin predicted in 1997 that 'over the next decade a system of regional self-government will evolve' within the Indigenous domain led by the Cape York Land Council and the ATSIC Peninsula Regional Council.[50] As he notes, 'the positions taken by Commonwealth, State and even local governments are of fundamental importance as to whether or not there is a climate conducive to negotiated regional approaches'.[51] He instanced the hostility of the Cook Shire Council and the Queensland Government to the 1996 Cape York Peninsula Heads of Agreement.[52]

In Smith's and Finlayson's view, Indigenous regionalism is a new challenge for all governments — a stimulus brought by Native Title legislation. With Native Title Representative Bodies seeking to negotiate regional agreements, they anticipate that State and Federal Governments will have to 'clarify their own policy approaches to regional agreements, including the formulation of preferred processes for government involvement'.[53] Local political interests are also significant. In her analysis of the political obstacles to Yorta Yorta negotiating a regional agreement over the management of timber and water resources and of heritage sites, Finlayson has portrayed the efforts of a 'rural elite' to discredit the very idea of native title and to dissociate native title from Indigenous 'heritage' rights.[54] Finlayson has elsewhere made the point that 'regionalism' is also an enormous challenge to Indigenous leaders. Her 'initial optimism for regionalism as a perspective from which to approach native title matters has been overtaken to some extent by the virulent and intense disputes about representation constantly surfacing and resurfacing in relation to what constitutes Indigenous traditions of land-based authority and what the Indigenous polity recognises as a legitimate claim'.[55]

New land tenures are not the only stimulus to regional political development. Westbury and Sanders have pointed out that the desire to improve service delivery can also provoke thoughts of regionalism. They advocate 'regional function-specific service agencies to complement and work with local councils ...'. In scale and ability, they would contribute to 'professional and systems expertise' that are not found in 'small multi-purpose organisations'. They give examples: 'Aboriginal Hostels Pty Ltd (delivering hostel care and accommodation), the Arnhem Land Progress Association (community store management and training), the Traditional Credit Union (banking and finance services), Nganampa Health (medical services) and the Centre for Appropriate Technology ...'[56] Wherever such regional agencies form, they are likely to find themselves talking to each of the three levels of government.

14
MODERNISING INDIGENOUS POLITICAL CULTURE

Has the Indigenous Sector developed Indigenous ways of doing political business? It is difficult to generalise about Indigenous political culture.[1] Most obviously, we must consider the possibility that there are regional variations, many of them occasioned by rather different histories of colonial contact. For example, Finlayson has suggested that in contrast with Indigenous people in the longer colonised regions, the people of remote and rural regions 'are often positively disposed toward the welfare state and expect the state to play a beneficent role …'.[2] Such differences in orientation towards government strategies of accommodation — urban scepticism vs rural/remote optimism — are consistent with regional differences in voter turn-out in ATSIC's non-compulsory elections, as Sanders, Taylor and Ross show.[3] Such differences are the opposite of what one might predict if one were to subscribe to the theory that the longer Indigenous Australians are exposed to the colonists' culture, the more they are disposed to embrace it.

Notwithstanding the perils of putting forward generalised models of 'Indigenous political culture', the CAEPR literature makes many observations about cultural dissonance between Indigenous ways and the formal procedures of the Indigenous Sector.

In their paper on the problems of reconciling 'self-determination' with 'accountability', Martin and Finlayson say that they seek to divine the 'cultural logics' of both the government bureaucracies and the Indigenous clients (that is, organisations) funded by governments. As they point out, 'many community organisations have the status of intermediary points between different cultural and political systems, as they attempt to negotiate between differing political positions and cultural imperatives while still maintaining legitimacy in both'.[4]

Their point applies not only to funded Indigenous organisations. ATSIC's own Regional Councils, according to Finlayson, are similarly intermediate. Early in ATSIC's history, the Regional Councils did not have the administrative support to undertake the community-based formulation of a regional plan, as required by ATSIC's Act. When such resources became available, it was important, argued Finlayson and Dale, to prevent them from imposing inappropriate formality on what they call the 'Aboriginal cultural practice of doing business conversationally'.[5] They complained that ATSIC was not living up to its mission to empower local constituencies; Regional Councils lacked 'financial or administrative support to operate with some independence'.[6] As well, they found tensions between the norms of accountable decision-making assumed by ATSIC officers and those assumed by their Indigenous clients. Notwithstanding these difficulties, they concluded that ATSIC's regional planning processes were important not merely as a statutory obligation on Regional Councils, but also as occasions of 'learning by doing'. Regional planning developed the capacities of the clients of those Councils, the Indigenous community organisations, strengthening them in their 'wider debates with the State' and in their consideration of local economic development options.[7]

The phrase 'learning by doing' indicates an appropriately dynamic conception of Indigenous political culture. If there is one generalisation in which we can have confidence it is that Indigenous political culture is subject to transforming pressures. Thus, it would misread the work of Martin and Finlayson to suppose that they are referring to the confrontation between two clearly defined 'political and cultural imperatives': the Indigenous and the non-Indigenous (bureaucratic). Their papers show that, while the demands of bureaucratic accountability may be relatively straightforward, the 'political and cultural imperatives' of Indigenous Australians are an unresolved mixture of dispositions and norms. Take for example Martin's account of the political culture of Cape York Aboriginal people.

In Queensland, local government bodies on Aboriginal land take their structures and powers from the *Community Services (Aborigines) Act 1984* or (in the case of Aurukun) the *Local Government (Aboriginal Lands) Act 1978*. According to Martin 'these Community and Aboriginal Shire Councils are elected through secret ballot by the residents of the area as a group — there is no provision, for example, for representation to be based upon Aboriginal political or land-based groupings or to reflect historical and traditional interests — and operate within complex administrative and financial accountability constraints which frequently place considerable strain upon Aboriginal values and mechanisms'.[8] In the 1990s, these Councils' control over Aboriginal lands became threatened. Under provisions of the *Aboriginal Land Act 1991* and the *Native Title Act 1993* portions of land now under Aboriginal municipal control could be vested in separate land trusts and native title holding corporations. Among the Cape's Aboriginal people, Martin explains, there are competing assessments of this possibility:

> In some Aboriginal townships significant proportions of the residents identify as 'historical' people — that is they are long-term residents whose ancestral lands lie elsewhere — and the assertion by others of rights based on traditional ownership or native title can be very threatening. Furthermore, it can not be assumed that there is a natural community of interests between Aboriginal Councils and native title holders or traditional owners, even though in many cases individual Councillors will also be traditional owners or native title holders of these areas. While the composition, structure, and functions of the Councils are predicated on principles drawn from those of the mainstream representative democracy, not the Aboriginal domain, *it is not sufficient to simply see them as institutions imposed by the state*. As probably the most important points of access to the cash economy (through their operating CDEP schemes for instance), as the focus of competition for material resources such as houses and vehicles, and as the locus of often intense politicking over relative power and status between different individuals and groupings, *they have become deeply embedded within the Aboriginal political domain*. Perceived threats to their spheres of influence — such as the break-up of 'community' lands — may lead Councils and their advisers to oppose, or at best warily assess, claims based on traditional ownership or native title.[9]

In this account, 'the Aboriginal domain' is not characterised by a single set of 'Aboriginal' political norms. Rather, on a matter of fundamental importance — land — there are competing norms which would sanction significantly different and rival codifications of land tenure.

The unresolved condition of Aboriginal political culture is a theme of other CAEPR writings. While recommending that 'welfare' must be open to 'self-determination', Finlayson has cautioned that 'at the local level in many remote communities, self-determination and self-management have no practical reality because Aboriginal people are structurally locked into long-term dependency'.[10] Somehow that induced dependency must be broken, she implies, if self-determination is to be practiced. In similar vein, when discussing the need to ground Indigenous education in Indigenous community perspectives, Schwab remarked that 'where the school is itself a foreign institution, communities certainly require help in understanding and implementing a structured reform effort'.[11] Both Finlayson and Schwab were pointing to the need, as they perceive it, for Indigenous people to develop the capacities to engage in the practices of 'self-determination'. There is a problem of interpretation to be confronted here. When Indigenous people are alienated from the structures of self-determination and do not engage with them, their behaviour may be interpreted either as self-determination (they have deliberately rejected practices of self-governance that they do not like) or as incapacity for self-determination (the practices of self-governance are available, but people require external assistance before they can use them).

Thus we can address in two different ways the problems of the Indigenous Sector's cultural articulation with wider Australian institutions. One approach takes as unproblematic the structures of self-determination that have developed in the last thirty years (the Indigenous Sector, as I have been calling it) and asks: in what ways do features of Indigenous political culture inhibit or facilitate the Indigenous use of these institutions? Thus Martin and Finlayson take as their object of inquiry 'the *capacity of Indigenous people* to realise their goals through various kinds of incorporated bodies'.[12] The second approach asks: what are the limits to reforming Indigenous political culture to ensure that the organisations of the Indigenous Sector can meet government and other expectations? Most of CAEPR's work on the cultural articulation of the Indigenous Sector has posed the first question. However, the second question haunts any answer to the first.

By 'Indigenous political culture' I mean the expectations and norms which Indigenous Australians bring to their participation in and contact with the institutions of Commonwealth, State, Territory and local government and the institutions of the Indigenous Sector. As I have illustrated by citing Martin on Cape York, Indigenous political culture may be a hybrid. On the one hand, Indigenous Australians apply to their political life the notions of mutual accountability and representation typical of a nomadic, hunter-gatherer, kinship-based social order; on the other hand, they draw on political concepts which are fundamental to the liberal-democratic, capitalist social order in which they are now encapsulated. Martin has argued that we should not assume the latter to be an exotic imposition on the former. The mix of these two traditions of value and behaviour probably varies greatly throughout the Indigenous population. While it is true to say that Indigenous Australians had no choice but to come to terms with alien political institutions, there is no doubt that, to various degrees, they have embraced these necessities — particularly under the encouragement of 'self-determination' policy — spurred by their fear of sanctions, by their material aspirations and by their changing understandings of fairness, entitlement and justice.

At times, their embrace of the new institutions and their norms can be seen as tactical moves within intra-Indigenous politics. Mantziaris and Martin have cited a number of recent instances of the Indigenous corporation being a site, a prize and a resource in political struggles among Indigenous Australians.[13] In Finlayson's view, to hold office in an Indigenous organisation is to possess a new form of 'social capital' and 'cultural capital' vis-à-vis older bases of Indigenous authority. Indigenous disputes may sometimes be couched as a contest between competing normative traditions, an issue of 'with which political domain should the principles of representation, accountability and authority be consistent'.[14]

Accordingly, to write of the contemporary 'hybridity' of Indigenous political culture is not to imply that it is a seamless synthesis of political norms from two different traditions. Rather, contemporary Indigenous political culture is better understood as a field of contested understandings of what is fair, right and culturally appropriate in the ordering of political relations among Indigenous Australians and between the Indigenous Sector and the wider political system.

Thus Macdonald's work among Wiradjuri people led her to conclude that 'intra-community Aboriginal politics are often played out as an uneasy tension between the potentially conflicting agendas of recognition and equity ...'.[15] The rhetoric of recognition is favoured by those who base their claims for resources on their identity as the 'traditional' people for the area in which they live. Those whose families migrated to where they now live cannot call upon such arguments from customary law. Instead, 'they have tended to emphasise social equity issues, capitalising on government agendas which continually emphasise the need for better education, housing, health and employment ...'. Their sense of equity is complex; it refers firstly to their position relative to other Indigenous people 'and secondly in relation to non-Indigenous people'.[16] They are advantaged by their use of 'equity' rhetoric, Macdonald suggests, because of its resonance with the notions of social justice more widely accepted in 'mainstream society'.[17] The difficulty for the Wiradjuri, she suggests, is that they must represent their interests in terms of two notions of social justice — that relating to their 'rights as Indigenous owners of country and culture' and that relating to 'citizenship and civil rights in a modern nation state'.[18]

Smith has noted at least one of the limits of 'equity' as a political norm for Indigenous Australians. In negotiations between Indigenous land-owners and other interests, it could be inappropriate to look for equity *among the Indigenous parties*, for 'if there is one thing that is not based on equity in Aboriginal societies, it is knowledge and the knowledge-based right to speak for land. Simply put, some people have the right to speak and others have the right to remain silent. Some do not want to actively participate and are happy to have others "look after" their interests'.[19] This observation takes us back to the defence, by Martin and others, of the pre-eminent position of the 'traditional owner' in Northern Territory land rights legislation. The reader will recall from Chapter 8 that when John Reeves QC proposed to reform the Land Rights Act by demoting the traditional owner to the status of 'resident', he relied partly on an argument about the virtue of 'equity' among residents on Aboriginal land — whether or not some residents were also 'traditional owners' of the land.

From the work of Smith, Finlayson, Macdonald and Martin we can conclude that the structures of Indigenous self-determination are, among other things, an intervention into the contest *among Indigenous Australians* between different political cultures. So too are these authors' writings an intervention. To the extent that their work has been prescriptive, not just descriptive, CAEPR writers have tended to accept the existing institutions of the Indigenous Sector and its public sector environment, and to take as problematic the orientations that Indigenous Australians bring to them.

In their first paper on these problems of political–cultural development, Martin and Finlayson put forward what they consider to be the 'core cultural themes' of Aborigines' approach to politics: 'the tendency of Aboriginal societies and groups towards "fission" and disaggregation rather than aggregation and corporateness', a tendency they call 'localism':

> The Aboriginal domain is typically highly factionalised, and characterised by the complex and often cross-cutting allegiances which people have to groupings based on families, clans, ancestral lands and so forth, as well as to contemporary forms such as Aboriginal organisations. A defining characteristic of this domain lies in its localism, in which the political, economic, and social imperatives lie, pre-eminently in more restricted forms and institutions rather than in broader and more encompassing ones. 'Local' can be either social or geographic or both, and the two are frequently related, for example, through relations based on affiliation to traditional lands. Localism is characterised by such features as a strong emphasis on individual autonomy, and by priority being accorded to values and issues which are grounded in the particular and local, rather than in the general and regional or national.[20]

Two points should be noted about this statement. First, 'localism' arguably subsumes the point, arising from Martin's description of Cape York, about the unresolved hybridity of Indigenous political culture. That is, if there are competing normative traditions through which Indigenous people can make claims on one another's loyalties and assert their differences with rivals and enemies, then the possibilities of 'fission' and 'disaggregation' are doubled. Localism, as Martin and Finlayson present it, has no fixed rhetorical or substantive expression.[21] Trigger's research on the politics of the Century Mine in Queensland illustrates this point well. His observations of intra-Aboriginal debates impressed upon him the *performative* dimensions of localism. That is, the positions that some people took on the mine were, in part, competitive demonstrations, to outsiders, of their standing within their own community, and manifestos, to their fellows, of their loyalty to certain kin. The substantive issues of the mine's development were at times simply the occasion for the playing out of these political dynamics.[22]

The second point to note is that 'aggregation' and 'corporateness' are, generally speaking, what the available institutions of self-determination demand of Indigenous people.[23] Martin and Finlayson are encouraged by the fact that Aboriginal people are heeding this call to 'aggregation':

> Organisations such as Land Councils and ATSIC itself are becoming powerful vehicles through which new forms of Aboriginal collective political and economic enterprises are being forged, at regional and national levels. Arguably, they have provided the institutional base from which both a regionally-based leadership and in informal coalition of Aboriginal leaders has emerged in recent years ...[24]

The forces ranged against the undermining potentials of 'localism' thus include not only non-Indigenous bureaucrats who solicit and encourage what they understand to be accountable and representative Indigenous political formations, but also Indigenous leaders (some of whom may be functionaries of government) who have embraced organised forms of Indigenous mobilisation that are 'unprecedented'.[25]

Martin's and Finlayson's consultancies for the review of the *Aboriginal Councils and Associations Act 1976* persuaded them that 'organisations which had developed broadly representative structures, and had instituted procedures to maximise equity in service delivery, participation in decision-making, and accountability to their constituencies in achieving their objectives had also achieved at least reasonable fiscal accountability'.[26] These organisations had found ways (possibly as statutory requirements or as conditions of funding) to reconcile the 'Aboriginal' with the 'bureaucratic' demands of accountability and representativeness.

Martin and Finlayson discuss three strategies for such reconciling:

- Identify the salient groupings ('major interest groups') within the organisation's clientele or constituency, and recognise them in the structures of election or nomination.

- Develop impersonal structures and procedures, which may or may not be written into constitutions: 'mechanisms to ensure equity in their service delivery and access to the particular resources they provide, measures to maximise the professionalism and accountability of their staff, procedures to ensure transparency in decision-making, and mechanisms by which decisions can be reassessed and conflicts arbitrated';[27]

- Avoid giving the phrase 'culturally appropriate' a prescriptive content that would prevent it from meaning different things in different circumstances.

In particular, they warn against presuming that the smaller the organisation the easier it will be to make it representative and accountable. Martin and Finlayson outline some ways that ATSIC could be a mentor for organisations seeking to reconcile internal and external accountability in these ways.

The importance of ATSIC's leadership in the reformation of Indigenous political culture is also a theme of Smith's and Finlayson's considerations of the problems of Native Title Representative Bodies. As Smith has observed:

> NTRBs are not based upon traditional authority structures, even though they are required to establish their public legitimacy partly in terms of being able to speak for, and on behalf of land-owning groups. First and foremost, they are a new class of legislatively created institutions located at the interface between Indigenous values in relation to land and aspirations, and those of the wider Australian political and economic system.[28]

For Finlayson, the plight of NTRBs in the second half of the 1990s exemplified the slow pace of the changes in Indigenous political culture which she thought essential. Reporting, from her own experience of Indigenous organisations, that the notions 'representation' and 'accountability' were of contested meaning within them, and citing ethnographic literature, Finlayson wrote that 'it is the culture of Indigenous community politics, rather than models of managerialism or technical knowledge, which determine[s] Indigenous organisational action and behaviour', and that 'community organisational accountability is very firmly (even too firmly) tailored to Aboriginal cultural conceptions of kin-based obligations and the necessary flow of goods and services'.[29] If there is to be reconciliation of this kind of accountability with that demanded by governments, she suggested, there must be a 'conceptual and cultural shift' in Indigenous political culture 'from exclusive to inclusive, from local to the regional, from the personal and familial to the wider general community'.[30] Cultural constructs such as 'impersonality' were strongly resisted by the governing committee of one NTRB with which she worked, causing tensions with the organisation's administrative arm, who were well socialised into 'impersonality'.[31] That organisation would benefit, she suggested, if its leaders were committed to following procedures — that is, to practical forms of 'impersonality'. It was also necessary to correct the misconception that a 'representative' body was one in which 'everyone gets everything'.[32] 'An NTRB is not fundamentally a grass-roots community organisation. It is a new creature which must operate according to statutory functions.'[33] In her view, prevailing notions of 'community-control' were overdue for review and reconstruction.

IS PUBLIC POLICY PART OF THE PROBLEM?

Though it is a minor theme in the CAEPR corpus, CAEPR researchers have not ignored the quality of the public sector culture within which 'self-determination' is being defined. Some have made the point, for example, that what Martin and Finlayson call 'localism' is *in part* an effect of the ways in which public policy has shaped the apparatuses of 'self-determination'. Merlan argued that fighting over country 'is produced not simply within the Aboriginal domain; the new conditions of claim as such ... are a major factor generating the general forms and intensity of conflict we now see'.[34] Sullivan also attributed conflict among Aborigines to defects in public policy. After outlining the structure of Rubibi Land Heritage and Development Council, he commented that its approach was:

> flawed ... not in its aspirations but in its lack of an appropriate statutory framework by which its members can live as a land-holding community with their own recognised laws, customs and local system of political authority. Yet, without such a framework, the authority to bind members to agreements with outside interests is lacking, and disputes and dissension can be expected to continue unchecked, confounding the wider community's pursuit of certainty in Aboriginal affairs.[35]

Fergie urged anthropologists to pay more attention to what she called the 'manners' of public institutions in which Indigenous Australians are called upon to represent themselves. She analysed an instance in which 'manners' were problematic: the 1995 Hindmarsh Island Bridge Royal Commission. In that process, the testimony elsewhere of some Aboriginal people (who boycotted the Commission) was critically evaluated against the testimony of rival Aboriginal people who welcomed the Commission. 'Judicial proceedings are an interpretive context in which the cues for assessing the truth of evidence are not simply verbal, embodied in the text of what is said, but embodied in *the way in which it is said* ...'[36] And, 'The enactment of the Hindmarsh Island Royal Commission relied as much on physical stances, verbal tone, emotional force and performative power as it did on reasoned or legal argument'.[37] She argued that this context enhanced the credibility of some Indigenous witnesses and degraded the credibility of others.

Anderson and Brady critically examined the terms in which Aboriginal Community Controlled Health Services (ACCHSs) were being required to account for themselves by ATSIC in the early 1990s. Aboriginal Health Services are complex bodies, and around their public funding there have emerged certain rhetorics defining their core purposes and the procedures for evaluating their effectiveness. Anderson and Brady argued that many of these procedures were inappropriate. Partly because they have community development as well as health-service delivery aspirations, there had been no agreement about the core functions of ACCHSs. They had developed according to the success of their many and various submissions for project funding, and no agreed and stable criteria for evaluating ACCHSs had evolved by 1995. Nonetheless, the introduction of program budgeting and management by objectives throughout the Australian public sector meant that, from the mid-1980s, they were compelled to behave as if their funding were ruled by a rational protocol of reporting and evaluation.[38]

Anderson and Brady gave examples of the bizarre demands for information to which these health services had been subjected by ATSIC. They warned that individual health services were unlikely to be able to measure the rates at which significant events (deaths, episodes of illness, clinical presentations, screenings, cures) occur within their fields of service because their base populations are difficult, if not impossible, to enumerate. In addition, the health of any Aboriginal client population is affected by multiple service providers, making it difficult to isolate the effectiveness of a particular health service. Finally, 'throughput indicators' do not measure quality of service (and to rely on them may even undermine it).

Poorly conceived initiatives in performance measurement are likely, they warned, to give a bad name to efforts to formulate national goals and strategies and thus to the development of defensible ways to evaluate ACCHSs' performance. What data would it be realistic and useful for these organisations to collect? asked Anderson and Brady. Their answer distinguished data relevant to enhancing the operation of a single ACCHS from both the data required for evaluation of the Commonwealth's Indigenous health program, and the data needed for planning the distribution of health care. The Indigenous health services should not be responsible for collecting the latter two kinds of information, argued Anderson and Brady, but they were entitled to be made aware of the results of any Commonwealth and State/Territory analyses of such data.

Having cast doubt on many performance measures, Anderson and Brady were left with the question: were there any objective ways in which Indigenous Health Services could establish their worth? They pointed to narrative accounts of planning and internal evaluation, to evidence of community participation and measures to guarantee community accountability, and to evidence of training and skills development. They mentioned research into the development of quality assurance protocols in the community health sector. It was necessary to undermine the 'hegemony of numbers' associated with the pre-eminence of the Department of Finance in furthering the Commonwealth government's quest for accountability. If some reliance on quantitative measures is inescapable, then let them be 'process indicators' and measures of risk reduction, they suggested.[39]

The 'culture' of public sector management manifests itself to Indigenous Australians not only in such protocols of accountability as those critically discussed by Anderson and Brady, but also in the day-to-day interactions between public sector officials and members of Indigenous communities. Julie Finlayson's ethnography of non-Indigenous officials delivering human services to a remote Queensland community furthers our understanding of the *local* cultural problems of articulating the Indigenous Sector with the wider institutions of governance. Fostering the emergence or elaboration of the Indigenous Sector was not a priority for the people whom she interviewed. 'A common sentiment from staff interviewed across all agencies was how inappropriate they saw self-determination as a community aspiration: many of them argued forcefully that Indigenous residents were incapable of effectively engaging with the present set of agencies and their services, let alone managing them.'[40] She found 'acceptance of the hopelessness of the Aboriginal situation' among such staff and noted their indifference to the many 'recommendations from project and program evaluations over the years'.[41]

EXPERIMENT AND ADVOCACY

Martin says that norms and practices of public sector management are changing the climate in which organisations of the Indigenous Sector must account for themselves. '[T]he hitherto largely unexamined claims that "community control" of service provision will necessarily lead to improved outcomes, whether for Aboriginal communities or mainstream ones, are likely to receive much closer scrutiny against the new criteria being developed within bureaucracies.'[42] Organisations able to prove themselves in this more demanding climate can make strong claims to better resources.

CAEPR writers have been not merely observers, but activists in that process, advocating reform and innovation in Indigenous political culture. They urge Indigenous institutions to try out new technologies of government in order to adhere to new political and organisational norms that are already emerging, so they argue, among Indigenous people. Finlayson, Martin and Smith suggest that already some Indigenous Sector institutions practically exemplify syntheses of different understandings of 'accountability' and 'representation'. The threat that 'localism' makes to the institutions of the Indigenous Sector is to be met by an alliance of: legislators, regulators, ATSIC and researchers such as those cited in this chapter. This alliance, under the banner of self-determination, is made up of both Indigenous and non-Indigenous personnel.

In the 1990s, the foremost theme of their agenda has been regionalism. Here ATSIC has been a most significant policy initiative. ATSIC's contribution to reform in Australian governance was not only that it vested money-spending powers in elected Indigenous Australians, but also that it has sought to do so through a regionalised structure. CAEPR's exploration of the significance of this experiment has generated two conclusions. First, that it is not possible (even if it were desirable) to make inter-regional ('horizontal') equity a principle of public policy towards Indigenous Australians because ATSIC is but one relatively small player among the public sector agencies responsible for service delivery to Indigenous Australians. Unless all other agencies can quantify that service delivery and make that information public, there is no empirical basis for calculating differences of 'desert' among the Indigenous regions. Second, CAEPR's account of Torres Strait political discussions suggests that at some stage in the evolution of Regional Authorities one must ask the question: what are the entitlements of non-Indigenous residents of the respective region? I do not prejudge answers to that question, but neither do I see how the cause of 'regionalism' can advance without it being discussed.

PART 5

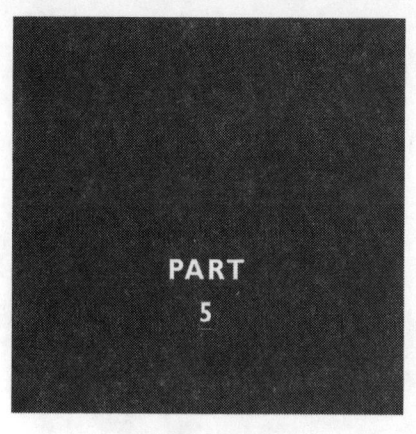

MAKING GOVERNMENTS ACCOUNTABLE

INTRODUCTION

CAEPR's researchers have revealed some of the many ways that the Indigenous Sector now forms part of the apparatus of Australian government. In asking how its institutions fit with the other institutions of Australia, we should avoid presuming that it is Indigenous Australians who must change in order to 'fit' better. CAEPR's considerations of the Indigenous Sector have sometimes implied that the onus to change rests also on the three levels of government: Commonwealth, State and local. How can Australian governments affirm and strengthen the Indigenous Sector?

15
THE INDIGENOUS SECTOR AND RELATIONS WITHIN AND AMONG GOVERNMENTS

In the very first CAEPR Discussion Paper, Altman and Sanders described the proliferation of government programs dedicated to helping Indigenous Australians. In an effort to set national program standards and goals and in order to achieve a measure of co-ordination, the Commonwealth founded the first national Indigenous welfare bureaucracy in 1973 — the Department of Aboriginal Affairs (DAA). DAA (1973–89) was responsible not only for service delivery, but also for policy advocacy. For example, it persistently pushed the Department of Social Security to develop its service-delivery capacities, so that all Indigenous Australians would receive the welfare payments for which they were eligible. DAA also tried to persuade other Commonwealth and State agencies to keep special Indigenous needs in mind.[1] On one interpretation, it is a measure of DAA's success in policy advocacy that 'mainstream' agencies, rather than dedicated 'Indigenous' agencies, are responsible for so many of the Commonwealth government programs from which Indigenous organisations draw their funds. Alternatively, such 'mainstreaming' is thought by some to renew the cultural logic of 'assimilation' policy. For Altman and Sanders 'mainstreaming' — its advantages and disadvantages to Indigenous Australians — is a central issue of 'self-determination' policy.

On the one hand, while there may be many benefits to Indigenous organisations in being able to access the programs of many government agencies, the wide distribution of Indigenous program responsibility detracts from the importance of the main organisational vehicle through which Indigenous Australians have entered the corridors of the Commonwealth government — ATSIC, preceded before 1989 by the DAA. However, ATSIC's political autonomy is limited; the Commonwealth can strip ATSIC of functions, without having to put a bill to Parliament. Such actions may even have the support of Indigenous people not satisfied with ATSIC. One of the more controversial episodes in ATSIC's early history was the rise of an Indigenous critique of ATSIC, leading to ATSIC's loss of responsibility for Indigenous health programs. DAA had held that responsibility exclusively (that is, without sharing responsibility with the Commonwealth Department of Health) since 1984. Inheriting this role, ATSIC sought to delegate some decisions about Indigenous health programs to the Regional Councils. Anderson and Sanders have narrated the development of dissatisfaction on the part of the Aboriginal Community Controlled Health Services (ACCHSs) with the consequences of this empowerment of Regional Councils. Their complaints culminated in a 1994 review which found that ATSIC had not effectively implemented the National Aboriginal Health Strategy. The ACCHSs' lobbying finally resulted in the transfer of Indigenous health programs from ATSIC to the Commonwealth Department of Human Services and Health in July 1995. In other words, some Indigenous leaders saw more value in the medical expertise of a 'mainstream' agency than in the cultural 'expertise' of an Indigenous agency. Discussions of the wisdom of this move have fuelled Indigenous debate about the long-term strategic utility of ATSIC to the project of Indigenous self-determination.[2]

In 1993 Sanders suggested that, from the point of view of funded Indigenous organisations, it may be a blessing that ATSIC was only one of many government departments with which they had to deal. He argued that the autonomy of local and regional Indigenous organisations would be reduced if they obtained their financial support from a single, all-embracing 'Indigenous' agency, such as DAA or ATSIC. As well, ATSIC is less vulnerable to blame for the inevitable failures in social policy towards Indigenous Australians if program responsibility can be sheeted home to other agencies. Third, Sanders argued that Indigenous Australians would be unlikely to get as much financial support were ATSIC the only agency with responsibilities. Fourth, Indigenous Australians are so diverse in aspiration that no single agency could be responsive to all their needs. His conclusion was that ATSIC should be strategically selective in deciding which programs it would like to have responsibility for, and that it should focus on ways to extend the delegation of decisions to Regional Councils and to maximise the autonomy of its client organisations.[3]

As both Arthur and Smith pointed out, it would not necessarily be a sign of ATSIC's strength were its program responsibilities to be wide and heavy. If ATSIC is spending a lot on some programs, it could well be a reflection of the State or Territory government's failure to take responsibility, with ATSIC 'substituting'.[4] The Commonwealth provides some funds to the States and Territories specifically to be spent on Indigenous Australians. While the Commonwealth views such funds as 'supplementary', and while 'the idea is that the funds should eventually become the responsibility of the States ..., the States view these funds as a substitute for their own funding responsibilities'.[5] ATSIC's activity in some circumstances could thus be a measure merely of the failure of its advocacy of other agencies' responsibilities.

STATE/TERRITORY GOVERNMENTS

Under the 1967 referendum modifications of the Australian federal compact, the Commonwealth government gained concurrent powers with the State governments in Indigenous affairs matters. Under the 1978 Northern Territory Self-Government Act, the Commonwealth retained certain powers over Northern Territory matters, notably Aboriginal land rights. Whatever its formal powers vis a vis States and Territories, the Commonwealth generally seeks co-operative rather than coercive relationships with their governments. In the ATSIC Act, the Commonwealth did not oblige State or Territory governments to co-operate with ATSIC. It has been ATSIC's hope that State and Territory agencies would expand their responsibility for delivery of services to Indigenous Australians. That responsibility could take three forms of State/Territory action: by offering programs through a State/Territory 'Indigenous Affairs' Department, by developing 'mainstream' agency programs to Indigenous Australians' benefit, or by subsidising Indigenous organisations' service delivery. Some States and Territories deal with Indigenous Australians through all three of these modes.

ATSIC, though responsible for advising on national policy, has no power to hold State or Territory governments accountable for their efforts. Nor do the Commonwealth's *Land Rights (Northern Territory) Act* and *Native Title Act* oblige State and Territory governments to co-operate with Land Councils and Native Title Representative Bodies. In the 1990s, developments in 'native title' and 'heritage' legislation have tended to reduce the power of the national government to hold State and Territory legislatures to certain standards.[6] Indeed, State and Territory governments have at times been very hostile to Commonwealth land rights and 'native title' initiatives. There are several examples in the CAEPR literature of the State and Territory governments not dealing in good faith with Indigenous land-owners.[7] There is no legislative basis by which any organisation within the Indigenous Sector might hold State or Territory governments accountable for the ways they approach servicing Indigenous people or the ways that they interact with the Indigenous Sector. However, when the Commonwealth funds the Indigenous Sector, it maintains the vitality of an organised constituency that can conduct a dialogue — at times highly critical — with State and Territory governments.

Each State or Territory government has some discretion about whether it encourages an Indigenous Sector. They may or may not choose to deliver services to Indigenous people by subsidising the work of Indigenous organisations. Some State and Territory governments have been wary of nurturing the Indigenous Sector, preferring to assume that their Indigenous citizens are adequately served by changes made to 'mainstream agencies'. Anderson and Sanders have noted the 'competition and even animosity', in the late 1970s, 'between the newly emerging Aboriginal Community controlled Health Services and the Aboriginal health services of the State (and Territory) health departments'.[8]

The States and Territories receive their funds from the Commonwealth in two roughly equal forms: General Revenue and Special Purpose Grants. How they spend General Purpose funds is not regulated by the Commonwealth. Tied or specific purpose payments are subject to Commonwealth conditions, but how effective is Commonwealth scrutiny? Arthur found that, in respect to Western Australia, there were no data which would allow an outsider to test the assumption or claim that Aboriginal and Torres Strait Islander people are satisfied by their access to the services offered by that State.[9] As Anderson and Sanders have reported, when the House of Representatives Standing Committee on Aboriginal Affairs inquired into Aboriginal health in 1979, it concluded that the States had 'simply availed themselves of Commonwealth funds on offer for Aboriginal health' without adequately resourcing the Aboriginal health units in their own Health Departments. State governments have been sceptical of Aboriginal community-controlled health service organisations.[10] Smith examined the Northern Territory's program expenditure, concluding that the Territory government was not, except for a small amount of 'tied' funding, financially accountable to the Commonwealth for its servicing of Aboriginal Territorians. In particular, the NT government was under little obligation to support the Indigenous Sector. 'While the NT Government expends a high total level of monies on services and programs having Aboriginal clients, it does so overwhelmingly through mainstream programs and service deliveries.'[11]

The Commonwealth Grants Commission (CGC) cannot bind States and Territories to spend portions of their (General Purpose) grant on meeting Aboriginal needs. However, as Smith argued, the CGC could demand more information of State and Territory governments about the nature and extent of Indigenous benefit from their programs.[12] ATSIC certainly has an interest in seeing the CGC extract from States and Territories the data needed for any evaluation of their servicing of Indigenous citizens. If ATSIC wished to 'negotiate bilateral funding agreements between the Commonwealth and the States regarding the funding and delivery of services to Aboriginal people' wrote Smith, it would 'need to commence negotiations for such comprehensive State expenditure data ...'.[13] However, it would not be fruitful, Sanders warned, to try to make untied CGC grants *conditional* on measured State/Territory performance, because State/Territory governments' opposition to such a reform would be overwhelming. It would be more effective to ask the federal government to make more 'specific purpose' grants to State/Territory governments. Sanders noted in 1995 that this had been ATSIC's recent strategy.[14] As well, Sanders urged Indigenous Sector leaders to seek from the CGC a formula-based 'General Purpose' grant for Aboriginal organisations.[15]

In short, through a combination of a permissive legal and constitutional framework and a lack of appropriate expenditure data, State and Territory governments have not been formally accountable to any institutions of the Indigenous sector — whether ATSIC or other publicly funded organisations — for equity in their delivery of services to Indigenous people, nor for their performance in resourcing, and negotiating seriously with, the Indigenous Sector.

Smith's studies of the Northern Territory government data were intended to illustrate the possible transparency of State/Territory government program expenditure data to the question of how much was spent on Indigenous Australians. Though she raised doubts about the Northern Territory's high commitment to mainstreaming, she did not argue that States and Territories should 'mainstream' less or more than they were.[16] However, her argument for transparency was relevant to making 'mainstreaming' an issue, for one of the main arguments for subsidising an Indigenous sector has been that Indigenous Australians are not served adequately by 'mainstream' programs. Such arguments are impossible to evaluate empirically if there are no data on Indigenous use of mainstream programs. She called for 'the introduction of [Aboriginal and Torres Strait Islander] identifiers into administrative data bases'.[17]

In CAEPR's body of research, it is only in relation to health policy that researchers have attempted to evaluate the fortunes of the Indigenous Sector (in this case, the Aboriginal Community Controlled Health Services) in winning a seat at the table with Commonwealth and State agencies. According to Anderson and

Sanders, both ATSIC and the Commonwealth Department of Human Services and Health have attempted to persuade State and Territory governments to commit themselves to plans to improve Indigenous health *and to involve both ATSIC and community-controlled health services in their planning.*[18] In another area of policy of interest to CAEPR, education, the political successes of the Indigenous Sector have been few. Schwab's account of the history of recommended changes in Indigenous education policy shows that Indigenous empowerment has been an intermittent concern of policy intellectuals. In 1975, the National Aboriginal Consultative Group recommended 'a national Aboriginal education body' which would advise the government, formulate policy and 'administer all Australian government expenditure related to Indigenous education'.[19] (In Chapter 4 I discussed the inadequacy of merely 'advisory' bodies in the Vocational Education and Training (VET) Sector.)

In 1992, the Council of Australian Governments formulated a National Commitment to Improved Outcomes in the Delivery of Services to Aboriginal Peoples. According to Sanders and Westbury, this has been in some respects an effective 'instrument for defining inter-governmental roles and financial responsibilities':

> In respect to Aboriginal health, Framework Agreements have been signed in all States and Territories between the respective State and Territory governments, State affiliates of the National Aboriginal Community Controlled Health Organisation, ATSIC and the Federal Minister for Health and Family Services. Under the Framework Agreements, regional planning processes have been established for improving access to health services, Aboriginal participation in decision making and priority determination, and the collection of improved data.[20]

They referred also to a 1995 agreement on Aboriginal housing between the Commonwealth, the Northern Territory government and ATSIC. In certain functional areas, they concluded, it has been possible for ATSIC, the States/Territories and the Commonwealth to collaborate. Over the issues of land and local governments, however, there remains an 'adversarial political culture'.[21]

LOCAL GOVERNMENT

The issue of the Indigenous Sector's relationship with local government takes two forms. Many of the institutions of the Indigenous Sector — typically in 'remote Australia' — are community councils with local government-type functions, in areas where there has never previously been a non-Indigenous local government. Other institutions of the Indigenous Sector do their work in shires and town councils which have long been local bastions of non-Indigenous interests. Sanders has considered both situations.

In remote parts of the continent, Aboriginal land and population are not, for the most part, within incorporated local government boundaries, leaving the way open for Indigenous organisations to become local governments, particularly in the Northern Territory, and in the northern parts of South Australia and Queensland. The organisations most likely to evolve into recognised local governments are the elected community councils typical of former missions and government settlements. However, as Davis and Arthur noted in their review of the literature, 'resource agencies' also have this potential.[22] The National Inquiry into Local Government Finance (NILGF) recommended in 1985 that the emergent Indigenous local governments be eligible to receive Commonwealth general purpose local government financial assistance. As a result of the Inquiry, 99 new Indigenous local governments were recognised throughout remote Australia by 1994: 60 in the Northern Territory, 33 in Queensland, five in South Australia and one in Western Australia.[23] Sanders has described the political controversies around these developments, making the point that the formation of Indigenous structures of local government may serve neo-colonial as well as 'self-determination' agendas.[24]

Mowbray has been alive to both possibilities in his studies of the Northern Territory government's effort to extend its system of local government onto Aboriginal land. In the constitutions of NT community governments, the customary political eminence of traditional owners is subverted by treating such owners as if they were individual voters, no more significant than other voters. Thus 'local government' has been part of the Northern Territory government's long struggle against the Land Rights Act's empowering of 'traditional owners' in land use decisions. According to Mowbray, Reeves' proposed Regional Land Councils were consistent in structure and dimensions with the Northern Territory government's desired pattern of municipal government on Aboriginal land.[25] In similar vein, Martin has described some of the ways that the Queensland government has promoted and retarded the powers of Indigenous local government structures on Cape York.[26]

Sanders has pointed to the fragility of the new Indigenous local government entities. Politically, their Indigenous legitimacy was not assured; financially, their revenue bases were slender and insecure, bolstered by CDEP funding, alcohol sales (though some communities refuse this option) and commercial use of their land.[27] Martin devoted a paper to the financial dilemmas of Aboriginal community councils in Cape York. Their alcohol canteens generated revenue, but they also created law and order problems. Estimating the Cape communities' alcohol consumption, he found an association between cycles of violence and of payment. He proposed that the Cape's community councils be funded from consolidated revenue, to break their financial dependence on alcohol sales, so that local authorities had a free hand to tackle the social problems of alcohol abuse.[28]

In those regions where Indigenous Australians find themselves a minority within long-established shires, cities and municipalities their aim is to make sure that the local government recognises and services their distinct needs. This may or may not include asking local governments to recognise local Indigenous Sector institutions, such as housing co-operatives. I am not aware of any research that tells us of the degree or pattern of local government recognition, across Australia, of Indigenous Sector institutions. Rather, research has raised the question of local governments' approach to ensuring equitable access to its services — an issue broached by the 1985 report of the National Inquiry into Local Government Funding (NILGF). Sanders has reviewed attempts, such as that in Western Australia and in a recommendation of the Royal Commission into Aboriginal Deaths in Custody, to ensure that local government bodies spend equitable portions of their federal grants on their Aboriginal populations. The Commonwealth has resisted such accountability measures, thus:

> defending the practice of making untied general purpose grants to local governments in recognition of their status as independent-elected democratic spheres of government. The fact that allocation of these grants was determined through exercises which made reference to Aborigines in the measurement of disability factors in order to achieve some degree of fiscal equalisation between local governments was clearly regarded as of secondary importance to the principle of general purpose funding.[29]

It surprised Sanders that no Indigenous organisations had taken up the National Inquiry's recommendation that Commonwealth funding, consolidating existing 'special purpose' programs, be set aside for Indigenous organisations to give them a stable financial base. He thought this idea was 'highly congruent with emerging ideas about the funding reforms required for Aboriginal self-government ...'.[30]

A number of reports and inquiries of the Commonwealth parliament have considered the options for improving relationships between Aboriginal people and local governments. Sanders' review of them concludes that it is difficult for Commonwealth or State governments to advocate the interests of Indigenous people and their organisations against the local political interests entrenched in shires and municipalities:

> It is in the end local governments and local Indigenous Australians themselves who must find ways of improving these relations. However, relations between these parties have been poor for so long

that self-directed improvement is hard to envisage or initiate. Gentle suggestions or prodding from Commonwealth or State governments can easily fall on deaf ears, while more concerted intervention risks being ineffective through local reaction to superordinate direction. Just how to proceed is a major dilemma for the Commonwealth and State levels of government.[31]

Nonetheless, he is encouraged by the formation of representative Aboriginal advisory committees in some municipalities, and the appointment of Indigenous liaison officers. The Australian Local Government Association has overseen the appointment of policy officers in most of its State affiliates.

Some Indigenous people living within mainstream shires and municipalities have had to confront the issue of the rateability of their land. And local governments have had to rethink their responsibilities to service those living on such land. In NSW the arguments about these mutual obligations have been vexed and protracted, as Sanders has shown.[32] With more purchases from the National Aboriginal Land Fund, Indigenous land-owners and local authorities in other States will also have to come to grips with their relationship. Sanders argued that the trend to regard Aboriginal land as subject to local government rates is unlikely to be reversed, at least in New South Wales. He urged Indigenous land-owners to be pragmatic. If they paid rates, he suggested, they would be better placed politically to make demands on their local governments. They could push for concessions, such as those given to 'charitable' institutions; or they could insist on communal, rather than household, rates.

THE COMMONWEALTH GRANTS COMMISSION'S REPORT (2001)

In November 1999, the Commonwealth Minister for Finance, John Fahey, directed the Commonwealth Grants Commission to inquire into 'the distribution of funding for programs that affect Aboriginal and Torres Strait Islander peoples'. The CGC was asked to develop 'measures of relative disadvantage that can be used to target resources more effectively to areas of greatest need'. Among the conclusions that the CGC reached were that Australian governments should render themselves more accountable for their delivery of services to Indigenous Australians. 'Programmes should be based on the views and aspirations of whole communities and Indigenous people themselves should have a central role in the design, planning and delivery of services.'[33] In the fifth chapter of its report, the CGC (without using the phrase 'Indigenous Sector') endorsed two rationales of that Sector's growth and continuing existence: representation of Indigenous need, and service delivery tailored to the Indigenous clientele:

We see a practical reason why Indigenous people must be involved in deciding how funds should be allocated to meet their needs — the need for judgment. There are two types of judgment that must be made in reaching decisions about resource allocations: (i) technical judgments — required to overcome data deficiencies; and (ii) value judgments — on issues including indicators of need, how they are measured, how the different aspects of need are weighted, how needs are best met, and how equity is to be achieved. Because judgment is an essential element of resource allocation, the allocation decisions must involve: (i) Indigenous people for whose benefit the services are being provided; and (ii) people with experience in delivering services.[34]

'Indigenous people' need not imply 'Indigenous organisations'. The 'Indigenous people' could be public servants, or specially constituted panels of advisers. However, by asserting the centrality of 'judgment', the CGC restates part of the rationale that organisations of the Indigenous Sector have always stated for themselves.

As well, the CGC saw another problem raised by CAEPR in the research summarised in this chapter: intergovernmental relations:

> Given the major role States play in service delivery, the Commonwealth should give priority to promoting the extension of collaborative decision making arrangements by: introducing and enforcing additional conditions for both mainstream and Indigenous-specific SPPs [Specific Purpose Payments], such as data collection, mandating performance reporting, Indigenous-specific performance criteria and greater Indigenous involvement in decision making; and seeking extra conditions that target some of the expenditure of mainstream SPPs to aspects of the services that are important to Indigenous people.[35]

CONCLUSION

The issue of the accountability of Indigenous organisations has been insistently canvassed in recent years, especially by critics of the Indigenous Sector who doubt its competence and honesty. Far less attention has been paid to the problems of making Australian governments — particularly the States and Territories — accountable to Indigenous organisations for the Consolidated Revenue that they receive in respect of their Indigenous populations. CAEPR's research into the latter issue has recently been followed and extended by the Commonwealth Grants Commission. Some of the CGC's recommendations help to renew the mandate of the Indigenous Sector.

CONCLUSION: CAEPR AND THE INDIGENOUS SECTOR

The policy of Indigenous self-determination builds on that which was emancipating in the policy era of assimilation. Assimilation, *at its best*, staged the withdrawal of 'protective' fetters on Indigenous Australians' liberties. Governments repealed legislation that restricted their movement, association, working, spending and civic participation. It was up to each individual and household to show that it merited the freedoms considered normal for Australians. Emancipation, in this sense, was to cost Indigenous Australians their attachment to certain ways of life and thought that unfitted them, so the authorities considered, for inclusion in the Australian way of life. Assimilation affirmed the individual and the family group that dared to 'progress' beyond the ties of kin and community.

Self-determination vindicated the senses of Indigenous social solidarity that assimilationist practices had found difficult to eradicate and to devalue. Governments began to solicit the incorporation of Indigenous groups and to endow Indigenous organisations with the funds to represent Indigenous Australians. The new policy respected the collective agency of Indigenous Australians and it invited them to make choices — as individuals, as family groups and as organisations — about the terms and the pace of their adaptation to the settler–colonial society that encapsulated them.

Three features of this policy transition (which took place in the first half of the 1970s) should be noted.

First, it coincided with a change in the structure of the economy that reduced the demand for rural and uncredentialled jobs. At the same time as Indigenous Australians' choices were significantly enhanced, they became economically superfluous to an unprecedented degree. Remote Indigenous populations, in particular, felt this paradox of new political and legal capacities overlaid on reduced opportunities for waged labour. Indigenous Australians were emancipated into welfare dependency. Some judge this result to be so adverse to real self-determination that they have condemned the 'self-determination' policy era as the most destructive in Australia's colonial history. In this view, 'the progressives' have a lot to answer for. My account of CAEPR's research is written from a more hopeful perspective. I emphasise the rise of new legal and political capacities, manifest in the Indigenous Sector and in land rights legislation, and I question the emphasis that has been placed on paid employment as the way to actualise Indigenous Australians' social participation and material well-being.

Second, I see 'self-determination' as complementing 'assimilation' in some important respects. I am aware of the more usual view that the principles of self-determination amount to a firm rejection of the principles of assimilation. To the extent that this conventional view determines our perception of the two periods of policy we overlook something important: that Indigenous Australians are empowered by capacities that they gained in both policy eras. Considering both policy eras in their best light — as promoting and rewarding Indigenous capacities to act autonomously — we can say that self-determination added to and built upon assimilation.

A third point follows from the second. Self-determination, no less than assimilation, implies Indigenous acculturation. Capacities are not culturally neutral. Self-determination affords new pressures and opportunities for Indigenous Australians to be more like non-Indigenous Australians, in many ways. This does not demand the surrender of Indigenous identity (quite the opposite), but it stimulates changes in Indigenous ways of reckoning their obligations to one another. The Indigenous Sector invites and provokes Indigenous Australians to adopt forms of *impersonal* association.

CAEPR researchers employ frameworks of analysis that have their characteristic patterns of shadow and illumination. In this book, I have attempted not merely to say something of 'self-determination' (that its defining product is the Indigenous Sector) but also to highlight CAEPR's characteristic idioms and frameworks, its means for representing the phenomena of 'self-determination'. The body of social science produced by CAEPR is implicated in two different ways in Indigenous self-determination. The CAEPR corpus is both descriptive and prescriptive.

My reading of CAEPR's work has been, at times, 'against the grain' of its researchers' consciously deliberated perspectives. Ostensibly, much of CAEPR's work — especially that which is devoted to evaluating the AEDP — records the failure of programs of self-determination to promote Indigenous economic development. From the angle at which I view CAEPR, their work is also about the rise of the Indigenous Sector.

I could make this point more critically by saying that CAEPR's tendency to privilege the categories of economics and the issues of economic development policy has dulled its political awareness. There are among CAEPR writings some missed opportunities to postulate the Indigenous Sector as self-determination's outcome. For example, CAEPR researchers have been bothered, at least twice, by some difficulties in applying the distinction between 'public' and 'private'. In each case, the difficulty might have provoked some theoretical creativity; anomalies usefully trigger paradigm shifts. In Chapter 6 I mentioned the issue raised by Altman: are mining royalty equivalents (the statutory payments from Consolidated Revenue to Aboriginal traditional owners in the Northern Territory under the Commonwealth Land Rights Act) public or private moneys? If they are 'public', their disposition is a matter for public policy. If they are private, it is nobody else's business if the recipients quickly expend them on goods that yield no income. Thoughtfully unsure of their answer to this question, CAEPR researchers had the opportunity to theorise royalty associations and land councils as being exemplary institutions of the Indigenous Sector — a sector *sui generis*, neither 'public' nor 'private' but some third thing, a semi-autonomous Indigenous jurisdiction that is emerging unheralded by treaty and untheorised by social science. The novelties and obscurities of this sector are consistent with the unavoidably experimental status of Australia's decolonising of certain lands since the mid-1970s.

Another public/private puzzle arose in the evaluation of the AEDP. As we saw in Chapter 3, among the 'equity' ambitions of the AEDP was to see Indigenous employment distributed across the private and public sectors in similar proportions to non-Indigenous employment. But were Indigenous community organisations, including CDEP schemes, to be classified as private or public sector employers? CAEPR answered this question by adopting a broad notion of 'public'. An alternative solution (or an additional line of investigation) would have started with a critique of the policy evaluation question itself: why presume that the Indigenous Sector fits neatly into either 'public' or 'private' sectors as those terms are usually understood? Might not these terms be a barrier to understanding the evolution of new institutions of governance — the suite of organisations that I call the Indigenous Sector? Social science has an opportunity, even a duty, to theorise such innovations, rather than to struggle to fit them onto the Procrustean bed of received languages of public policy. In both cases, the unresolvable problem of classification (public/private) is symptomatic of the political experiment that is the politics of recognition. When a liberal democratic society seeks to deal more respectfully with the differences between Indigenous Australians and other Australians, both sides are forced to innovate in ways that they may be slow to understand.

CAEPR researchers have made use of a number of intellectual tools in order to recognise cultural difference. For example, CAEPR literature finds in the notions of 'human capital' and 'social capital' ways to think about 'choice' and 'culture' respectively. I showed in Chapter 3 that CAEPR's use of 'human capital' has been intelligently uneasy. Can Indigenous behaviour be modelled as 'investment' in education, training and job-seeking? If so, are we to conceive the investing subject as individual (seeking an improved employment outcome) or as collective (seeking to reproduce certain forms of social life)? What rewards and incentives are we to impute to such Indigenous calculators? Again, as I argued in Chapters 3 and 4, CAEPR's posing of these questions presented opportunities for inferring that 'the Indigenous Sector' has been *both the ground and the emergent effect* of individual and collective trade-offs between economic advancement and continuity in ways of life.

'Social capital' is a relatively new term in the CAEPR corpus. In Chapter 2, I placed it in a line of CAEPR investigation that has tried to evoke the Indigenous social worlds that lie beyond the formal labour market. When Hunter sifted the 'helpful' from the 'unhelpful' elements of Indigenous social capital, he seemed to me to evoke two kinds of ambivalence. On the one hand, he refreshed a lurking CAEPR ambivalence about 'Indigenous culture' — ennobling tradition and/or 'culture of poverty'? On the other hand, Hunter's thoughts on social capital can be read as evoking the ambivalence that many Indigenous Australians must feel about realising their personal and household autonomy through paid employment. His own clarity about what was helpful and unhelpful in Indigenous 'social capital' was contingent on his preferring the 'social participation' afforded by paid employment to that made possible by not being in the labour force. The grounds for *that* preference seem to me to strengthen or weaken according to the gender and morale attributed to the imagined Indigenous person. Is the alternative to paid employment the anomie of Noel Pearson's deracinated men or the nurturant home-centredness of Julie Finlayson's women?

My question is intended to illustrate the ways that our apprehensions for, or admiration of, the ways of life of Indigenous Australians are conditioned by the circulation, in public debate, of vignettes of pathology or of wholesomeness. The rhetorical power of Noel Pearson's speeches owes much to his public status as an unimpeachable witness to scenes of pathology among his own people. (This is not to say that he has no cause for alarm.) Similarly, the rhetorical power of ethnographic generalisation in the CAEPR literature is that, unlike the Census 'snapshot', ethnography can attest process and agency. Ethnography has been vital to CAEPR's ability to ask whether the categories of the labour market were adequate to an assessment of Indigenous well-being. What was their experience of being 'employed', 'unemployed' or 'not in the labour force'? Should we not include answers to that question in any evaluation of the AEDP? Were Indigenous choices intelligible without answers to that question? CAEPR's studies of particular CDEP schemes have made it impossible — without conspicuous closure of the official mind — to see them simply as 'labour market programs'.

If ethnographic investigation (or sometimes merely ethnographic questions) have helped to illuminate the individual and the organised collective agency of Indigenous Australians, the same can not be said of CAEPR's efforts to construct an Indigenous agent that is neither an individual nor an organisation: the household/family. In CAEPR's consideration of Indigenous domestic processes the analyses based on the Census were under continuing reproach for their insensitivity to flows of goods, money and people between hearths and dwellings. As I noted in Chapter 9, while researchers could present very persuasively the tension between static boundedness (Census categories) and lived experience of flow (ethnographic evocations of demand sharing), that tension was not resolved in a conceptual synthesis. Instead we saw a research program that both picked away at its own empirical and conceptual foundations while confidently postulating categories (for example, the 'single parent family') as if no such picking was taking place. Not only that, but when all the evocations of demand sharing were assembled within the space of a few pages (in Chapter 10), it became clear that interpretive choice (predation or reciprocity? equilibrium or anarchy?) enjoyed a high degree of autonomy from evidentiary base.

This problem of arbitrariness in some applications of ethnographic knowledge in the CAEPR research program owed much to the ambition to produce a policy relevant cultural model. As I have noted, the 'self' of self-determination is postulated by governments and researchers as emerging at the individual, domestic and organisational levels. CAEPR sought to substantiate the 'domestic' self by developing a model of Indigenous domestic life. True, it is the possibility of constructing such models that lifts ethnography above the level of merely telling a story about particular people in a particular place at a particular moment. However, in the CAEPR context, ethnography has sometimes been asked to bear a much greater burden. Public policy, in the era of self-determination, invites a discourse on difference in which the categories of difference are the gross categories — non-Indigenous, Aboriginal (subdivided sometimes as urban and remote) and Torres Strait Islander — of identity politics and demography. So CAEPR went looking for, but could not find, a model of the 'Aboriginal' family/household.

The categories in which Indigenous identity politics have been mobilised give effective form and language to national institutions of the Indigenous Sector, but they are far too clumsy to serve all the needs of a social science of cultural difference. The language of political recognition has to be interrogated by researchers, rather than adopted as the organising terms of a research program. 'Aboriginal' and 'Torres Strait Islander' are better understood as demographic than as 'cultural' terms. 'Aboriginal people' is a category based on an affirmation of identity in a particular context (the Census) in which the affirmers are (quite properly) subject to no scrutiny as to their 'cultural' characteristics. Observations of people who live in Aurukun or Maningrida should not serve as cameos of what 'Aboriginal people' do in Inala, Kuranda or Leeton. The commonality among these 'Aboriginal people' is a real one — affirmed identity — but that is only one item in their repertoires of behaviours and belief.

Are such demographic and Census categories as 'Aboriginal' and 'Torres Strait Islander' of any use to policy relevant social science? The Indigenous population (or the 'Aboriginal population' or the 'Torres Strait Islander population') is an artefact of one specific interaction between government and household: the state's attribution of responsibility to 'household head', in the administration of the Census, to nominate householders' identity. That artefact is of great importance in *one* version of the politics of recognition. That is, social analysis requires the enumeration of the Indigenous population in order to have a denominator in the calculation of Indigenous rates of this or that. Only when this artefact became available in a credible way (since the Censuses of the 1970s) have statistical Indigenous/non-Indigenous comparisons of well-being been possible. This has resulted in the most influential version of the politics of recognition: the politics of (what the AEDP called) 'equity'. The imperative of this version of the politics of difference is that the differences (in employment rates, mortality and morbidity, educational attainment) should be overcome by greater governmental effort.

However, the categories of a politics of 'equity' are not suited to *all* policy relevant mobilisations of cultural difference. Sometimes the politics of recognition is at odds with a politics of 'equity' because to be 'different' is more a chosen destiny than a misfortune. At what level are such choices being made? To answer this question requires social analysis using categories much finer than those that serve a national politics of identity, that serve demographic analysis and that serve the kind of AEDP evaluation summarised in Chapter 1. A social analysis attentive to the kinds of cultural 'difference' that people choose to defend must be more fine-grained; it must highlight distinctions of locality, class and gender. It must attend to differences *within* the Indigenous population, and/or it must ask about how Indigenous and non-Indigenous people differ in particular circumstances of their co-existence.[1]

In my reading — incomplete and deliberately interpretive — of CAEPR's work, I have made a plea for understanding 'self-determination' as an addition of new collective Indigenous capacities to the individual capacities favoured by the reforms of 'assimilation'. I began the book by asserting that the state now seeks to realise Indigenous agency at three levels, or three modes: individual, domestic and organisational. CAEPR has contributed — sometimes inadvertently and obscurely — to our understanding of each of these modes. The terms in which Indigenous domestic agency is to be conceived are elusive. Social policy has difficulty imagining and bringing into being a generalised model of domestic process. The only way in which the domestic Indigenous agent is substantiated in the work of government is in the administration of the Census — a crucial realisation of Indigenous agency, nonetheless, providing the knowledge base (the Indigenous denominator) for a politics of 'equity'.

However, as I pointed out in my Introduction, many Indigenous Australians aspire to go beyond a politics of equity. They see 'equity' as a limited and ambiguous form of the politics of recognition because of its strong implication that 'difference' is a 'deficit' to be remedied, rather than a 'choice' to be respected. If 'choice' is not to be terminally buried beneath 'deficit' in current policy debates about what Indigenous Australians are entitled to, there must be a persistent and organised articulation of the Indigenous right to choose. Such choices will be made individually and collectively. The Indigenous Sector is an ensemble of types of organisations, each born out of a specific governmental necessity: the localised labour market intervention, the title-holding body, the representative structure, royalty accountancy, educational and medical service delivery. I wish to promote the Indigenous Sector to the attention of those who describe Australia's institutions of government, including to policy-makers Indigenous and non-Indigenous. They and we must ask (as CAEPR has done): what are the distinctive conditions of existence, tasks and problems of each of these types of organisation? Across these varieties of organisation there are cultural continuities. However, these are not the commonality of 'Indigenous political culture' (a term that would plunge us back in our demographic identity category), but the commonality of their subjection to the rationalising cultural imperative that is integral to 'self-determination' policy.

NOTES

INTRODUCTION
FROM ASSIMILATION TO SELF-DETERMINATION
1   I have provided a political narrative of these years in the early chapters of Rowse (2000a).
2   Attwood and Markus (1997) and Taffe (2001: Chapter 3)
3   See Senate Standing Committee on Legal and Constitutional Affairs (1983).
4   I am grateful to Judith Brett for pointing out to me the multiple senses of 'disadvantage' in Australian policy discourse.
5   Manne (2001)
6   Sewell (1993: 33)
7   Miller (1985)
8   Commonwealth of Australia (1987)
9   Taylor (1991a: 27)
10 Altman and Smith (1992: 20, emphasis added)
11 Daly (1991b: 13)
12 Daly (1991a: 16)
13 Daly (1991a: 16)
14 Taylor (1992: 14, emphasis added)
15 Neutze, Sanders and Jones (2000: 16)
16 Musharbash (2001: 17, 25)
17 Henry and Daly (2001: 11, emphasis added)
18 Smith (1991a: 31, emphasis added)
19 Schwab (1996d: 87–88)
20 Rowse (2001a)
21 Sutton (2001)
22 Sandall (2001: 17)
23 Sutton (2001: 146)
24 Yeatman (2001)
25 Sutton (2001: 151–52, emphasis added)
26 Taylor (1989: 159)
27 Yeatman (2000: 1508)

PART I
INTERPRETING THE ABORIGINAL EMPLOYMENT DEVELOPMENT POLICY

INTRODUCTION
1   Miller (1985: 39)
2   Miller (1985: 5, my emphasis)
3   Miller (1985: 6)
4   Miller (1985: 9, my emphasis)
5   Commonwealth of Australia (1987: iii)
6   Commonwealth of Australia (1987: iii, my emphasis)
7   Altman and Sanders (1991b: 7–8)
8   Commonwealth of Australia (1987: 3–4)
9   Commonwealth of Australia (1987: 5)

1   SOME OUTCOMES OF THE ABORIGINAL EMPLOYMENT DEVELOPMENT POLICY
10 Taylor (1993a: 1993b)
11 Taylor (1993a: 46)
12 Taylor (1993a: 43)
13 Taylor (1993b: 62)
14 Taylor (1993b: 65)
15 Taylor (1993b: 65–66)
16 Taylor (1993b: 66)
17 Taylor (1993b: 66)
18 Taylor (1993b: 67)
19 Taylor and Altman (1997)
20 Taylor (1997: 1)
21 Taylor (1997: 13)
22 Hunter (1998: 15)
23 Taylor (1998a, 1998b, 1998c, 1998d, 1998e, 1999), Taylor and Roach (1998)
24 Taylor and Hunter (1998)
25 Taylor and Hunter (1998: Tables 4, 5, pp. 14–16)
26 Taylor and Hunter (1998: 5)

2   INDIGENOUS CULTURE AND INDIGENOUS CHOICE
1   Smith (1991c: 21)
2   Smith (1994a: 5)
3   Smith (1994a: 7)
4   Smith (1994a: 7)
5   Smith (1994a: 12).
6   Smith (1994a: 11, my emphasis)
7   Smith (1994a: 13, emphasis added)
8   Altman and Allen (1991, 1992), Altman, Bek and Roach (1995)
9   Arthur (1991a: 13–14, 1991b)
10 Martin (1995: abstract,7)
11 Martin (1995: 6)
12 Martin (1995: 17)
13 Schwab (1995b: 12–13)
14 Schwab (1995b: 15–16)
15 Smith and Roach (1996: 73)
16 Daly (1991b)
17 Hunter and Daly (1998: 14)
18 Hunter and Daly (1998: 17, emphasis added)

19 Altman and Sanders (1991a: 14)
20 Altman and Smith (1992: 1)
21 Fraser and Gordon (1994)
22 Altman and Smith (1992: 18)
23 Altman and Smith (1992: 19)
24 Smith (2000c: 94)
25 Daly and Hawke (1993: 16)
26 Daly (1991c: 13)
27 Daly (1991a: 16)
28 Daly (1991c: 13)
29 Daly (1991a: 16)
30 Altman and Hunter (1997: Table 3), Ross and Mikalauskas (1996: 15, Table 5)
31 Altman and Hunter (1997: 8), Hunter (2001: 129–30)
32 Altman and Hunter (1997: 8–12)
33 Hunter (1996a: 12)
34 Hunter (1996a: 13)
35 Hunter and Borland (1997: 1)
36 Hunter and Borland (1997: 9)
37 Hunter and Borland (1997: 17)
38 Hunter (2001: 151)
39 Hunter (2001: 155)
40 Hunter (2001: 155)
41 Hunter and Hawke (2000: ix)
42 Hunter (2000: 2, 4)
43 Hunter (2000: 6)
44 Hunter (2000: 7)
45 Hunter (2000: Appendix A)
46 Hunter (2000: 36–37)
47 Hunter (2000: 37)
48 Schwab (1995b), Martin (1995), Smith (1992c: 75, 1994)
49 Hunter (2000: 37)
50 Altman and Sanders (1991b: 9–10)
51 Altman and Sanders (1991b: 10)
52 ATSIC (1994: 62, emphasis added)

3 THE PROBLEM OF MOTIVATION IN EDUCATION, TRAINING AND EMPLOYMENT

1 Daly (1992: 9–10)
2 Daly and Liu (1995: 14–15)
3 Hunter (1996b)
4 Taylor and Hunter (1996: 6)
5 Taylor and Hunter (1996: 13)
6 Taylor and Hunter (1996: 16)
7 Taylor and Hunter (1996: 1)
8 Gray, Hunter and Schwab (1998: 15–16)
9 Gray, Hunter and Schwab (1998: vi)
10 Schwab (1995a: 24)
11 Schwab (1995a: 20)
12 Schwab (1996a: 16)
13 Schwab (1995a: 22–23)
14 Schwab (1995a: 24)
15 Schwab (1995a: 24)
16 Chapman (1991: 133)
17 Chapman (1991: 133)
18 Chapman (1991: 138)

19 Daly (1991b: 14), Tesfaghiorghis (1991b: 3), Daly, Allen, Aufflick, Bosworth and Caruso (1993), Daly (1993: 36), Daly (1994: 13–14)
20 Daly (1993: 36)
21 Taylor (1991b: 19)
22 Taylor (1992: 11)
23 Taylor (1992: 13)
24 Taylor (1992: 14)
25 Taylor (1992: 14)
26 Altman and Taylor (1994: 1)
27 Altman and Taylor (1994: 2, 4)
28 Altman and Taylor (1994: 11)
29 Taylor (1995: 3)
30 Taylor (1995: Table 4)
31 Taylor (1995: 21–22)
32 Taylor and Liu (1995: 1996)
33 Taylor and Liu (1995: 21)
34 Taylor and Liu (1995: 22–23)
35 Taylor and Liu (1996: 21)
36 Taylor (1992: 14)
37 Daly (1992: 14)
38 Schwab (1997a: 8)
39 Schwab (1996c: 11)
40 Schwab (1997a: 8)
41 Schwab (1996c: 15, 18)
42 See for example his recommendations 3 and 5 in Schwab (1999: xi).
43 Schwab (1997a: 9)
44 Schwab (1997a: 1)
45 Schwab (1998: 11)
46 Schwab (1998: 7)
47 Schwab (1998: 10)
48 Schwab (1998: 15)
49 Schwab (1998: 17)
50 Schwab (1996a: 4)
51 Arthur and David-Petero (2000b: vii)
52 Schwab (1996a: 4)
53 Schwab (1997b: 1)
54 Schwab (1997b: 6)
55 Schwab (1997b: 17)
56 Campbell (2000: 3)
57 Arthur and David-Petero (2000b: 10–12)
58 Schwab (1996a: 4–5)

4 INDIGENOUS INSTITUTIONS AND THE LABOUR MARKET
1 Morony (1991: 105)
2 Altman and Sanders (1991b: 12)
3 Arthur (1991a: 10)
4 Arthur (1991a: 15)
5 Altman and Sanders (1991c: 4)
6 Smith (1991c: 24–25)
7 Altman and Smith (1992: 20), Altman (1991a: 3)
8 Altman and Smith (1993: 4)
9 Altman and Hawke (1993: 12)
10 Altman and Hawke (1993: 12–13)
11 Altman and Smith (1993: 7)
12 Altman (1997b: 2)
13 See in particular Altman and Sanders (1991c).

14 Sanders (1993c: 4–5)
15 Sanders (1993c: 10)
16 Sanders (1993c: 14)
17 Madden (2000: 1, 6)
18 Hunter and Borland (1997: 9)
19 ABS (1996: 4)
20 For example, Taylor (1998e: Table 9)
21 Taylor (1998e: 14)
22 Smith (1994b: 3)
23 Altman and Hunter (1996a: 12)
24 Arthur (1999a: 16)
25 Altman and Hunter (1996a: 10–11)
26 Altman and Hunter (1996b: 18)
27 Altman and Gray (2000: 19)
28 Altman (1997b: 13)
29 Altman and Smith (1993: 12)
30 Smith (1994b, 1995a, 1996a)
31 Smith (1996a: 16)
32 Smith (1994b: 24)
33 Smith (1994b: 19, 1995a: 7, emphasis in original)
34 Smith (1995a: 7)
35 Gray and Thacker (2000: 3)
36 Arthur and David-Petero (2000a: 20–21)
37 Arthur and David-Petero (2000a: 24–25)
38 Arthur and David-Petero (2000b: 20)
39 For an extended presentation of this argument, see Rowse (2001a).
40 Office of Evaluation and Audit (ATSIC) (1997: 17)
41 Arthur (1999: 16), Altman and Johnson (2000: 30)
42 Smith (1994b: 14)
43 Gray and Thacker (2000: 11, 18)
44 Altman and Johnson (2000: 15)
45 Gray and Thacker (2000: 7)
46 Madden (2000: 7)
47 Altman and Johnson (2000: 27)
48 Altman and Johnson (2000: 18)
49 Taylor, Bern and Senior (2000: 42)
50 Altman and Johnson (2000: 28)
51 Boughton (1998)
52 Schwab and Anderson (1999)
53 Schwab and Anderson (1998: vii)
54 Schwab (1996a: 10)
55 Campbell (2000: 7)
56 Campbell (2000: 8–9)
57 Campbell (2000: 21)
58 Campbell (2000: 9)
59 Campbell (2000: 31)
60 Campbell (2000: 37)

PART 2
LAND, SEA AND ECONOMIC DEVELOPMENT

INTRODUCTION
1 Pollack (2001: ix)
2 Miller (1985: 317, 318)
3 Miller (1985: 321)

4   Miller (1985: 324)
5   Altman and Allen (1991: 2–4), Altman, Bek and Roach (1995: 2–7)
6   Altman, Bek and Roach (1995: 17)
7   Trigger (1997: 114)
8   Trigger (1997: 115–16)
9   Smith (1998: 22)
10 Finlayson (1999b: 13)
11 Levitus (1999: 128)
12 Altman and Allen (1991: 2)
13 Altman (1991d: 165)
14 For a discussion of the embeddedness of the 'economic' in traditional Aboriginal society and of the 'economic' as a feature of capitalist social relations, see Godelier (1972).

5 HUNTING, GATHERING AND TOURISM

15 Altman and Smith (1992: 18)
16 Taylor (1991a: 28)
17 Altman and Allen (1991: 4)
18 Altman and Allen (1991: 9)
19 Altman and Allen (1992: 140, 138)
20 Altman, Bek and Roach (1995: 12–13)
21 Altman, Bek and Roach (1995: 18)
22 Altman, Roach and Liddle (1997: 4)
23 Altman, Roach and Liddle (1997: 6)
24 Arthur (1991a: 15)
25 Altman, Arthur and Bek (1994: Table 5)
26 Davis (1995: 25)
27 Altman (1993: 1–4)
28 Altman and Finlayson (1992: 8, my emphasis)
29 Altman and Finlayson (1992: 8–9, 12)
30 Altman and Finlayson (1992: 15)
31 Altman and Finlayson (1992: 18)
32 Altman (1993: 7)
33 Altman (1993: 10)
34 Finlayson (1995a: 13, 14)
35 Finlayson (1995a: 16)
36 Altman (1995b: 15 5)
37 Altman (1995b: 14, my emphasis)
38 Altman (1995b: 22)
39 Altman (1995b: 18)

6 MINING INCOMES

1   O'Faircheallaigh (1995b: 1)
2   Altman and Pollack (1998a: 7)
3   O'Faircheallaigh (1995a: 19)
4   O'Faircheallaigh (1995a: 19)
5   Trigger (1997)
6   O'Faircheallaigh (1995b: 6)
7   O'Faircheallaigh (1995b)
8   Quiggin (1999: 137)
9   Altman (1996c: 6–7)
10 Altman (1996c: 9)
11 Altman (1994a: 9, 1996c: 9)
12 Altman (1994a: 10)
13 Altman (1994a: 10)
14 Altman (1994a: 14)

15 Altman (1994a: 10, 1994b: 67–68)
16 Quiggin (1999: 137)
17 Altman and Pollack (1998a: 7)
18 Altman and Smith (1994: 8)
19 Altman and Smith (1994: 9–11)
20 Altman and Smith (1994: 19)
21 Altman and Smith (1994: 20)
22 Altman and Smith (1994: 22)
23 Altman (1997a: 180)
24 Altman (1997a: 183)
25 Altman (1997a: 176)
26 Altman and Smith (1999: 10)
27 Altman and Smith (1999: 15–16)
28 Altman and Smith (1999: 17)
29 Altman (1996c: 10)
30 Levitus (1999: 124)
31 Levitus (1999: 125)
32 Altman and Levitus (1999)
33 Altman and Pollack (1998b: 45)
34 Altman and Pollack (1998b: 45)
35 Altman and Pollack (1998a: 8)
36 Altman and Levitus (1999: 18)

7 NATIVE TITLE
1 Mantziaris and Martin (2000: 44)
2 Wootten (1995: 107)
3 Wootten (1995: 112)
4 Mantziaris and Martin (2000: 87)
5 Smith (1996b: 11)
6 Altman (1996b: 2)
7 Whether that is his personal view or an analytic device is not clear, see Altman (1995a: 1–2).
8 Altman (1995a: 2)
9 Altman (1994a: 15–16)
10 McKenna (1995)
11 Altman (1995a)
12 Altman (1996a: 9)
13 Altman (1994a: 15–16)
14 Altman (1996b: 12)
15 Altman (1995a: 10)
16 Altman (1996b: 10)
17 Altman (1996a: 5)
18 Altman (1996a: 9)
19 Altman (1996b: 10–12)
20 Sullivan (1995: 11)
21 Smith (1996b: 20), and see Clarke (1997) for a more detailed exposition and critique of the proposed amendments.
22 Smith (1996b: 22)
23 Clarke (1997: 34)
24 Smith (1998: 17)
25 Altman and Pollack (1998a: 11–12)
26 Smith (1998: 21)
27 Smith (1998: 21)
28 Mantziaris and Martin (2000)
29 Altman and Pollack (1998c: 9)
30 Altman and Pollack (1998c: 19–20)

31 Altman and Pollack (1998c: 18)
32 Altman and Pollack (1998c: 18)

8 REPRESENTING THE LAND-OWNER INTEREST

1 Finlayson (1999: 3)
2 Quoted in Finlayson (1999: 11)
3 See Nettheim (1999)
4 Stead (1995: 77)
5 Stead (1995: 77)
6 Stead (1997: 173)
7 Morton (1997: 89)
8 Morton (1997: 89–90)
9 Reeves (1998: xix–xxi)
10 Galligan (1999: 20)
11 Peterson (1999: 28)
12 Sutton (1999: 41–45)
13 Sutton (1999: 41)
14 Martin (1999: 160, emphasis in original)
15 Martin (1999: 160)
16 Pollack (1999)
17 Altman (1999: 113)
18 Levitus, Martin and Pollack (1999)
19 Levitus, Martin and Pollack (1999: 11)
20 Smith (1995b: 59)
21 Smith (1995b: 64)
22 Smith (1995b: 70)
23 Martin (1997b: 11–12)
24 Trigger (1997: 126)
25 Munster (1997: 192)
26 Altman (1996b: 6)
27 Altman (1996b: 11)
28 Munster (1997: 193–99)
29 Munster (1997: 199)
30 Lewington, Roberts and Brownley (1997: 207)
31 Sullivan (1997: 136)
32 Sullivan (1997: 136–38)
33 Lewington, Roberts and Brownley (1997: 207)
34 Altman (1996b: 8)
35 Finlayson (1997a: 2)
36 Finlayson (1997a: 7)
37 Finlayson (1997a: 10)
38 Finlayson (1997a: 14)
39 Smith (1998: 18)
40 Smith (1998: 20)
41 Smith (1998: 19–20)
42 Finlayson (1998: 7)
43 Finlayson (1998: 12–13)

PART 3
DOMESTIC CHOICES: CHILDREN, GENDER AND IDENTITY

INTRODUCTION

1 Rose (1987) gives an account of Aboriginal society as nomadic 'households'.
2 Henry and Daly (2001: 5)
3 Finlayson and Auld (1999: 19)

9 FAMILIES AND WELFARE

4 Smith (2000b: 8)
5 Smith (1991a, 1991b)
6 Smith (1991a, 19991b)
7 Gray and Tesfaghiorghis (1991: 3, 34)
8 Jones (1994: 2–3)
9 Gray and Tesfaghiorghis (1991: 1–2)
10 Altman and Smith (1992: 8, 16)
11 Smith (1991b: 24)
12 Altman and Smith (1992: 16, 18)
13 Smith (1991b: 5–6)
14 Smith (1991b: 6)
15 Smith (1991b: 8)
16 Smith (1991b: 10)
17 Smith (1991b: 10)
18 Taylor (1988)
19 Smith (1991b: 11–12)
20 Martin and Taylor (1995: 14)
21 Martin and Taylor (1995: 17)
22 Daly and Smith (1995: 3)
23 Daly and Smith (1995: 3)
24 Smith (1991b: 10), Smith and Daly (1996: 2)
25 Daly and Smith (1995: 10)
26 See Henry and Daly (2001: 10) for acknowledgment of this point.
27 Daly and Smith (1995: 10)
28 Daly and Smith (1995: 20)
29 Finlayson (1995b: 11)
30 Smith and Daly (1996: 6)
31 Smith and Daly (1996: 9)
32 Smith and Daly (1996: 6)
33 Smith and Daly (1996: 14)
34 Smith (1991b: 24, emphasis added)
35 Smith (1992c: 75, emphasis added)
36 Daly and Smith (1997: Table 4)
37 Daly and Smith (1997: 13)
38 Daly and Smith (1997: 14)
39 Daly and Smith (1997: 11)
40 Daly and Smith (1997)
41 Daly and Smith (1997: 23)
42 Daly and Smith (1997: 24)
43 Taylor and Westbury (2000: 22)
44 Daly and Smith (1998: 7)
45 Daly and Smith (1998: 7)
46 Daly and Smith (1999: 2, my emphasis)
47 Daly and Smith (1999: 3)
48 Daly and Smith (1999: 3)
49 Daly and Smith (1999: 13)
50 Daly and Smith (1999: Table 6)
51 Daly and Smith (1999: 13–14, my emphasis)
52 Smith (1992c: 75)
53 Smith (2000b: 1–2)
54 Smith (2000b: 8)
55 Daly and Smith (2000: 11)
56 Daly and Smith (2000: 21)
57 Daly and Smith (2000: 13, 21)
58 Henry and Daly (2001: 5)

59 Daly and Smith (2000: 13)
60 Daly and Smith (2000: 13)
61 Finlayson, Daly and Smith (2000: 26)
62 Finlayson, Daly and Smith (2000: 43)
63 Finlayson, Daly and Smith (2000: 28)
64 Musharbash (2000: 58)
65 Musharbash (2000: 62)
66 Musharbash (2000: 57–58)
67 Musharbash (2000: 60)
68 Musharbash (2001: 10–17)
69 Finlayson, Daly and Smith (2000: 35)
70 Musharbash (2000: 66)
71 Finlayson, Daly and Smith (2000: 35)
72 Musharbash (2000: 67)
73 Finlayson, Daly and Smith (2000: 43)
74 Finlayson, Daly and Smith (2000: 44)
75 Finlayson, Daly and Smith (2000: 46)
76 Finlayson, Daly and Smith (2000: 46)
77 Finlayson, Daly and Smith (2000: 50)
78 Smith (2000c: 87, 89)
79 Smith (2000c: 90)
80 Smith (2000c: 90)
81 Henry and Daly (2001: 11)
82 Indeed, at the July 2001 Social Policy Research Centre's Conference, Centrelink's Pat Turner outlined additional steps recently taken to ensure that remote Indigenous Australians understood their entitlement and received their due.
83 Finlayson and Auld (1999: 16)
84 Finlayson and Auld (1999: 16)
85 Henry and Daly (2001: 18, 6)
86 See Peterson (1993)
87 Finlayson and Auld (1999: 19)
88 For details see Henry and Daly (2001: 12–13, 16, 18–21), Musharbash (2001: 22–26).
89 Musharbash (2001: 25)
90 Henry and Daly (2001: 20)

10 GENDER REFORMING

1 Peel (2000: 138)
2 Peel (2000: 139–40)
3 Lawrence and Gray (2000: 43)
4 Pearson (2000: 17, my emphasis)
5 Finlayson (1989: 95)
6 Finlayson (1989: 100)
7 Finlayson (1989: 105)
8 Finlayson (1989: 111)
9 Finlayson (1989: 112, endnote 17)
10 Finlayson (1989: 115–16)
11 Daly and Hawke (1993)
12 Daly and Hawke (1994: Table 1)
13 Daly and Hawke (1993 : Table 3), Daly and Hawke (1994: Table 4)
14 Taylor (1993b: Table 5.3, 1998a: Table 12, 1998b: Table 13, 1998c: Table 12, 1998d: Table 12, 1998e: Table 12, 1999: Table 8)
15 Gregory (1991: 150–51)
16 Tesfaghiorghis and Altman (1991 : Table 6)

17 Taylor (1993b: Table 3.11)
18 Taylor (1993a: Tables 3.2a, 3.7)
19 Taylor (1993a: Table A4a, A4b)
20 Taylor (1993a: Tables A7a, A7b)
21 Daly (1996: 100, Table 9.3)
22 Daly (1996: 102, Table 9.5)
23 Daly (1996: 101, Table 9.4, 103, Table 9.6)
24 Taylor and Roach (1998: Table 7), Taylor (1998a: Table 6, 1998b: Table 5, 1998c: Table 6, 1998d: Table 6, 1999a: Table 3, 1998e: Table 6)
25 Daly (1991a: Table 4)
26 Hunter (1996c: 54)
27 Daly (1994: Table 4)
28 Hunter and Daly (1998: vi)
29 Taylor and Hunter (1996: 7)
30 Taylor and Hunter (1996: 11)
31 Taylor and Hunter (1996: 12–13)
32 Taylor and Hunter (1996: 14)
33 Hunter and Gray (1999: Table 3)
34 Hunter and Gray (1999: Tables 5 and 6)
35 Arthur and David-Petero (2000a: 22)
36 Gray (1992: 115)
37 But see Burbank (1988) and Burbank and Chisholm (1989).
38 Gaminiratne (1992b: 15)
39 Gray and Gaminiratne (1993)
40 Tesfaghiorghis (1996: 14)
41 Tesfaghiorghis (1996: 17)
42 Gray (1997a: Table 1)
43 Taylor (2000: 5)
44 Smith (1991c, 1992c)
45 Smith and Roach (1996: Table 6.1)
46 Hunter (2000: Tables 2a and 2b)
47 Smith and Roach (1996)
48 Schwab (1996d: 88)
49 ABS (1996: Table I)
50 Memmott, Stacey, Chambers and Keys (2001: 29–30)
51 Memmott et al. (2001: 38)
52 Memmott et al. (2001: 45)
53 Smith (1992c: 75)
54 Daly and Hawke (1994)
55 Smith and Daly (1996: 14)
56 Schwab (1995b: 9, emphasis added)
57 Schwab (1995b: 9, emphasis added)
58 Finlayson and Auld (1999: 19)
59 Martin (1995: 10)
60 Martin (1995: 14)
61 Martin (1995: 15)
62 Finlayson and Auld (1999: 16)
63 Finlayson and Auld (1999: 20)

11 HOUSEHOLDS, INDIVIDUALS AND THE INDIGENOUS POPULATION

1 Smith (1980: 44)
2 Smith (1980: 277)
3 Gray and Tesfaghiorghis (1991: 2)
4 In this passage the points that I make about 'Aboriginal' apply equally to 'Torres Strait Islander'.

5   Gray (1998: viii)
6   Gray and Tesfaghiorghis (1991: 2)
7   Gray (1998: 14)
8   Gray and Gaminiratne (1993: 5)
9   Taylor (2000: 9)
10 Taylor (1997b: 1)
11 Gray (1997a: 17)
12 Taylor (1997b: 3, 10–11)
13 Taylor (1997b: 13)
14 Hunter (1998: v)
15 Hunter (1998: 15)
16 Taylor and Bell (1998: 6)
17 Taylor (2000: 7)
18 Taylor (in press)

PART 4
INDIGENOUS AGENCIES OF COLLECTIVE CHOICE

INTRODUCTION
1   Sanders, Taylor and Ross (2000: Table 8)
2   Charles Taylor makes this distinction when he differentiates 'advocacy issues' from 'ontological issues' (Taylor 1989).
3   Rowse (1998: 96–97)
4   Hindess (1988: 105)
5   Post (2000: 200–201)
6   Commonwealth Parliamentary Debates (House of Representatives) v.99, pp. 2946–47
7   See Fingleton (1996). For commentaries on Fingleton's review see Mantziaris (1997a, 1997b) and Rowse (2000b).
8   See Johnston (1991) Volume Four, recommendations nos 192–97.

12 ATSIC'S REGIONS: THE 'EQUITY' ISSUE
9   Sanders (1993b: 8)
10 Sanders (1993b: 8)
11 Sanders (1993b: 11–12)
12 Sanders (1993b: 14)
13 Sanders (1993b: 18)
14 Ivanitz (2000)
15 Hand (1999: 24)
16 Tesfaghiorghis (1991b: 1)
17 Smith (1996c: 24)
18 Taylor and Bell (1994b: 22)
19 Altman and Gaminiratne (1992: 2)
20 Altman and Gaminiratne (1992: 17)
21 Martin and Taylor (1995: 19)
22 Martin and Taylor (1995: 22)
23 Tesfaghiorghis (1991: 12)
24 Smith (1993a: 12)
25 Smith (1993a: 12)
26 Smith (1996c: 18–24)
27 Smith (1993a: 13)
28 Smith (1993a: 13)
29 Smith (1993a: 14)
30 Smith (1993b: 12)
31 Smith (1993b: 12)

32 Smith (1993a: 14)
33 Altman and Liu (1994: 25)
34 Altman and Liu (1994: 25)
35 Gray and Auld (2000: 17)

13 ATSIC'S REGIONS: THE IDENTITY ISSUE
1 Arthur (1992: 57)
2 Gaminiratne (1992a: 6)
3 Gaminiratne (1992a: 9–10)
4 Jeremy Beckett (personal communication, 11 April 2001)
5 Taylor and Arthur (1992: 2–5)
6 Taylor and Arthur (1992: 7–9)
7 Taylor and Arthur (1992: 14)
8 Arthur (1996a: 166)
9 Arthur and Taylor (1994)
10 Arthur and Taylor (1994: 14)
11 Arthur and Taylor (1994: 15)
12 Arthur (1996a: 167)
13 Gaminiratne (1993: 17)
14 Taylor (1997: 3)
15 Gray (1997b)
16 Taylor and Bell (1999)
17 Sanders (1994a: 6)
18 Sanders (1994a: 10)
19 Arthur (1994: 15–16)
20 Davis (1995: 25)
21 Arthur and Taylor (1994: 14)
22 Sanders (1994a: 16)
23 Sanders (1994a: 22)
24 Arthur (1997: 17)
25 Altman, Arthur and Sanders (1996: 7)
26 Altman, Arthur and Sanders (1996: 13)
27 Arthur (19971)
28 Arthur (1998: 9)
29 Sanders and Arthur (1997: 2)
30 Sanders and Arthur (1997: 6)
31 Arthur (1997: 11)
32 Arthur (1997: 17)
33 Arthur (1998: v, my emphasis)
34 Arthur (1998: 7)
35 Arthur (1998: 10)
36 Sanders (1999)
37 Sanders (1999: 6–7)
38 Sanders and Arthur (2001: 7)
39 Sanders (1999: 9)
40 Sanders and Arthur (2001: 9)
41 Sanders (1999: 12)
42 ATSIC (2000: 18)
43 ATSIC (2000: 19)
44 ATSIC (2000: 20–21, 23)
45 ATSIC (2000: 25)
46 Cited in (ATSIC 2000: 36, emphasis added)
47 Sanders and Arthur (2001: 12)
48 Sullivan (1995: 9)
49 Martin (1997b: 25)
50 Martin (1997b: 11)

51 Martin (1997b: 15)
52 Martin (1997b: 20)
53 Finlayson and Smith (1995: xxi)
54 Finlayson (1997e)
55 Finlayson (1997b: 143)
56 Westbury and Sanders (2000: 7)

14 MODERNISING INDIGENOUS POLITICAL CULTURE

1 For an historical and sociological consideration of the suggestion that Indigenous Australians have a distinct approach to democratic representation, see Rowse (2001b).
2 Finlayson (1995b: 4)
3 Sanders, Taylor and Ross (2000)
4 Martin and Finlayson (1996: 2)
5 Finlayson and Dale (1996: 79)
6 Finlayson and Dale (1996: 81)
7 Finlayson and Dale (1996: 87), Finlayson (1995a: 19)
8 Martin (1997b: 9, 1997a)
9 Martin (1997b: 21, my emphasis)
10 Finlayson (1995b: 8–9)
11 Schwab (1996b: 19)
12 Martin and Finlayson (1996: 2, my emphasis)
13 Mantziaris and Martin (2000: 277–80)
14 Finlayson (1997b: 149)
15 Macdonald (1997: 73)
16 Macdonald (1997: 74–75)
17 Macdonald (1997: 76–77)
18 Macdonald (1997: 79)
19 Smith (1997: 103)
20 Martin and Finlayson (1996: 5)
21 Martin and Finlayson (1996: 5)
22 Trigger (1997: 119, 121)
23 Martin and Finlayson (1996: 6)
24 Martin and Finlayson (1996: 8)
25 Martin and Finlayson (1996: 8)
26 Martin and Finlayson (1996: 12–13)
27 Martin and Finlayson (1996: 15)
28 Smith (1995b: 68)
29 Finlayson (1998: 9)
30 Finlayson (1998: 10)
31 Finlayson (1997a: 5, 7)
32 Finlayson (1997a: 12)
33 Finlayson (1997a: 10)
34 Merlan (1997: 1–2, 7, 13)
35 Sullivan (1997: 139)
36 Fergie (1997: 49, emphasis in original)
37 Fergie (1997: 59)
38 Anderson and Brady (1995)
39 Anderson and Brady (1995)
40 Finlayson (1997c: 9)
41 Finlayson (1997c: 13–14)
42 Martin (1997b: 23)

PART 5
MAKING GOVERNMENTS ACCOUNTABLE

15 THE INDIGENOUS SECTOR AND RELATIONS WITHIN AND AMONG GOVERNMENTS

1. Altman and Sanders (1991a)
2. Anderson and Sanders (1996)
3. Sanders (1993a), Westbury and Sanders (2000)
4. Smith (1992b: 25)
5. Arthur (1991b: 6)
6. See Clarke (1997: 14–18) on Native Title, Finlayson (1997e: 5–6) on Heritage.
7. Smith (1997: 99), Finlayson (1997d)
8. Anderson and Sanders (1996: 7)
9. Arthur (1991b)
10. Anderson and Sanders (1996: 7–8)
11. Smith (1992a: 26)
12. Smith (1992a)
13. Smith (1992a: 27)
14. Sanders (1995b: 7–8)
15. Sanders (1995b: 9–10)
16. Smith (1992b: 23–24)
17. Smith (1992b: 27)
18. Anderson and Sanders (1996: 15–16)
19. Schwab (1995a: 10–11)
20. Westbury and Sanders (2000: 9)
21. Westbury and Sanders (2000: 11)
22. Davis and Arthur (1998: 7). 'Resource agencies' typically supply networks of remote outstations with certain essential goods (fuel, basic foods) and services (bookkeeping, mechanical repairs, government liaison).
23. Sanders (1995b: 3)
24. Sanders (1995a)
25. Mowbray (1999)
26. Martin (1997b: 8–10)
27. Sanders (1995a: 22–24)
28. Martin (1998)
29. Sanders (1995b: 4)
30. Sanders (1995b: 5)
31. Sanders (1995a: 15)
32. Sanders (1995a: 7–11)
33. CGC (2001: 73–74)
34. CGC (2001: 89)
35. CGC (2001: 103)

CONCLUSION: CAEPR AND THE INDIGENOUS SECTOR

1. For a fine example of a study of the local working out of senses of 'difference' over time, see Cowlishaw (2000).

REFERENCES

CAEPR monographs and discussion papers are published by the Centre for Aboriginal Economic Policy Research, Australian National University, Canberra.

Aboriginal and Torres Strait Islander Commission (ATSIC) (1994) *Review of the AEDP*. ATSIC, Canberra.
—— (1997) *Evaluation of the Community Development Employment Projects Program: Final Report, September 1997*. ATSIC Office of Evaluation and Audit, ATSIC, Canberra.
—— (2000) *Report on Greater Regional Autonomy*. ATSIC Strategic Planning and Policy Branch, ATSIC, Canberra.
Altman, JC (1991a) 'Appropriate income support for Aboriginal Australians: Options for the 90s'. CAEPR Discussion Paper 12.
—— (ed.) (1991b) *Aboriginal Employment Equity by the Year 2000*. CAEPR Research Monograph 2.
—— (ed.) (1992) *A National Survey of Indigenous Australians: Options and Implications*. CAEPR Research Monograph 3.
—— (1993) 'Indigenous Australians in the National Tourism Strategy: Impact, sustainability and policy issues'. CAEPR Discussion Paper 37.
—— (1994a) 'Implementing native title: Economic lessons from the Northern Territory'. CAEPR Discussion Paper 64.
—— (1994b) 'Economic implications of native title: Dead end or way forward?'. In W Sanders (ed.) *Mabo and Native Title: Origins and Institutional Implications*. CAEPR Research Monograph 7, pp. 61–77.
—— (1995a) '*Native Title Act 1993*: Implementation issues for resource developers'. CAEPR Discussion Paper 88.
—— (1995b) 'Coping with locational advantage: The economic development potential of tourism as Seisia community, Cape York Peninsula'. CAEPR Discussion Paper 98.
—— (1997a) 'Fighting over mining moneys: The Ranger Uranium Mine and the Gagudju Association'. In DE Smith and J Finlayson (eds) *Fighting over Country: Anthropological Perspectives*. CAEPR Research Monograph 12, pp. 175–86.
—— (1997b) 'The CDEP scheme in a new policy environment: Options for change?'. CAEPR Discussion Paper 148.

—— (1999) 'The proposed restructure of the financial framework of the Land Rights Act: A critique of Reeves'. In JC Altman, F Morphy and T Rowse (eds) *Land Rights at Risk? Evaluations of the Reeves Report*. CAEPR Research Monograph 14, pp. 109–121.

—— (2000–01) 'Aboriginal economy and social process'. *Arena Magazine* 56(December–January): 38–39.

Altman, JC and Allen, LM (1991) 'Living off the land in national parks: Issues for Aboriginal Australians'. CAEPR Discussion Paper 14.

—— (1992) 'Indigenous participation in the informal economy: Statistical and policy implications'. In JC Altman (ed.) *A National Survey of Indigenous Australians: Options and Implications*. CAEPR Research Monograph 3, pp. 138–51.

Altman, JC and Finlayson, J (1992) 'Aborigines, tourism and sustainable development'. CAEPR Discussion Paper 26.

Altman, JC and Gaminiratne, KHW (1992) 'Establishing trends in ATSIC regional council populations using Census data: A cautionary note'. CAEPR Discussion Paper 20.

Altman, JC and Gray, MC (2000) 'The effects of the CDEP scheme on the economic status of Indigenous Australians: Some analyses using the 1996 Census data'. CAEPR Discussion Paper 195.

Altman, JC and Hawke, AE (1993) 'Indigenous Australians and the labour market: Issues for the Union Movement in the 1990s'. CAEPR Discussion Paper 45.

Altman, JC and Hunter, B (1996a) 'The comparative economic status of CDEP and non-CDEP community residents in the Northern Territory in 1991'. CAEPR Discussion Paper 107.

—— (1996b) 'The geographic distribution of unemployment-related benefits and CDEP scheme employment'. CAEPR Discussion Paper 112.

—— (1997) 'Indigenous poverty since the Henderson Report'. CAEPR Discussion Paper 127.

Altman, JC and Jin Liu (1994) 'Socioeconomic status at the ATSIC regional level, 1986 and 1991: Data for regional planning?'. CAEPR Discussion Paper 76.

Altman, JC and Johnson, V (2000) 'CDEP in town and country Arnhem Land: Bawinanga Aboriginal Corporation'. CAEPR Discussion Paper 209.

Altman, JC and Levitus, RI (1999) 'The allocation and management of royalties under the Aboriginal Land Rights (Northern Territory) Act: Options for reform'. CAEPR Discussion Paper 191.

Altman, JC and Pollack, DP (1998a) 'Native title compensation: Historic and policy perspectives for an effective and fair regime'. CAEPR Discussion Paper 152.

—— (1998b) 'Financial aspects of Aboriginal land rights in the Northern Territory'. CAEPR Discussion Paper 168.

—— (1998c) 'The Indigenous Land Corporation: A new approach to land acquisition and land management'. CAEPR Discussion Paper 169.

Altman, JC and Sanders, W (1991a) 'From exclusion to dependence: Aborigines and the welfare state in Australia'. CAEPR Discussion Paper 1.

—— (1991b) 'Government initiatives for Aboriginal employment: Equity, equality and policy realism'. In JC Altman (ed.) *Aboriginal Employment Equity by the Year 2000*. CAEPR Research Monograph 2, pp. 1–18.

—— (1991c) 'The CDEP scheme: Administrative and policy issues'. CAEPR Discussion Paper 5.

Altman, JC and Smith, DE (1992) 'Estimating the Reliance of Aboriginal Australians on welfare: Some policy implications'. CAEPR Discussion Paper 19.

—— (1993) 'Compensating Indigenous Australian "losers": A community-oriented approach from the Aboriginal social policy arena'. CAEPR Discussion Paper 47.

—— (1994) 'The economic impact of mining moneys: The Nabarlek case, Western Arnhem Land'. CAEPR Discussion Paper 63.

—— (1999) 'The Ngurratjuta Aboriginal Corporation: A model for understanding Northern Territory royalty associations'. CAEPR Discussion Paper 185.

Altman, JC and Taylor, J (1994) 'Estimating Indigenous Australian employment in the private sector'. CAEPR Discussion Paper 70.

—— (eds) (1996) *The National Aboriginal and Torres Strait Islander Survey: Findings and Future Prospects.* CAEPR Research Monograph 11.

Altman, JC, Arthur, WS and Bek, HJ (1994) 'Indigenous participation in commercial fisheries in Torres Strait: A preliminary discussion'. CAEPR Discussion Paper 73.

Altman, JC, Arthur, WS and Sanders, W (1996) 'Towards greater autonomy for Torres Strait: Political and economic considerations'. CAEPR Discussion Paper 121.

Altman, JC, Bek, HJ and Roach, LM (1995) 'Native title and Indigenous Australian utilisation of wildlife: Policy perspectives'. CAEPR Discussion Paper 95.

Altman, JC, Morphy, F and Rowse, T (eds) (1999) *Land Rights at Risk? Evaluations of the Reeves Report.* CAEPR Research Monograph 14.

Altman, JC, Roach, LM and Liddle, LE (1997) 'Utilisation of wildlife by Indigenous Australians: Commercial considerations'. CAEPR Discussion Paper 135.

Anderson, I and Brady, M (1995) 'Performance indicators for Aboriginal health services'. CAEPR Discussion Paper 81.

Anderson, I and Sanders, W (1996) 'Aboriginal health and institutional reform within Australian federalism'. CAEPR Discussion Paper 117.

Arthur, WS (1991a) 'Indigenous economic development in the Torres Strait: Possibilities and limitations'. CAEPR Discussion Paper 4.

—— (1991b) 'Funding allocations to Aboriginal people: The Western Australia case'. CAEPR Discussion Paper 15.

—— (1992) 'The Provision of statistics about Torres Strait Islanders'. In JC Altman (ed.) *A National Survey of Indigenous Australians: Options and Implications.* CAEPR Research Monograph 3, pp. 57–67.

—— (1994) 'The relative economic status of Indigenous Australians within the jurisdiction of the Torres Strait Regional Authority, 1986–91'. CAEPR Discussion paper 71.

—— (1996) 'Torres Strait Islanders'. In JC Altman and J Taylor (eds) *The National Aboriginal and Torres Strait Islander Survey: Findings and Future Prospects.* CAEPR Research Monograph 11, pp. 165–72.

—— (1997) 'Towards a comprehensive regional agreement: Torres Strait'. CAEPR Discussion Paper 147.

—— (1998) 'Access to government programs and services for mainland Torres Strait Islanders'. CAEPR Discussion Paper 151.

—— (1999) 'Careers, aspirations and the meaning of work in remote Australia: Torres Strait'. CAEPR Discussion Paper 190.

Arthur, WS and David-Petero, J (2000a) 'Job-searching and careers: Young Torres Strait Islanders, 1999'. CAEPR Discussion Paper 205.

—— (2000b) 'Education, training and careers: Young Torres Strait Islanders, 1999'. CAEPR Discussion Paper 207.

Arthur, WS and Taylor, J (1994) 'The comparative economic status of Torres Strait Islanders in Torres Strait and mainland Australia'. CAEPR Discussion Paper 72.

Attwood, B and Markus, A (1997) *The 1967 Referendum: Or when Aborigines didn't get the Vote.* Aboriginal Studies Press, Canberra.

Australian Bureau of Statistics (ABS) (1996) *National Aboriginal and Torres Strait Islander Survey: Employment Outcomes for Indigenous Australians.* ABS Catalogue No. 4199.0, AGPS, Canberra.

Boughton, B (1998) *Alternative VET Pathways to Indigenous Development.* National Centre for Vocational Education and Training, Melbourne.

Burbank, V (1988) *Aboriginal Adolescence: Maidenhood in an Australian Community.* Rutgers University Press, New Brunswick.

Burbank, V and Chisholm, J (1989) 'Old and new inequalities in a southeast Arnhem Land community: Polygyny, marriage age, and birth spacing'. In JC Altman (ed.) *Emergent Inequalities in Aboriginal Australia. Oceania* Monograph 38, University of Sydney, Sydney, pp. 85–94.

Campbell, S (2000) 'The reform agenda for vocational education and training: Implications for Indigenous Australians'. CAEPR Discussion Paper 202.

Chapman, BJ (1991) 'Aboriginal employment, income and human capital: Towards a conceptual framework'. In JC Altman (ed.) *Aboriginal Employment Equity by the Year 2000*. CAEPR Research Monograph 2, pp. 133–39.

Clarke, J (1997) 'The Native Title Amendment Bill 1997: A different order of uncertainty?'. CAEPR Discussion Paper 144.

Commonwealth of Australia (1987) *Aboriginal Employment Development Policy Statement: Policy Paper 1*. AGPS, Canberra.

Commonwealth Grants Commission (2001) *Indigenous Funding Inquiry: Final Report*, volume 1. AGPS, Canberra.

Cowlishaw, G (1999) *Rednecks, Eggheads and Blackfellas*. Allen & Unwin, Sydney.

Daly, AE (1991a) 'The participation of Aboriginal people in the Australian labour market'. CAEPR Discussion Paper 6.

—— (1991b) 'The Impact of welfare on the economic status of Aboriginal women'. CAEPR Discussion Paper 7.

—— (1991c) 'The employment of Aboriginal Australians in the labour market'. CAEPR Discussion Paper 16.

—— (1992) 'The determinants of Aboriginal employment income'. CAEPR Discussion Paper 32.

—— (1993) 'Education and employment for young Indigenous Australians, 1986–91'. CAEPR Discussion Paper 50.

—— (1994) 'Self-employed Indigenous Australians in the labour market'. CAEPR Discussion Paper 67.

—— (1996) 'Post-secondary qualifications and training for Indigenous Australians'. In JC Altman and J Taylor (eds) *The National Aboriginal and Torres Strait Islander Survey: Findings and Future Prospects*. CAEPR Research Monograph 11, pp. 96–105.

Daly, AE and Hawke, AE (1993) 'Work and welfare for indigenous Australians'. CAEPR Discussion Paper 48.

—— (1994) 'The impact of the welfare state on the economic status of Indigenous Australian women'. CAEPR Discussion Paper 65.

Daly, AE and Lin Jiu (1995) 'Estimating the private rate of return to education for Indigenous Australians'. CAEPR Discussion Paper 97.

Daly, AE and Smith, DE (1995) 'The economic status of Indigenous Australian families'. CAEPR Discussion Paper 93.

—— (1997) 'Indigenous sole-parent families: Invisible and disadvantaged'. CAEPR Discussion Paper 134.

—— (1998) 'The continuing disadvantage of Indigenous sole parents: A preliminary analysis of 1996 Census data'. CAEPR Discussion Paper 153.

—— (1999) 'Indigenous household demography and socio-economic status: The policy implications of 1996 Census data'. CAEPR Discussion Paper 181.

—— (2000) 'Research methodology'. In DE Smith (ed.) *Indigenous Families and the Welfare System: Two Community Case Studies*. CAEPR Research Monograph 17, pp. 11–23.

Daly, AE, Allen, B, Aufflick, L, Bosworth, E and Caruso, M (1993) 'Determining the labour force status of Aboriginal people using a multinomial logit model'. CAEPR Discussion Paper 44.

Davis, R (1995) 'Looking beyond the borderline: Development performance and prospects of Saibai Island, Torres Strait'. CAEPR Discussion Paper 80.

Davis, R and Arthur, WS (1998) 'Homelands and resource agencies since the

Blanchard Report: A review of the literature and an annotated bibliography'. CAEPR Discussion Paper 165.

Fergie, D (1997) 'Having it out over Hindmarsh: An essay on the significance of manners'. In DE Smith and J Finlayson (eds) *Fighting over Country: Anthropological Perspectives*. CAEPR Research Monograph 12, pp. 46–64.

Fingleton, J (1996) *Final Report: Review of the Aboriginal Councils and Associations Act 1976*, volume 1. Australian Institute of Aboriginal and Torres Strait Islander Studies, Canberra.

Finlayson, JD (1989) 'Welfare incomes and Aboriginal gender relations'. In JC Altman (ed.) *Emergent Inequalities in Aboriginal Australia*. Oceania Monograph 38, University of Sydney, Sydney, pp. 95–117.

—— (1995a) 'Aboriginal employment, native title and regionalism'. CAEPR Discussion Paper 87.

—— (1995b) 'Equity for Aboriginal families in the 1990s: The challenges for social policy'. CAEPR Discussion Paper 94.

—— (1997a) 'Native title representative bodies: The challenge of strategic planning'. CAEPR Discussion Paper 129.

—— (1997b) 'Aboriginal tradition and Native Title Representative bodies'. In DE Smith and J Finlayson (eds) *Fighting over Country: Anthropological Perspectives*. CAEPR Research Monograph 12, pp. 141–52.

—— (1997c) 'Service provision and service providers in a remote Queensland community'. CAEPR Discussion Paper 133.

—— (1997d) 'The right to negotiate and the miner's right: A case study of native title future act processes in Queensland'. CAEPR Discussion Paper 139.

—— (1997e) 'Indigenous heritage protection, native title and regional agreements: The changing environment'. CAEPR Discussion Paper 145.

—— (1998) 'New and emerging challenges for Native Title Representative Bodies'. CAEPR Discussion Paper 167.

—— (1999) 'Northern Territory land rights: Purpose and effectiveness'. CAEPR Discussion Paper 180.

Finlayson, JD and Auld, AJ (1999) 'Shoe or stew? Balancing wants and needs in indigenous households: A study of appropriate income and support payments and policies for families'. CAEPR Discussion Paper 182.

Finlayson, JD and Dale, A (1996) 'Negotiating Indigenous self-determination at the regional level'. In P Sullivan (ed.) *Shooting the Banker: Essays on ATSIC and Self-determination*. North Australia Research Unit, Darwin, pp. 70–88.

Finlayson, J and Smith, DE (eds) (1995) *Native Title: Emerging Issues for Research, Policy and Practice*. CAEPR Research Monograph 10.

Finlayson, JD, Daly, AE and Smith, DE (2000) 'The Kuranda community case study'. In DE Smith (ed.) *Indigenous Families and the Welfare System: Two Community Case Studies*. CAEPR Research Monograph 17, pp. 25–51.

Finlayson, JD, Rigsby, B and Bek, HJ (eds) (1999) *Connections in Native Title: Genealogies, Kinship and Groups*. CAEPR Research Monograph 13.

Fisk, E K (1985) *The Aboriginal Economy in Town and Country*. Allen & Unwin, Sydney.

Fraser, N and Gordon, L (1994) 'A Genealogy of "Dependency": A keyword of the welfare state'. In P James (ed.) *Critical Politics: From the Personal to the Global*. Arena Publications, Melbourne, pp. 59–75.

Galligan, B (1999) 'The Reeves Report as public policy'. In JC Altman, F Morphy and T Rowse (eds) *Land Rights at Risk? Evaluations of the Reeves Report*. CAEPR Research Monograph 14, pp. 11–23.

Gaminiratne, KHW (1992a) 'First counts, 1991 Census: A Comment on Aboriginal and Torres Strait Islander population growth'. CAEPR Discussion Paper 24.

—— (1992b) 'Estimating Aboriginal and Torres Strait Islander fertility from Census data'. CAEPR Discussion Paper 31.

—— (1993) 'Change in Aboriginal and Torres Strait Islander population distribution, 1986–91'. CAEPR Discussion Paper 49.
Godelier, M (1972) *Rationality and Irrationality in Economics*. New Left Books, London.
Gray, A (1992) 'Health and housing in Aboriginal and Torres Strait Islander communities'. In JC Altman (ed.) *A National Survey of Indigenous Australians: Options and Implications*. CAEPR Research Monograph 3, pp. 109–23.
—— (1997a) 'The explosion of Aboriginality: Components of Indigenous population growth 1991–6'. CAEPR Discussion Paper 142.
—— (1997b) 'Growth of the Aboriginal and Torres Strait Islander population, 1991–2001 and beyond'. CAEPR Discussion Paper 150.
—— (1998) 'Parentage and Indigenous population change'. CAEPR Discussion Paper 166.
Gray, A and Gaminiratne, KHW (1993) 'Indicative projections of the Aboriginal and Torres Strait Islander population to 2011'. CAEPR Discussion Paper 52.
Gray, A and Tesfaghiorghis, H (1991) 'Social indicators of the Aboriginal population of Australia'. CAEPR Discussion Paper 18.
Gray, MC and Auld, AJ (2000) 'Towards an index of relative Indigenous socio-economic advantage'. CAEPR Discussion Paper 196.
Gray, MC and Thacker, E (2000) 'A case study of the Bungala CDEP: Economic and social impacts'. CAEPR Discussion Paper 208.
Gray, M, Hunter, B and Schwab, RG (1998) ' A critical survey of Indigenous education outcomes, 1986–1996'. CAEPR Discussion Paper 170.
Gregory, RG (1991) '"The American dilemma" down under: A comparison of the economic status of US Indians and Blacks and Aboriginal Australians'. In JC Altman (ed.) *Aboriginal Employment Equity by the Year 2000*. CAEPR Research Monograph 2, pp. 141–54.
Hand, G (1999) 'The Aboriginal and Torres Strait Islander Commission: A sophisticated model — a decade of experience' (with questions and discussion). *Canberra Bulletin of Public Administration* 94(December): 17–27.
Havnen, O (1999) 'Regional Councils: Roles and functions'. *Canberra Bulletin of Public Administration* 94(December): 28–30.
Henry, R and Daly, A (2001) 'Indigenous families and the welfare system: The Kuranda community case study, Stage Two'. CAEPR Discussion Paper 216.
Hindess, B (1988) *Choice, Rationality and Social Theory*. Unwin Hyman, London.
Hunter, B (1996a) 'Indigenous Australians and the socioeconomic status of urban neighbourhoods'. CAEPR Discussion Paper 106.
—— (1996b) 'The determinants of Indigenous employment outcomes: The importance of education and training'. CAEPR Discussion Paper 115.
—— (1996c) 'Indigenous Australians in the labour market: The NATSIS and beyond'. In JC Altman and J Taylor (eds) *The National Aboriginal and Torres Strait Islander Survey: Findings and Future Prospects*. CAEPR Research Monograph 11, pp. 53–64.
—— (2000) 'Social exclusion, social capital, and Indigenous Australians: Measuring the social costs of unemployment'. CAEPR Discussion Paper 204.
—— (2001) 'Tackling poverty among Indigenous Australians'. In R Fincher and P Saunders (eds) *Creating Unequal Futures? Rethinking Poverty, Inequality and Disadvantage*. Allen & Unwin, Sydney, pp. 129–57.
Hunter, B and Borland, J (1997) 'The interrelationships between arrest and employment: More evidence on the social determinants of Indigenous employment'. CAEPR Discussion Paper 136.
Hunter, B and Daly, AE (1998) 'Labour market incentives among Indigenous Australians: The cost of job loss versus the gains from employment'. CAEPR Discussion Paper 159.

Hunter, B and Gray, MC (1999) 'Further investigations into Indigenous labour supply: What discourages discouraged workers?'. CAEPR Working Paper 2.

Hunter, B and Hawke, AE (2000) 'Industrial relations in workplaces employing Indigenous Australians'. CAEPR Discussion Paper 200.

Ivanitz, M (2000) 'The demise of ATSIC: Accountability and the Coalition government'. *Australian Journal of Public Administration* 59(1) March: 3–12.

Johnston, E (1991) *National Report.* Royal Commission into Aboriginal Deaths in Custody, AGPS, Canberra.

Jones, R (1994) *The Housing Needs of Indigenous Australians, 1991.* CAEPR Research Monograph 8.

Lawrence, G and Gray, I (2000) 'The myths of modern agriculture: Australian rural production in the 21st century'. In B Pritchard and P McManus (eds) *Land of Discontent: The Dynamics of Change in Rural and Regional Australia.* UNSW Press, Sydney, pp. 33–51.

Levitus, R (1999) 'Local organisations and the purpose of money'. In JC Altman, F Morphy and T Rowse (eds) *Land Rights at Risk? Evaluations of the Reeves Report.* CAEPR Research Monograph 14, pp. 123–29.

Levitus, R, Martin, DF and Pollack, DP (1999) 'Regionalisation of Northern Territory Land Councils'. CAEPR Discussion Paper 192.

Lewington, J, Roberts, S and Brownley, Y (1997) 'Multiplicity and complexity: The Goldfields Land Council's native title experience'. In DE Smith and J Finlayson (eds) *Fighting over Country: Anthropological Perspectives.* CAEPR Research Monograph 12, pp. 203–214.

Macdonald, G (1997) '"Recognition and justice": The traditional/historical contradiction in New South Wales'. In DE Smith and J Finlayson (eds) *Fighting over Country: Anthropological Perspectives.* CAEPR Research Monograph 12, pp. 65–82.

McKenna, SL (1995) 'Assessing the relative allocative efficiency of the Native Title Act 1993 and the Aboriginal Land Rights (Northern Territory) Act 1976'. CAEPR Discussion Paper 79.

Madden R (2000) '"If it wasn't for CDEP": A case study of Worn Gundidj CDEP, Victoria'. CAEPR Discussion Paper 210.

Manne, R (2001) 'Aboriginal debate makes a sharp right'. *Sydney Morning Herald,* 4 June.

Mantziaris, C (1997a) 'Beyond the Aboriginal Councils and Association Act'. *Indigenous Law Bulletin* 4(5): 10–14.

—— (1997b) 'Beyond the Aboriginal Councils and Association Act'. *Indigenous Law Bulletin* 4(6): 7–15.

Mantziaris, C and Martin, D (2000) *Native Title Corporations: A Legal and Anthropological Analysis.* Federation Press, Sydney.

Martin, DF (1995) 'Money, business and culture: Issues for Aboriginal economic policy'. CAEPR Discussion Paper 101.

—— (1997a) 'The incorporation of "traditional" and "historical" interests in Native Title Representative Bodies'. In DE Smith and J Finlayson (eds) *Fighting over Country: Anthropological Perspectives.* CAEPR Research Monograph 12, pp. 153–63.

—— (1997b) 'Regional agreements and localism: A case study from Cape York Peninsula'. CAEPR Discussion Paper 146.

—— (1998) 'The supply of alcohol in remote Aboriginal communities: Potential policy directions from Cape York'. CAEPR Discussion Paper 162.

—— (1999) 'The Reeves Report's assumptions on regionalism and socio-economic advancement'. In JC Altman, F Morphy and T Rowse (eds) *Land Rights at Risk? Evaluations of the Reeves Report.* CAEPR Research Monograph 14, pp. 155–66.

Martin, DF and Finlayson, JD (1996) 'Linking accountability and self-determination in Aboriginal organisations'. CAEPR Discussion Paper 116.

Martin, DF and Taylor, J (1995) 'Enumerating the Aboriginal population of remote Australia: Methodological and conceptual issues'. CAEPR Discussion Paper 91.

Memmott, P, Stacy, R, Chambers, C and Keys, C (2001) *Violence in Indigenous Communities*. Report to the Crime Prevention Branch of the Attorney-General's Department, Canberra.

Merlan, F (1997) 'Fighting over country: Four commonplaces'. In DE Smith and J Finlayson (eds) *Fighting over Country: Anthropological Perspectives*. CAEPR Research Monograph 12, pp. 1–14.

Miller, M (1985) *Report of the Committee of Review of Aboriginal Employment and Training Programs*. AGPS, Canberra.

Morony, R (1991) 'The Community Development Employment Projects (CDEP) Scheme'. In JC Altman (ed.) *Aboriginal Employment Equity by the Year 2000*. CAEPR Research Monograph 2, pp. 101–106.

Morton, J (1997) 'Why can't they be nice to one another? Anthropology and the generation and resolution of land claim disputes'. In DE Smith and J Finlayson (eds) *Fighting over Country: Anthropological Perspectives*. CAEPR Research Monograph 12, pp. 83–92.

Mowbray, M (1999) 'Municipalising land councils: Land rights and local governance'. In JC Altman, F Morphy and T Rowse (eds) *Land Rights at Risk? Evaluations of the Reeves Report*. CAEPR Research Monograph 14, pp. 167–79.

Munster, J (1997) 'Dispute management strategies: Suggestions from the Central Land Council'. In DE Smith and J Finlayson (eds) *Fighting over Country: Anthropological Perspectives*. CAEPR Research Monograph 12, pp. 187–202.

Musharbash, Y (2000) 'The Yuendumu community case study'. In Smith DE (ed.) *Indigenous Families and the Welfare System: Two Community Case Studies*. CAEPR Research Monograph 17, pp. 53–84.

—— (2001) 'Indigenous families and the welfare system: The Yuendumu community case study, Stage Two'. CAEPR Discussion Paper 217.

Nettheim, G (1999) 'Statehood, land rights and Aboriginal law'. In JC Altman, F Morphy and T Rowse (eds) *Land Rights at Risk? Evaluations of the Reeves Report*. CAEPR Research Monograph 14, pp. 89–98.

Neutze, M, Sanders, W and Jones, R (2000) 'Estimating Indigenous housing need for public funding allocation: A multimeasure approach'. CAEPR Discussion Paper 197.

O'Faircheallaigh, C (1995a) 'Mineral development agreements negotiated by Aboriginal communities in the 1990s'. CAEPR Discussion Paper 85.

—— (1995b) 'Negotiations between mining companies and Aboriginal communities: Process and structure'. CAEPR Discussion Paper 86.

Pearson, N (2000) *Our Right to Take Responsibility*. Noel Pearson and Associates, Cairns.

Peel, M (2000) 'Decency and justice: Voices from the Australian margins'. 30th Anniversary Lecture, *Australian Academy of Humanities Proceedings 1999*, pp.133–53.

Peterson, N (1993) 'Demand sharing: Reciprocity and pressure for generosity among foragers'. *American Anthropologist* 95(4): 860–74.

—— (1999) 'Reeves in the context of the history of land rights legislation: Anthropological aspects'. In JC Altman, F Morphy and T Rowse (eds) *Land Rights at Risk? Evaluations of the Reeves Report*. CAEPR Research Monograph 14, pp. 25–31.

Pollack, D (1999) 'Smaller land councils: Value for money?'. In JC Altman, F Morphy and T Rowse (eds) *Land Rights at Risk? Evaluations of the Reeves Report*. CAEPR Research Monograph 14, pp. 141–53.

—— (2001) 'Indigenous land in Australia: A quantitative assessment of Indigenous landholdings in 2000'. CAEPR Discussion Paper 221.

Post, RC (2000) 'Democratic constitutionalism and cultural heterogeneity'. *Australian Journal of Legal Philosophy* 25(2): 185–204.
Quiggin, J (1999) 'Delays and uncertainties in the negotiations for mining on Aboriginal land'. In JC Altman, F Morphy and T Rowse (eds) *Land Rights at Risk? Evaluations of the Reeves Report*. CAEPR Research Monograph 14, pp. 131–40.
Reeves, J (1998) *Building on Land Rights for the Next Generation* (two volumes). AGPS, Canberra.
Rose, FGG (1987) *The Traditional Mode of Production of the Australian Aborigines*. Angus & Robertson, Sydney.
Ross, RT and Mikalauskas, A (1996) 'Income poverty among Indigenous families with children: Estimates from the 1991 Census'. CAEPR Discussion Paper 110.
Rowse, T (1994) 'Representing the "Aboriginal interest" in alcohol policy reform'. *Australian Aboriginal Studies* 1: 14–26.
—— (1996) *Traditions for Health: Studies in Aboriginal Reconstruction*. NARU, Darwin.
—— (1998) 'Indigenous citizenship and self-determination: The problem of shared responsibilities'. In N Peterson and W Sanders (eds) *Citizenship and Indigenous Australians: Changing Conceptions and Possibilities*. Cambridge University Press, Melbourne, pp. 79–100.
—— (2000a) *Obliged to be Difficult: Nugget Coombs' Legacy in Indigenous Affairs*. Cambridge University Press, Melbourne.
—— (2000b) 'Culturally appropriate Indigenous accountability'. *American Behavioral Scientist* 43(9): 1514–32.
—— (2001a) 'The political dimensions of community development'. In F Morphy and W Sanders (eds) *The Indigenous Welfare Economy and the CDEP Scheme*. CAEPR Research Monograph 20, pp. 39–46.
—— (2001b) '"Democratic systems are an alien thing to Aboriginal culture"'. In M Sawer and G Zappala (eds) *Speaking for the People*. Melbourne University Press, Melbourne, pp. 103–33.
Sandall, R (2001) *The Culture Cult*. Westview Press, Boulder.
Sanders, W (1993a) 'Rethinking the fundamentals of social policy towards indigenous Australians: Block grants, mainstreaming and the multiplicity of agencies and programs'. CAEPR Discussion Paper 46.
—— (1993b) 'Reconciling public accountability and Aboriginal self-determination/self-management: Is ATSIC succeeding?'. CAEPR Discussion Paper 51.
—— (1993c) 'The rise and rise of the CDEP scheme: An Aboriginal "workfare" program in times of persistent unemployment'. CAEPR Discussion Paper 54.
—— (1994a) 'Reshaping governance in Torres Strait: The Torres Strait Regional Authority and beyond'. CAEPR Discussion Paper 74.
—— (ed.) (1994b) *Mabo and Native Title: Origins and Institutional Implications*. CAEPR Research Monograph 7.
—— (1995a) 'Local governments and Indigenous Australians: Developments and dilemmas in contrasting circumstances'. CAEPR Discussion Paper 84.
—— (1995b) 'Australian fiscal federalism and Aboriginal self-government: Some issues of tactics and targets'. CAEPR Discussion Paper 90.
—— (1999) 'Torres Strait governance structures and the Centenary of Australian Federation: A missed opportunity?'. CAEPR Discussion Paper 184.
Sanders, W and Arthur, WS (1997) 'A Torres Strait Islanders Commission? Possibilities and issues'. CAEPR Discussion Paper 132.
—— (2001) 'Autonomy rights in Torres Strait: From whom, for whom, for or over what?'. CAEPR Discussion Paper 215.
Sanders, W, Taylor, J and Ross, K (2000) 'Participation and representation in ATSIC elections: A ten-year perspective'. CAEPR Discussion Paper 198.
Schwab, RG (1995a) 'Twenty years of policy recommendations for Indigenous education: Overview and research implications'. CAEPR Discussion Paper 92.

—— (1995b) 'The calculus of reciprocity: Principles and implications of Aboriginal sharing'. CAEPR Discussion Paper 100.
—— (1996a) 'Having it "both ways": The continuing complexities of community-controlled Indigenous education'. CAEPR Discussion Paper 111.
—— (1996b) 'Community involvement in education: An exploration of American Indian policy and implications for Australia'. CAEPR Discussion Paper 120.
—— (1996c) 'Indigenous participation in higher education: Culture, choice and human capital theory'. CAEPR Discussion Paper 122.
—— (1996d) 'Indigenous participation in schooling: A preliminary assessment of the NATSIS findings'. In JC Altman and J Taylor (eds) *The National Aboriginal and Torres Strait Islander Survey: Findings and Future Prospects*. CAEPR Research Monograph 11, pp. 84–95.
—— (1997a) 'Post-compulsory education and training for Indigenous Australians'. CAEPR Discussion Paper 131.
—— (1997b) 'Indigenous TAFE graduates: Patterns and implications'. CAEPR Discussion Paper 138.
—— (1998) 'Educational "failure" and educational "success" in an Aboriginal community'. CAEPR Discussion Paper 161.
—— (1999) *Why Only One in Three? The Complex Reasons for Low Indigenous School Retention*. CAEPR Research Monograph 16.
Schwab, RG and Anderson, I (1998) 'Indigenous participation in health sciences education: Recent trends in the higher education sector'. CAEPR Discussion Paper 171.
—— (1999) 'Trends in Indigenous participation in health sciences education: The vocational education and training sector, 1994–7'. CAEPR Discussion Paper 179.
Senate Standing Committee on Legal and Constitutional Affairs (1983) *After Two Hundred Years*. AGPS, Canberra.
Sewell, WH (1993) 'Towards a post-materialist rhetoric for Labor History'. In LR Berlanstein (ed.) *Rethinking Labor History*. University of Illinois Press, Urbana and Chicago, pp. 15–38.
Smith, DE (1991a) 'Aboriginal expenditure patterns: An analysis of empirical data and its policy implications'. CAEPR Discussion Paper 9.
—— (1991b) 'Towards and Aboriginal household expenditure survey: Conceptual, methodological and cultural considerations'. CAEPR Discussion Paper 10.
—— (1991c) 'Aboriginal unemployment statistics: Policy implications of the divergence between official and case study data'. CAEPR Discussion Paper 13.
—— (1992a) 'An analysis of the Aboriginal component of Commonwealth fiscal flows to the Northern Territory'. CAEPR Discussion Paper 29.
—— (1992b) 'Estimating Northern Territory Government program expenditure for Aboriginal people: Problems and implications'. CAEPR Discussion Paper 30.
—— (1992c) 'The cultural appropriateness of existing survey questions and concepts'. In JC Altman (ed.) *A National Survey of Indigenous Australians: Options and Implications*. CAEPR Research Monograph 3, pp. 68–85.
—— (1993a) 'ATSIC's mechanisms for resource allocation: Current policy and practice'. CAEPR Discussion Paper 41.
—— (1993b) 'The fiscal equalisation model: Options for ATSIC's future funding policy and practice'. CAEPR Discussion Paper 42.
—— (1994a) 'The cross-cultural validity of labour force statistics about Indigenous Australians'. CAEPR Discussion Paper 69.
—— (1994b) '"Working for CDEP": A case study of the Community Development Employment Projects scheme in Port Lincoln, South Australia'. CAEPR Discussion Paper 75.
—— (1995a) 'Redfern works: The policy and community challenges of an urban CDEP scheme'. CAEPR Discussion Paper 99.
—— (1995b) 'Representative politics and the new wave of native title organisations'. In J Finlayson and DE Smith (eds) *Native Title: Emerging Issues for*

Research, Policy and Practice. CAEPR Research Monograph 10, pp. 59–74.
—— (1996a) 'CDEP as urban enterprise: The case of Yarnteen Aboriginal and Torres Strait Islanders Corporation'. CAEPR Discussion Paper 114.
—— (1996b) 'The right to negotiate and native title future acts: Implications of the Native Title Amendment Bill 1996'. CAEPR Discussion Paper 124.
—— (1996c) 'From cultural diversity to regionalism: The political culture of difference in ATSIC'. In P Sullivan (ed.) *Shooting the Banker: Essays on ATSIC and Self-determination.* North Australia Research Unit, Darwin, pp. 17–41.
—— (1997) 'From humbug to good faith? The politics of negotiating the right to negotiate'. In DE Smith and J Finlayson (eds) *Fighting over Country: Anthropological Perspectives.* CAEPR Research Monograph 12, pp. 93–109.
—— (1998) 'Indigenous land use agreements: The opportunities, challenges and policy implications of the amended Native Title Act'. CAEPR Discussion Paper 163.
—— (ed.) (2000a) *Indigenous Families and the Welfare System: Two Community Case Studies.* CAEPR Research Monograph 17.
—— (2000b) 'The project research and policy context'. In DE Smith (ed.) *Indigenous Families and the Welfare System: Two Community Case Studies.* CAEPR Research Monograph 17, pp. 1–9.
—— (2000c) 'Kuranda and Yuendumu: Comparative conclusions'. In DE Smith (ed.) *Indigenous Families and the Welfare System: Two Community Case Studies.* CAEPR Research Monograph 17, pp. 85–96.
Smith, DE and Daly, AE (1996) 'The economic status of Indigenous Australian households: A statistical and ethnographic analysis'. CAEPR Discussion Paper 109.
Smith, DE and Finlayson, J (eds) (1997) *Fighting over Country: Anthropological Perspectives.* CAEPR Research Monograph 12.
Smith, DE and Roach, LM (1996) 'Indigenous voluntary work: NATSIS empirical evidence, policy relevance and future data issues'. In JC Altman and J Taylor (eds) *The National Aboriginal and Torres Strait Islander Survey: Findings and Future Prospects.* CAEPR Research Monograph 11, pp. 65–76.
Smith, LR (1980) *The Aboriginal Population of Australia.* Australian National University Press, Canberra.
Stead, J (1995) 'Lessons from Northern territory land claims: A Land Council perspective'. In J Finlayson and DE Smith (eds) *Native Title: Emerging Issues for Research, Policy and Practice.* CAEPR Research Monograph 10, pp. 75–82.
—— (1997) 'Disputes in land: The Northern Land Council experience'. In DE Smith and J Finlayson (eds) *Fighting over Country: Anthropological Perspectives.* CAEPR Research Monograph 12, pp. 164–74.
Sullivan, P (1995) 'Beyond native title: Multiple land use agreements and Aboriginal governance in the Kimberley'. CAEPR Discussion Paper 89.
—— (1997) 'Dealing with native title conflicts by recognising Aboriginal political authority'. In DE Smith and J Finlayson (eds) *Fighting over Country: Anthropological Perspectives.* CAEPR Research Monograph 12, pp. 129–40.
Sutton, P (1999) 'The Reeves Report and the idea of the "community"'. In JC Altman, F Morphy and T Rowse (eds) *Land Rights at Risk? Evaluations of the Reeves Report.* CAEPR Research Monograph 14, pp. 39–51.
—— (2001) 'The politics of suffering: Indigenous policy in Australia since the 1970s'. *Anthropological Forum* 11(2): 125–73.
Taffe, S (2001) The Federal Council for the Advancement of Aborigines and Torres Strait Islanders, 1958–73: The politics of inter-racial coalition in Australia. PhD thesis, Monash University, Melbourne.
Taylor, C (1989) 'Cross-purposes: The liberal-communitarian debate'. In NL Rosenblum (ed.) *Liberalism and the moral life.* Harvard University Press, Cambridge (Mass) and London, pp. 159–82.
Taylor, J (1988) 'Aboriginal population mobility and urban development in the Katherine region'. In D Wade-Marshall and P Loveday (eds) *Contemporary Issues in Development.* North Australia Research Unit, Darwin, pp. 201–24.

—— (1991a) 'Geographic location and Aboriginal economic status: A Census-based analysis of outstations in Australia's Northern Territory'. CAEPR Discussion Paper 8.
—— (1991b) 'Spatial mobility of working age Aborigines in settled and remote Australia: A preliminary analysis'. CAEPR Discussion Paper 17.
—— (1992) 'Industry segregation among employed Aborigines and Torres Strait Islanders'. CAEPR Discussion Paper 22.
—— (1993a) *The Relative Economic Status of Indigenous Australians, 1986–91*. CAEPR Research Monograph 5.
—— (1993b) *Regional Change in the Economic Status of Indigenous Australians, 1986–91*. CAEPR Research Monograph 6.
—— (1995) 'Indigenous employment and job segregation in the Northern Territory labour market'. CAEPR Discussion Paper 83.
—— (1997) 'Changing numbers, changing needs? A preliminary assessment of Indigenous population growth 1991–6'. CAEPR Discussion Paper 143.
—— (1998a) 'The relative economic status of Indigenous people in Western Australia, 1991 and 1996'. CAEPR Discussion Paper 157.
—— (1998b) 'The relative economic status of Indigenous people in Tasmania, 1991 and 1996'. CAEPR Discussion Paper 159.
—— (1998c) 'The relative economic status of Indigenous people in Queensland, 1991 and 1996'. CAEPR Discussion Paper 172.
—— (1998d) 'The relative economic status of Indigenous people in New South Wales, 1991 and 1996'. CAEPR Discussion Paper 173.
—— (1998e) 'The relative economic status of Indigenous people in Victoria, 1991 and 1996'. CAEPR Discussion Paper 174.
—— (1999) 'The relative economic status of indigenous people in the Australian Capital Territory, 1991 and 1996'. CAEPR Discussion Paper 175.
—— (2000) 'Transformations of the Indigenous population: Recent and future trends'. CAEPR Discussion Paper 194.
—— (in press) 'Indigenous enumeration in the late twentieth century: Emerging issues for population analysis'. *Aboriginal History*.
Taylor, J and Altman, JC (1997) *The Job Ahead: Escalating Economic Costs of Indigenous Employment Disparity*. ATSIC Office of Public Affairs, Canberra.
Taylor, J and Arthur, WS (1992) 'Patterns and trends in the spatial diffusion of the Torres Strait Islander population'. CAEPR Discussion Paper 25.
Taylor, J and Bell, M (1994) 'The mobility status of Indigenous Australians'. CAEPR Discussion Paper 78.
—— (1998) 'Estimating intercensal Indigenous employment change, 1991–96'. CAEPR Discussion Paper 155.
—— (1999) 'Changing places: Indigenous population movement in the 1990s'. CAEPR Discussion Paper 189.
Taylor, J and Hunter, B (1996) 'Indigenous participation in labour market and training programs'. CAEPR Discussion Paper 108.
—— (1997) 'A profile of Indigenous workers in the private sector'. CAEPR Discussion Paper 137.
—— (1998) *The Job Still Ahead: Economic Costs of Continuing Indigenous Employment Disparity*. ATSIC Office of Public Affairs, Canberra.
Taylor, J and Liu Jin (1995) 'Change in the relative distribution of employment by industry, 1986–91'. CAEPR Discussion Paper 96.
Taylor, J and Roach, L (1998) 'The relative economic status of Indigenous people in the Northern Territory, 1991–6'. CAEPR Discussion Paper 156.
Taylor, J and Westbury, N (2000) *Aboriginal nutrition and the Nyirranggulung Health Strategy in Jawoyn Country*. CAEPR Research Monograph 19.
Taylor, J, Bern, J and Senior, KA (2000) *Ngukurr at the Millennium: A Baseline Profile for Social Impact Planning in South-East Arnhem Land*. CAEPR Research Monograph 18.

Tesfaghiorghis, H (1991) 'Aboriginal economic status by ATSIC regions: Analyses of 1986 Census data'. CAEPR Discussion Paper 11.
—— (1996) 'Further policy implications of rising Aboriginal fertility in the 1990s'. CAEPR Discussion Paper 103.
Tesfaghiorghis, H and Altman, JC (1991) 'Aboriginal socio-economic status: Are there any evident changes?'. CAEPR Discussion Paper 3.
Trigger, D (1997) 'Reflections on Century Mine: Preliminary thoughts on the politics of Indigenous responses'. In DE Smith and J Finlayson (eds) *Fighting over Country: Anthropological Perspectives*. CAEPR Research Monograph 12, pp. 110–28.
Westbury, N and Sanders, W (2000) 'Governance and service delivery for remote Aboriginal communities in the Northern Territory: Challenges and opportunities'. CAEPR Working Paper 6.
Wootten, H (1995) 'The end of dispossession? Anthropologists and lawyers in the native title process'. In J Finlayson and DE Smith (eds) *Native Title: Emerging Issues for Research, Policy and Practice*. CAEPR Research Monograph 10, pp. 101–18.
Yeatman, A (2000) 'Who is the subject of human rights?' *American* Aboriginal Benefits Account (ABA) 92, 94–96

INDEX

Aboriginal Benefits Reserve (ABR) 92, 94–96, 101, 110
Aboriginal Benefits Trust Account (ABTA) 92, 94–96, 113–14
Aboriginal Community Controlled Health Services 213, 221, 224
Aboriginal Development Commission (ADC) 182
Aboriginal Education Policy 10, 54
Aboriginal Employment Development Policy (AEDP) x, 8–9, 19–20, 26–27, 29–35, 36, 37, 47–49, 50, 52, 54, 58, 65, 75, 152, 158, 175, 232, 235–36
Aboriginal Hostels Pty Ltd 203
Aboriginal and Torres Strait Islander Commission (ATSIC) x, 1, 48–49, 66, 67, 71, 99, 109, 114, 122, 176, 182–83, 184–91, 194–201, 204–205, 210–11, 213, 215, 220–22, 224–25
   Office of Evaluation and Audit 73, 184, 185, 188
   Office of Torres Strait Islander Affairs 196, 198
   Torres Strait Islander Advisory Board 196, 200
Aboriginal Councils and Associations Act 1976 (Cwealth) 181–82, 210
Aboriginal Land Act 1991 (Qld) 206
Aboriginal Land Rights (Northern Territory) Act 1976 (Cwealth) 82, 84, 92–102, 105–106, 111–17, 119, 122, 181, 209, 222, 232

accountability 73–74, 77, 97, 99–101, 111–23, 184–86, 189, 205, 207, 210–12, 213, 214, 224
alcohol 154, 156, 162, 178–89, 226–27
Allen, L 83, 85–86
Altman, JC 9, 32, 38, 40–41, 42, 47–48, 56, 66–67, 69, 70, 73, 75, 81, 83, 84, 85–86, 87–88, 89–91, 95–102, 105–10, 111–12, 118, 119, 120, 131, 157, 186, 189, 197, 220, 232
Anderson, I 176, 213–24, 223–25
Anindilyakwa Land Council (NT) 114
Antonios, Z 178
Arnhem Land Progress Association (NT) 203
Arthur, W 61–62, 66, 69–70, 72, 87–88, 159, 191–93, 195–201, 221, 223, 226
assimilation, policy 1–2, 5–6, 16, 19, 180, 220, 230–36
   mainstreaming 220, 224–25, 230–31
Atkinson, J 163
Auld, T 128, 148, 164–65, 189
Aurukun (Qld) 205
Australian Bureau of Statistics (ABS) 68, 70, 131–34, 136–37, 139–42, 144–45, 167, 187
Australian Local Government Association 228
Australian National Audit Office (formerly Auditor General) 67, 184

Australian National University vii–viii, 5
Australian Petroleum, Production and Exploration Association 107
Australian Workplace Industrial Relations Survey 44

Badu Island (Qld) 72
Bamaga (Qld) 195
Barn Islands (Qld) 195
Barron Falls National Park (Qld) 90
Bawinanga (NT) 73, 74, 75
Beckett, J 192, 196
Bek, H 86, 88
Bell, M 171, 186, 194
Bolger, A 163
Borland, J 43
Brady, M 213–14
Bungala (SA) 73, 74

CAEPR vii–xii, 5, 230–36
  and choice 8–13
Cairns (Qld) 166
Campbell, S 63, 77–78
Cape York (Qld) 90–91, 154–56, 202, 205–207, 209, 226–27
Cape York Land Council (Qld) 118, 202
Carpentaria Land Council (Qld) 119
Central Land Council (NT) 111, 114, 117
Centre for Appropriate Technology 203
Centrelink 146
Century Mine (Qld) 82
Chapman, B 53–54
children 42, 43, 47, 126–27, 140–41, 144–51, 154, 162, 168–69
choice 5–17, 19, 26–28, 36–49, 50–64, 65, 84, 89, 171–72, 236; *see also* self-determination, individual negotiation 92–94, 104–109
Clarke, J 108
Commonwealth Grants Commission (CGC) 21, 189, 223–24, 228–29
Community Development Employment Projects (CDEP) 1, 9, 13, 19–20, 28, 29–35, 44, 54, 65–77, 88–89, 147, 158, 165, 166, 176–77, 193, 226, 234
Community Services (Aborigines) Act 1984 (Qld) 205
Cook Shire Council (Qld) 202
Coombs, HC viii
Council for Aboriginal Reconciliation 201

Crab Island (Qld) 195
criminality 42–44, 68, 161–62
culture, Indigenous 4–5, 10–11, 13–17, 18–19, 21, 26, 28, 31, 42–46, 47, 48, 54–55, 60–61, 62, 77, 89–91, 123, 150, 180, 181, 233, 234–36
'localism' 204–15

Dale, A 205
Daly, A 9, 11, 39–40, 41–42, 50, 54, 58, 128, 131, 133–44, 146, 148–51, 156, 158–59, 163
data, problems, opportunities and limits; *see also* evaluation
  Census 30, 32–33, 36–38, 70, 131–37, 138–40, 142, 145–46, 149, 167–72, 192–94, 235
  ethnographies 37, 46, 60–61, 88–89, 131–38, 143, 149–50, 154–56, 162–66, 234–36
  NATSIS 39, 42–43, 159, 160–62
  performance indicators 82–83, 213–14, 224
Indigenous Sector 186–87
David-Petero, J 61–62, 72, 159
Davis, R 88–89, 195, 226
Department of Aboriginal Affairs (DAA) vii–viii, 67, 97, 186, 201, 220–21
Department of Employment, Education and Training (and Youth Affairs) (DEETYA) 51, 76, 159, 183
Department of Employment, Workplace Relations and Small Business (DEWSRB) 183
Department of Family and Community Services (DFACS) 144, 183
Department of Finance (DOF) 67, 195, 214
Department of Health (and Human Services) 221, 225
Department of Immigration 185
Department of Prime Minister and Cabinet 185
Department of Social Security 67, 163
development, notions of 83–84, 89
Dillon, M 111–12
disadvantage, problem of 2–4, 61, 235–36; *see also* equity (equality)
Djabugay Tribal Corporation (Qld) 90
Dodson, M 179, 201

economy, Indigenous 37–39, 41, 46, 99–100, 162

education 8–9, 11–12, 15, 19–20, 27, 44, 50–55, 59–64, 75–78, 140, 152, 158–59, 162, 225
employers 41, 44, 58, 77–78
enterprise 67, 71, , 88, 91, 101, 109–10, 179
Environment Australia 183
equity (equality) 8–9, 26–27, 31–32, 34, 36, 52–54, 58, 61, 67, 96, 108, 163, 188–90, 208–209, 215, 235–36
evaluation, problems of 27–28, 32, 37, 50, 53, 66–71, 89, 101, 185, 207, 213–14, 224

Fahey, J 228
Federal Court 113
federal relations 21, 196, 222–25, 228–29
Fergie, D 212
fertility 160–61, 168–69
Finlayson, J 82, 89–90, 111, 120–22, 128, 136, 146, 148, 154–56, 162, 164–65, 202–206, 208–209, 211–12, 214–15, 233
fisheries 87–89
Fraser, M (government) 111, 182
Fraser, N 40

Gagudju Association (NT) 98
Gale, F 163
Galligan, B 114
Gaminiratne, KHW 160, 169, 186, 192, 193
gender relations 20, 51, 58, 128, 130, 152–66, 233 *see also* children, fertility, violence
Goldfields Land Council (WA) 120
Goolburri Land Council (Qld) 119
Gordon, L 40
Gray, A 160–61, 168–70, 194
Gray, G 153–54
Gray, M 52, 70, 73, 130–31, 159, 189
Great Barrier Reef Marine Park Authority (Qld) 118
Gregory, R 157

Hand, G 186
Hawke, A 41, 44, 67, 156, 163
Hawke, R (government) 25–27, 184
health 13, 43, 76, 213–14, 221, 223, 225
Henderson, R 42
Henry, R 11, 128, 148–51
Heron Island (Qld) 195
High Court 3, 103, 117

Hindess, B 179
Hindmarsh Island Bridge Royal Comission (SA) 212
Hope Vale (Qld) 93
House of Representatives Standing Committee on Aboriginal and Torres Strait Islander Affairs (HORSCATSIA) 196–200
household (including 'family') 5, 11, 13–14, 19–20, 130–72, 230, 234–35
  definition problems 131–36, 145, 234–35
  identity choice 167–72
  reciprocity, demand sharing and nurturance 155–56, 162–66; *see also* visitors
  'sole parent' 138–44, 150, 234
  visitors 132–33, 137–38, 142–43, 145–46, 149
housing 10–11, 13, 43, 131
Howard, J (government) 34, 68, 108, 120–21
human capital 10, 28, 31, 52–55, 58–59, 61–62, 63–64, 75–76, 158, 233
human rights 16, 18–19
Hunter, B 33–34, 39–40, 42–47, 51, 52, 68, 69, 158–59, 161–62, 170, 233
Hunter, E 161

identity, Indigenous 20, 26, 167–72, 235–36
Inala (Qld) 235
income 8, 10, 27, 31–34, 39–40, 43, 46, 54, 56, 58, 59, 67, 86, 88–89, 90, 127, 136–37, 139, 152, 156–57, 159; *see also* poverty, royalties, welfare payments, household
Indigenous Land Fund 103, 109–10, 202, 228
Indigenous Land Use Agreements 108, 121
Indigenous Sector, institutions of 1–4, 13, 17, 19–21, 28, 58, 176–83, 209, 223, 227–29, 230–36; *see also* ATSIC, CDEP, land councils, Native Title Representative Bodies, Prescribed Bodies Corporate, royalties and royalty associations
individual 5, 13–14, 17–18, 19–20, 28, 52, 103–104, 148, 177–78, 230, 233, 234
  as royalty recipient 98, 101
Industries Commission 97

investment 95–101; *see also* human capital
Island Coordinating Council (Qld) 195–96
Ivanitz, M 185

Jabiluka (NT) 82
Johnson, V 73, 75
Johnston, E 181–82
Jones, R 10, 131

Kakadu National Park (NT) 82
Kakadu Region Social Impact Study 102
Katherine (NT) 132, 141
Keating, P (government) 69
Kimberley (WA) 107, 201–202
Kimberley Land Council (WA) 120
kinship 14, 37–39, 41, 58, 83, 127, 133–34, 138, 149, 159; *see also* children, gender relations
Kunwinjku Association (NT) 97–98
Kuranda (Qld) 11, 90, 128, 144–51, 165, 235

labour market (including employment, unemployment and labour force participation) 8–10, 13, 17–18, 19, 25, 27–28, 29–35, 68–72, 75, 86, 152, 157–58, 161, 171, 234
    education and 50–64, 158
    occupation and industry structure 10, 55–58, 77, 157–58, 232
    social context of 36–49, 86, 161–62
land as resource 81–84, 103–8; *see also* property rights
Land Enterprise Australia 109
land rights 1, 20, 81–82, 89–91, 103–104, 208–209, 226, 232
Land Trust 115
Langton, M 163, 179
Lawrence, G 153–54
Leeton (NSW) 235
Levitus, R 82–83, 100–102, 116
liberalism 2
Liu Jin 50, 57, 58, 189
local government 225–28

Macdonald, G 208–209
Madden, R 68, 74–75
Maningrida (NT) 60–61, 73, 74, 75, 78, 235
Manne, R 5–7, 13, 14–15
Mantziaris, C 103–104, 109, 208
Mapoon (Old and New) (Qld) 93
Martin, D 38, 46, 103–104, 109, 115–16, 132, 165–66, 187, 202, 204–12, 214–15, 226

McKenna, S 105–106
McMahon, W (government) 1
Memmott, P 163
Merlan, F 212
Miller, Mick (committee chair) vii, 8, 25–27, 37, 46, 48–49, 67, 81, 83
mining 82, 92–102, 105–107
Morton, J 113
Mount Todd (NT) 106
Mowbray, M 226
Munster, J 119–20
Musharbash, Y 11, 145–46, 150–51

Nabarlek Traditional Owners Association (NT) 97–98
Napranum (Qld) 93
National Aboriginal Congress (NAC) 182
National Aboriginal Consultative Committee (NACC) 182
National Aboriginal Consultative Group 225
National Inquiry into Local Government Finance 226–27
national parks 82, 86. 90
native title 84
National Native Title Tribunal 120, 122
Native Title Act 1993 (Cwealth) 103–10, 117–22, 202, 206, 222
Native Title Representative Bodies (NTRBs) 20, 105, 107, 109, 110, 117–22, 175–76, 202, 211–12, 222
National Aboriginal and Torres Strait Islander Survey (NATSIS) 11–12, 39, 43, 47, 51, 64, 76, 158–62, 176, 193
Newcastle (NSW) 71
New South Wales Land Council 119
Neutze, M 10
Nganampa Health Council (NT) 203
Ngukurr (NT) 75
Ngurratjuta Aboriginal Corporation (NT) 99–100
Northern Land Council (NT) 97–98, 111, 113, 114, 117, 121
Northern Territory government 112, 200, 222–23
Northern Territory Self-Government Act 1978 (Cwealth) 222

Oceania viii
outstations 9, 99, 187
O'Faircheallaigh, C 93–94
Olney, J 113

Papua New Guinea 88
Pearson, N 118, 154–56, 166, 233–24
Peel, M 153
Peterson, N 115
Pitjantjatjara Council (NT) 178
Pollack, D 96, 100–102, 108–10, 116
population 32–34, 48, 129, 167–72, 176, 186–87, 191–93, 235–36
Port Lincoln (SA) 71, 73
Post, R 179
poverty 42–44, 48, 127–28, 149–50
Prescribed Bodies Corporate 109, 120, 176
Prince of Wales Island (Qld) 195
property rights 83, 87, 89, 94, 95–96, 105
public/private distinction 56, 96–97, 100–101, 232–33

Queensland Mines Limited 97
Quiggin, J 94, 95–96

reconciliation, policy 2–3
Redfern (NSW) 71
Reeves, J 96, 100–101, 114–17, 209, 226
regional differences 30–33, 37, 42–43, 51, 69–71, 170, 184–90, 204, 215, 225–26
regions as Indigenous political units 107, 116–17, 191–203, 215
Roach, L 39, 86, 161
Ross, K 204
Royal Commision into Aboriginal Deaths in Custody 67, 181, 227
royalties 82, 92, 94–102, 106–107
Rubibi Land Heritage and Development Council (WA) 120, 212
'Rubyville' (Kuranda) (Qld) 155

Saibai (Qld) 88–89, 195
Sandall, R 15–16
Sanders, W 10, 40, 47–48, 66, 67–68, 184–85, 196–201, 203, 204, 220–21, 223–28, 225, 226–28
Schwab, J 12, 38–39, 46, 52–53, 59–64, 76, 164–66, 206, 225
Seisia (Qld) 90–91, 195
Seisia Island Council 91
self-determination, policy 1, 4–5, 6, 17, 19–21, 46, 58, 75, 77, 95, 98, 163, 175, 180–83, 191, 206–207, 214, 230–36
Senate Standing Committee on Legal and Constitutional Affairs 3

Sewell, W 7–8
Smith, D 9, 36–38, 39, 40–41, 45, 46, 66–67, 69, 70–71, 73, 82, 84, 97–98, 100, 104–105, 108, 118, 121, 130–44, 146–49, 161, 163–64, 166, 188–89, 202, 208–209, 215, 221, 223–24
Smith, L 167, 169
social capital 45–46, 47, 162, 208, 221, 233
Stead, J 112
subsistence production 38–39 , 83, 85–87 (see also Indigenous economy)
substitute funding 68, 74–75, 100, 101–102, 222
Sullivan, P 107, 201–202, 212
Sutton, P 14–17, 115
Sydney Morning Herald 6

TAFE 62–63, 76
Taylor, C 17
Taylor, J 9, 10, 29–34, 51, 55–58, 68–69, 85, 132–33, 157–59, 161, 169–71, 186–87, 192–95, 204
Tesfaghiorghis, H 130–31, 157, 160, 168, 186–88
Tenneco Gas International 119
Thacker, E 73
Thursday Island (Qld) 195, 198
Tiwi Land Council (NT) 114
Tjakupai Dance Theatre (Qld) 90
Torres Shire Council (Qld) 197–99
Torres Strait Islanders
  economic development 61–62, 66, 69, 72, 91, 195–96
  definition 191–92
  demography 192–94
  identity 191, 194, 196–201
  political development 194–201
Torres Strait Protected Zone 89
Torres Strait Regional Assembly (proposed) 197–98
Torres Strait Regional Authority 87, 185, 195–98, 200
tourism 86, 89–91
trade unions 67, 179
Traditional Credit Council 203
treaty 3–4, 232
Trigger, D 82, 93, 119, 210

Viner, I 181
violence 152, 154–56, 227
Vocational Education and Training (VET) 28, 63, 75–78, 225

Warlpiri (NT) 11
welfare payments 19, 25, 31, 32, 38–42, 47, 70, 84, 88, 138–44, 148, 154–56, 157, 165–66
Westbury, N 203, 225
Whitlam, EG 1, 111, 182
Wiradjuri (NSW) 208
Woodward, E 82, 107, 111, 114, 115, 118
Wootten, H 103–104, 107
work; *see also* labour market
   as social experience 37–39, 44–45, 55–58, 71, 161
   conceptions of 37, 39, 72,
   voluntary 39, 162
Worn Gundidj (Vic) 68, 74

Yeatman, A 16, 18
Yorta Yorta (people) (Vic) 202
Yuendumu (NT) 144–51
Yunupingu, M 61–64
Scientist 43(9): 1498–1513.